# The Philosophy of Nietzsche

## Continental European Philosophy

This series provides accessible and stimulating introductions to the ideas of continental thinkers who have shaped the fundamentals of European philosophical thought. Powerful and radical, the ideas of these philosophers have often been contested, but they remain key to understanding current philosophical thinking as well as the current direction of disciplines such as political science, literary theory, comparative literature, art history, and cultural studies. Each book seeks to combine clarity with depth, introducing fresh insights and wider perspectives while also providing a comprehensive survey of each thinker's philosophical ideas.

### Published titles

*The Philosophy of Gadamer*
Jean Grondin

*The Philosophy of Merleau-Ponty*
Eric Matthews

*The Philosophy of Nietzsche*
Rex Welshon

### Forthcoming titles include

*The Philosophy of Deleuze*
Peter Sedgwick

*The Philosophy of Kant*
Jim O'Shea

*The Philosophy of Derrida*
Mark Dooley

*The Philosophy of Kierkegaard*
George Pattison

*The Philosophy of Habermas*
Andrew Edgar

*The Philosophy of Marx*
Mark Neocleous

*The Philosophy of Hegel*
Allen Speight

*The Philosophy of Rousseau*
Patrick Riley, Sr and Patrick Riley, Jr

*The Philosophy of Heidegger*
Jeff Malpas

*The Philosophy of Sartre*
Anthony Hatzimoysis

*The Philosophy of Husserl*
Burt Hopkins

*The Philosophy of Schopenhauer*
Dale Jacquette

# The Philosophy of
# Nietzsche

*Rex Welshon*

McGill-Queen's University Press
Montreal & Kingston • Ithaca

ISBN 0-7735-2776-1  (hardcover)
ISBN 0-7735-2777-X  (paperback)

Legal deposit second quarter 2004
Bibliothèque nationale du Québec

Published simultaneously outside North America
by Acumen Publishing Limited

McGill-Queen's University Press acknowledges the financial support of
the Government of Canada through the Book Publishing Development
Program (BPIDP) for its activities.

**National Library of Canada Cataloguing in Publication Data**

Welshon, Rex, 1955-
    The philosophy of Nietzsche / Rex Welshon.

Includes bibliographical references and index.
ISBN 0-7735-2776-1 (bound).—ISBN 0-7735-2777-X (pbk.)

    1. Nietzsche, Friedrich Wilhelm, 1844-1900.  2. Philosophy,
German—19th century.  I. Title.

B3317.W44 2004                    193              C2004-901042-5

Designed and typeset by Kate Williams, Swansea.
Printed and bound by The Cromwell Press, Trowbridge.

For my parents, Donald and Eleanor,
and my brothers, Douglas and Lawrence

# Contents

# Acknowledgements

I would like to thank the following people for direct and indirect help in this project: Frederic Bender, Perrin Cunningham, Steve Hales, Bernard Reginster, Richard Schacht and Christopher Shields. I would like to thank the Department of Philosophy at the University of Colorado at Colorado Springs and the Office of the Dean of the College of Letters, Arts, and Sciences at the University of Colorado at Colorado Springs, Linda Nolan, Dean, for their support. I would also like to thank series editor John Shand, and Steven Gerrard at Acumen, for their patience, and Kate Williams for her judicious copy-editing.

# Abbreviations

I use the following abbreviations for in-text citations to Nietzsche's works. Full bibliographical information for Nietzsche's works, including those not cited in the text, is supplied in the Guide to Further Reading.

    AC  *The Anti-Christ: Curse on Christianity*
   BGE  *Beyond Good and Evil: Prelude to a Philosophy of the Future*
    BT  *Birth of Tragedy*
     D  *Daybreak: Reflections on Moral Prejudices*
    EH  *Ecce Homo: How One Becomes What One Is*
    GM  *On the Genealogy of Morals: A Polemic*
    GS  *The Gay Science*
   HAH  *Human, All Too Human: A Book for Free Spirits*
    TI  *Twilight of the Idols, or How One Philosophizes with a Hammer*
    UM  *Untimely Meditations*
    WP  *The Will to Power*

References to specific passages follow *International Studies in Philosophy* style. For example, *BGE* 230 refers to *Beyond Good and Evil*, section 230 and *TI* III 1 refers to *Twilight of the Idols*, Chapter III, section 1. All emphasis in extracts is Nietzsche's, unless otherwise indicated.

*The Will to Power* is a degenerate book. Edited by Nietzsche's sister, Elisabeth, from unpublished notes she found in Nietzsche's possession, *The Will to Power* is less a book by Nietzsche than a collection of Elisabeth's favourite passages from his notebooks. The notebooks – Nietzsche's *Nachlass* – are arranged chronologically. In this book I sometimes use the *Nachlass* notes that appear in *The Will to Power*. They are identified as *Nachlass* notes with references to *The Will to Power*.

# Introduction

## Reading and writing about Nietzsche

Friedrich Nietzsche (1844–1900) is the world's most controversial philosopher. He is also the world's most relentlessly interesting philosopher. There is no other philosopher who writes as beautifully about as many topics as does Nietzsche, and no other philosopher whose ideas are more notorious. For all his notoriety, however, Nietzsche is increasingly remembered for his trenchant criticisms of the Western philosophical and theological traditions, for his celebration of creativity and flourishing, and for his tireless campaign to replace woolly-minded metaphysics with a philosophical view that is naturalistic and closely aligned with science. This change is welcome. For a century, Nietzsche has reigned as the one philosopher whose work should perhaps be banned, the one philosopher the mere mention of whose name is likely to raise the hackles on most of those within earshot. We shall, in due course, uncover the reasons why Nietzsche has this effect on otherwise reasonable people. In the vast majority of cases his villainous reputation is not deserved, and in the one case where it is deserved – his scathing criticism of Christianity – his reputation misleads by focusing attention away from the substance of his concerns, which have, in some cases, been raised by Christians themselves.

In writing a book of this sort I bear the double burden of introducing the reader to this controversial and interesting philosopher and showing that his bad reputation, even where deserved, should not be a reason not to read him. I shall try to accomplish both goals in the same way, by laying out what I think is the philosophical core of Nietzsche's thought. Now, it is to be admitted that introducing Nietzsche's philosophical thought is difficult, for there are two obvious and unavoidable obstacles. First, regardless of the range of topics covered, many others cannot be covered. Nietzsche is the most wide-ranging philosopher in the Western philosophical tradition, with the possible exception of Aristotle. No other philosopher writes on the variety of topics that Nietzsche does, and no other philosopher recognizes the logical, historical, causal, normative and epistemological relations between these topics as well as Nietzsche. Indeed, Nietzsche is something of a freak. Unlike most philosophers, who specialize on some small area or cluster of areas, Nietzsche writes on a huge number of issues and writes interestingly on the vast majority of them – but not all of them. He has some appalling blind spots and delivers some laughably bad arguments, which, for a philosopher who prized precise expression and rigour, is disappointing. Still, his philosophical vision roams over vast territories with incredible acuity and, for that reason, no single book on Nietzsche shorter than several thousand pages could begin to canvass all that with which he concerns himself.

Secondly, regardless of the depth of coverage on any one of the topics chosen, it is never deep enough. This problem is more severe than the first. Although Nietzsche writes about many different topics, there is a core set of issues to which he returns over and over again, with fresh insights, better arguments and refined, often amended, thoughts. There is something to the claim that there is no "real" Nietzsche. One has only to investigate what he says about morality to confirm that his views deepened over time and sometimes changed quite noticeably. There is little the commentator can do about this, except note it and try to reconcile the various threads of argument.

It is not an exaggeration to say that Nietzsche is the greatest philosophical writer ever. Unlike so much of philosophy, Nietzsche's work is a pleasure to read, even if, as is sometimes the case, what he has to say is not pleasant. He has an uncanny sense of the rhythm of language and of the etymological connections between words. Even when we read him in English, his talents as a writer come through, thanks to the respect shown him by most of his English translators. For all his talents, however, what sets Nietzsche apart from most other philosophical writers is his engagement with his topics. We never get the impression that the topic of discussion is for Nietzsche just an idle philosophical problem, and at no place in his work are we likely to think that he's just going through the motions. He obviously cares, not just about how to live a good life in a banal culture, but how the logical law of identity, for instance, plays a role in sustaining social practices that squash creativity.

Another facet that can intimidate is the extent of Nietzsche's knowledge and his willingness to unleash it. He is one of those people of whom it can accurately be said that he probably forgot more than most of us will ever know. He was trained in Latin and Greek, he was a voracious reader of all kinds of books, including Christian theology, anthropology, Eastern philosophy, physics, chemistry and physiology, and he was a close observer of German and European culture. He brings all this knowledge to bear in his work, peppering the most abstruse chain of argument with cultural asides and interspersing abstract discussions of virtue with cracks about the connection between morality and one's digestive tract. This is intentional and more than a little perplexing to the first-time reader; we feel as though we are dancing with a whirlwind.

As Nietzsche himself remarks in *Ecce Homo*, he writes so that his readers can dip into his books as if they were jumping into a glacial stream: in and out quickly, with the expectation that the experience will be remembered for a long time. He is a great aphorist and a master of turning phrases. But this virtue of Nietzsche's work poses another problem for his interpreters, who come loaded with their own philosophical baggage. We can try to emulate his style, knowing a priori that we shall fail; our style will never match his. We can try to take a philosophical sledgehammer to his work to get it to agree with the latest philosophical fad, knowing a priori that we shall fail; he is immensely subtle and will not be contained by any theoretical framework. We can try taking a balanced approach to his work, knowing a priori that we shall fail; many of his most compelling reflections are his most outrageous.

In the end, the best way to get to know Nietzsche's work is to read Nietzsche. But reading Nietzsche entails another kind of failure, for we have to admit up front that, no matter how often we look through his books, we shall always miss something. Of course, this is a source of pleasure too, for no matter how much we think we know his work there will always be some chain of argument or nuance that we can look forward to discovering in the future. In this book I hope to introduce you to some of the main philosophical themes to be found in Nietzsche's work, so that when you read Nietzsche you will be prepared for some of those chains of arguments and some of those nuances. This book does not pretend to be a guide to all Nietzsche's work; rather, I hope that it provokes acknowledgement that Nietzsche's thought is deep, knowledgeable, rigorous, challenging, maddening and fascinating. In short, I hope that this book allows you to find a way into the work of Nietzsche so that your engagement with it becomes a lifelong affair.

## Nietzsche's life

Nietzsche may be the world's most notorious philosopher, but his notoriety does not stem from the way he lived. He was, by all accounts, a well-mannered and engaging person, a little formal and stiff, but not someone from whom one would expect the wild rhetoric for which he is infamous. And if anything characterizes his life it is that he was increasingly alone with his thoughts and apart from other people, and not that he was sought-after or famous.

Nietzsche was born in Röcken, Prussia (a part of Germany), in 1844, to a devout Lutheran family. His father, Karl Ludwig, was a member of the Lutheran clergy, and his mother, Franziska, and sister, Elisabeth, were both pious women. Some have speculated that Nietzsche's break from Christianity was a result of rejecting his early home life. However, there is little evidence to suggest that his childhood was unhappy and plenty of evidence to suggest that it was quite contented. The speculation is ungrounded.

Nietzsche's father died at the age of 36 in 1849, when Nietzsche was 5, of what was then known as "softening of the brain", a condition character-ized by convulsive attacks and debilitating depression. Thereafter, Nietzsche lived with his mother and sister and two aunts in a town called Naumburg. He attended school there, receiving a rigorous liberal education. Upon graduation he enrolled at the University of Bonn, fully expecting to follow his father into the clergy. Yet he soon tired of his theological studies and gravitated towards philology, the study of language. Indeed, his primary intellectual mentors at Bonn were the philologists Friedrich Ritschl and Otto Jahn. Nietzsche's family did not greet Nietzsche's turn to philology warmly, and the rift formed then with his sister and mother never completely healed. A sequence of letters between Nietzsche and Elisabeth makes it apparent that his break with Christianity, so significant in his work, was the result of an intellectual decision to forgo happiness in favour of the search for truth. In those letters he freely admits that contentment and happiness were best found by being a Christian. For him, however, the cost was too high, for it required abandoning the search for what was true. It was during this time as a student that Nietzsche paid his one and only known visit to a brothel, in Bonn, perhaps contracting syphilis.

Before obtaining his doctorate from the University of Leipzig, where he had transferred when Ritschl accepted a position there, Nietzsche served briefly in the Prussian army. Upon returning to Leipzig, he learned that Ritschl had recommended him for the chair of philology at the University of Basel to begin the following academic year. He arrived in 1869, at the age of 24, and within a year was promoted to the rank of full professor, an achievement virtually unheard of in German university life. Nietzsche's Basel years – from 1869 to 1879 – were a mixture of success and frustration. On the one hand, he befriended Franz Overbeck, a historian of Christianity, and Jakob Burkhardt, a historian of the Greek classical period, and remained close to them until he went mad. It was also while he was a professor at Basel that he published his first books, *The Birth of Tragedy*, *Untimely Meditations* and *Human, All Too Human*, and came to know the German composer Richard Wagner. Wagner's influence on Nietzsche was immense, both because Nietzsche found Wagner compelling and because, on reflection, he found him despicable. Nietzsche was initially attracted to Wagner because he thought he found in him a model for being a creative and significant human being. In possessing a musical talent of the highest order, Wagner was someone whom Nietzsche, himself a composer of middling talent, admired. In addition, Wagner was a brilliant and witty conversationalist and cultural impresario and led an undeniably attractive example of the kind of flourishing life that Nietzsche championed in his work. Moreover, Wagner's wife, Cosima von Bülow, provided another model for Nietzsche, that of an intellectual comrade. He would search in vain to replicate her in his own life.

Nietzsche became a fixture at the Wagners' home from 1869 until 1875. He participated in Wagner's plans for the Bayreuth festival, consulted with Wagner about philosophy (they both admired the German philosopher Arthur Schopenhauer) and spent many days in conversation with Wagner's inner circle. Yet by 1875 Nietzsche was growing restless in Wagner's shadow, and in 1876 he broke with him altogether. Nietzsche was appalled at the first Bayreuth festival's commercialism and banality, and he grew weary of the toadying sycophants Wagner surrounded himself with and tired of Wagner's egomaniacal tendencies. Worse, Wagner indulged himself in anti-Semitism and a virulent form of German nationalism, both of which Nietzsche despised. Nietzsche looked upon Wagner no longer with fascination and admiration but with contempt and disappointment, and he ridiculed himself for ever having been duped. By 1877, his break with Wagner was as complete and as certain as his friendship had been four years earlier.

Nietzsche had suffered migraines for years and had taken medical leaves of absence from his teaching post at Basel in 1871 and 1877. In 1879, he finally resigned his position altogether. Thereafter, he survived on a small pension he received from Basel, renting rooms in houses in various Swiss mountain towns in the summer and various Italian towns the rest of the year. Among other places, his travels took him to Nice, Turin, Genoa, Recoaro, Messina, Rapallo, Florence, Venice, Rome, Sils-Maria and Leipzig. When his health permitted it, he wandered the hills and mountains, jotting thoughts down before returning to his room to rework them into manuscripts. As he slid into his late thirties and early forties, he suffered from intestinal difficulties and steadily worsening eyesight. Despite his lonely and peripatetic life, for him the 1880s were a period of philosophical creativity rarely matched by anyone at any time. He wrote *Daybreak* in 1881, the first four books of *The Gay Science* in 1882, *Thus Spoke Zarathustra* from 1883 to 1885, *Beyond Good and Evil* in 1886, *On the Genealogy of Morals* (henceforth *The Genealogy of Morals*) and Book V of *The Gay Science* in 1887 and, in 1888, *Twilight of the Idols*, *The Anti-Christ* and *Ecce Homo*. In addition, he composed hundreds of notes that never came to press during this time, many of them collected after his collapse by his sister Elisabeth into the infamous *Will to Power*. (All of these notes have subsequently been published, together with all his published work, in a single German collection as *Sämtliche Werke: Studienausgabe in 15 Bänden*, and an English translation of this collection under the editorship of Ernst Behler is currently underway.)

Occasionally, during these lonely years, Nietzsche sought out friendship and even fell in love at least once. In Rome in 1882, Nietzsche met Lou Salomé, a 21-year-old Russian studying philosophy in Zurich. He fell hopelessly in love and proposed marriage to her, not once, but twice. On both occasions she declined. Years later, she became an associate of Sigmund Freud.

Nietzsche returned to Italy in 1888 to finish what he thought would become his masterwork: a book begun in 1886, tentatively called *The Will to Power: A Revaluation of all Values*. But by late summer he abandoned the project as unfinishable. The material he had already composed found its way into print as *Twilight of the Idols* and *The Anti-Christ*. Sadly, as he was realizing that his ambitious project for a revaluation of all values could not be completed, his psychological grip began to loosen. By October of 1888, he had taken to signing his letters with various *noms de plume*, usually "Dionysus" or "The Crucified", and the few friends to whom he still wrote noticed that his handwriting was deteriorating and that the content of his letters was increasingly histrionic. The final break came on 3 January 1889. As was his custom, he left his lodgings in Turin for a mid-morning walk and happened upon a tradesman beating a horse. Nietzsche attempted to intercede to prevent the cruelty and collapsed. He was helped back to his rooms and, in the next few days, he danced around them naked and dashed off letters, one to Jacob Burkhardt comparing himself to God and another to Franz Overbeck. Overbeck became alarmed, travelled to Turin and found Nietzsche huddled in a corner of his room holding the manuscript of *Nietszsche Contra Wagner*. Together, they returned to Germany.

Back in Germany, Nietzsche was diagnosed with a progressive brain disorder and placed in the care of the Jena psychiatric clinic, where he remained for about a year. But he made no improvement; he sat still for hours on end only to erupt into terrifying explosions of rage that ended as inexplicably as they had begun. He was finally released to his mother's care in late 1890 and they returned to Naumburg together. His sister Elisabeth soon joined them and, following their mother's death in 1897, she moved Nietzsche from Naumburg to Weimar, where she had established the Nietzsche archive. By the mid-1890s, his celebrity was increasing and numerous visitors came to pay their respects. What they found was a pathetic shell of a human, uncaring, incompetent and silent. He died in Weimar on 25 August 1900.

No autopsy was performed, so the cause of his insanity has never been determined. Two theories compete for explaining his collapse. Some claim that Nietzsche suffered from syphilis and that his collapse was the result of tertiary symptoms of that disease. Others claim he had a brain tumour. For neither theory is there ironclad evidence. It is an open question whether Nietzsche was treated for syphilis and, if he was, whether the treatment was properly prescribed. After all, his sexual life was, by his own admission, exceedingly limited. For decades it has been popular to repeat the story of his one visit to a brothel when he was in his early twenties and to mention that he sometimes travelled to Italian seaside resorts. But from these snippets virtually no inferences can be drawn. We know nothing of his sex life other than these stories. Concerning the second hypothesis, we do not know whether he inherited a disease from his father or whether he had cancer. Lacking an autopsy, we shall never know.

## Nietzsche's philosophical development

Nietzsche's first book was published in 1872, three years after he took up his appointment at Basel. Entitled *The Birth of Tragedy: Out of the Spirit of Music*, it presented a conception of ancient Greek culture at odds with the then-popular understanding of it in Germany. Instead of seeing in ancient Greece a culture of nobility and rationality, Nietzsche saw in it an amoral energy that was actively being suppressed by the forces of logic, reason and civility. He called the suppressed energy Dionysian and the suppressing force Apollonian, and reviewed the history of Western culture as the overthrow of the Dionysian by the Apollonian. To our own detriment, the Apollonian forces have, Nietzsche argues, won out in our culture. *The Birth of Tragedy* is a work heavily influenced by Schopenhauer, and Nietzsche later distanced himself from its simplistic dichotomy.

Between 1873 and 1878, Nietzsche wrote a collection of essays in which he engaged with German culture from an increasingly critical distance. Some of these essays eventually found their way into his

*Untimely Meditations*, published in 1876. But at least one essay, "On Truth and Lies in an Extra-moral Sense", from 1873, was never printed in Nietzsche's lifetime. This is an interesting essay, for in it Nietzsche rejects universal and absolute truth, claiming instead that truth is a metaphor. Against the philosophical claim that there must be absolute truths, Nietzsche suggests that human experience is shot through with arbitrariness and that our conceptual frameworks routinely camouflage their capricious origins because to reveal and accept them would shatter our comfort and security.

In 1876, Nietzsche published his *Untimely Meditations*, four lengthy essays on German culture. In the first two essays – *David Strauss, the Confessor and the Writer* and *On the Uses and Disadvantages of History for Life* – Nietzsche trades German cultural self-congratulation for merciless criticism of that culture. He tempers this critique with two essays – *Schopenhauer as Educator* and *Richard Wagner in Bayreuth* – that point to some reason for hope. The first two essays attack the heroes and heroic assumptions of German culture. The essay on David Strauss, whose works were quite popular in Germany in the mid-nineteenth century, holds Strauss's faith in science and history up to ridicule. The second essay surveys various ways to write history and discusses how some of them are irredeemably harmful while others can contribute to a society's health. The third and fourth essays argue that Schopenhauer and Wagner might be able to be vanguards for a healthy German culture. As in the case of *The Birth of Tragedy*, Nietzsche later distanced himself from both of these claims and thinkers. By the mid-1880s, both Schopenhauer and Wagner were just two more in a long line of decadents for Nietzsche.

Two years later, in 1878, Nietzsche published the first of his "middle" or "positivistic" period books, *Human, All Too Human*. In 1879 he added a second section to the book, entitled *Mixed Opinions and Maxims*, and in 1880 he added a third section, entitled *The Wanderer and his Shadow*. The three parts were published together for the first time in 1886 as *Human, All Too Human: A Book for Free Spirits*. In *Human, All Too Human*, Nietzsche develops the aphoristic style he would use in most of his subsequent books. Admittedly, some of his aphorisms run to two pages, so it is not simply one pithy slogan after another. Still, there is no extended philosophical argument that runs for more than two pages, there are no chapters and there is no single theme. Nietzsche's wide-ranging intellect focuses on a variety of topics, many of them directly philosophical, and for the first time his fascination with power emerges. Nietzsche followed *Human, All Too Human* with *Daybreak: Reflections on Moral Prejudices*. Published in 1881, *Daybreak* is the first of Nietzsche's really great books. Again written in aphoristic style, *Daybreak* is remarkable for its clarity, intellectual insight and graceful command of the subject matter. The many subtle social and psychological analyses make the book a real eye-opener and, as an added bonus, it gives us Nietzsche's first direct discussions of power. Nietzsche's turn to power marks a crucial break with nineteenth-century moral philosophy, which, in the hands of the British utilitarians, had focused on pleasure and happiness as the goal of human behaviour.

Nietzsche's next work, *The Gay Science*, published in 1882, finds him unleashing his talents in a spectacular way. *The Gay Science* is a transitional work from his middle period to his mature work, yet, as a book, *The Gay Science* has few equals in all Western culture. Learned, playful, poetic, lyrical, devastatingly critical and surprisingly optimistic in the face of nihilism, *The Gay Science* is a *tour de force*. Nietzsche treats us to, among other things, the announcement that God is dead, the doctrine of the eternal recurrence, the perspectivity of science, a critique of Christianity, and page after page of fascinating, sometimes profound, analyses of philosophical, psychological, social and cultural phenomena. In 1887, Nietzsche added a preface, a fifth Book, and an appendix of songs to a second edition.

In 1883, Nietzsche dropped into the world *Thus Spoke Zarathustra: A Book for All and None*. *Thus Spoke Zarathustra* is probably Nietzsche's most famous work; Nietzsche himself regarded it as unequalled in human history. There is no way accurately to describe it. Unlike all his other work, *Thus Spoke Zarathustra* is written as poetry. It is, in turns, prophetic, mystical, obscure, mythological, hectoring and just plain weird. It is full of allusions to the Bible and to sacred texts from Buddhism, Hinduism and Islam, and full, too, of metaphors using nature and natural beasts and plants. *Thus Spoke Zarathustra* is a kind of anti-Bible, using parables, metaphors, allusions, sermons, songs and moral stories to describe the spiritual path of Zarathustra, a solitary sage who preaches self-overcoming, reflection, ironic detachment and Dionysian ecstasy. Zarathustra also teaches the "*Übermensch*", an individual who overcomes himself and his culture. *Thus Spoke Zarathustra* is unique, both in Nietzsche's *oeuvre* and in all European letters. Because it is unique, and because many of the philosophical issues it deals with are covered in his other works, we shall not mention it again in this book.

His next book, *Beyond Good and Evil: Prelude to a Philosophy of the Future*, published in 1886, is also generally considered one of his great works. Here, for the first time, Nietzsche unfurls his mature philosophy in a single work. He attacks Western philosophy and philosophers with a vengeance, arguing that their metaphysical, moral and psychological theories are anti-life and pernicious. Against them he offers another kind of philosophizing and another kind of philosopher. Nietzsche champions originality, a life committed to ruthless critical engagement with one's culture, a life without God or morality, a life of creating values. And it is in *Beyond Good and Evil* that the doctrine of the will to power really comes to the fore.

Intended as a commentary and exegesis to some of the claims made in *Beyond Good and Evil*, his 1887 work *The Genealogy of Morals* is composed of three essays, each of which expands on a crucial component of his critique of European morality. The first essay is devoted to an explanation of the emergence of slave or herd moralities; the second, to the development of guilt; and the third, to the attraction of what Nietzsche calls "ascetic ideals". Although no single book of Nietzsche's presents all his thinking on any of the topics he took an interest in, *The Genealogy of Morals* comes closest to capturing the general aim of his mature work. It is sober, detailed, psychologically astute, historically challenging, scholarly and a joy to read. The third essay in particular gathers such momentum that, in the final seven sections or so, Nietzsche's ideas tumble out at an utterly fantastic rate, leaving any but the most unengaged reader exhilarated but exhausted.

Nietzsche's final year of sanity, 1888, saw him publish three books and send one more off to the printer. The first, *The Case of Wagner: A Musician's Problem*, is, according to Nietzsche himself, a declaration of war against Richard Wagner. In it, he savages Wagner as a musical and cultural decadent. Next came *Twilight of the Idols, or How One Philosophizes with a Hammer*, published in September 1888. Playing off the title of Wagner's opera, *The Twilight of the Gods*, Nietzsche comes as close as possible in print to simply blasting away at Western philosophy and European cultural figures, spraying criticism around like buckshot. Finally, he published *The Anti-Christ: Curse on Christianity*. Here, Nietzsche's style degenerates somewhat. Although it is a brutal critique of Christianity, *The Anti-Christ* is shrill and, especially towards the end, somewhat discontinuous. As one of his last sane acts, he sent the manuscript of *Ecce Homo: How One Becomes What One Is* to the publisher in December 1888. Whatever else one may say about this work, it cannot be denied that it is hilarious and dumbfounding. How many other authors would dare to present their intellectual autobiography with Nietzsche's over-the-top self-love and flair, as exemplified by the titles of its first three sections: "Why I Am So Wise", "Why I Am So Clever" and "Why I Write Such Good Books"? Nietzsche then reviews all his published works and concludes the book with the accurate, albeit vain, self-prophecy, "Why I Am a Destiny". He collapsed a month after sending *Ecce Homo* to the printer. When Overbeck found him in January, Nietzsche was clutching the manuscript of *Nietzsche Contra Wagner: Out of the Files of a Psychologist*. This is a collection of snippets from his published work that Nietzsche put together with some new observations thrown in. Most concern Wagner, of course, and most are nasty. However, Nietzsche talks also about his own beliefs and his undying fondness for Wagner's abilities to express loneliness and sorrow in music. It is a sad and poignant acknowledgement of the losses Nietzsche endured in becoming who he was.

## Interpretation styles

In the past twenty years, two distinct strands of Nietzsche scholarship have emerged. With the sedimentation of the so-called analytic–continental split in philosophy (a split that developed with the split between Husserl and Frege over truth), Nietzsche scholarship became a starting point for debates of philosophical method. Competing Nietzsche societies were formed, competing Nietzsche journals began publication and competing conferences were held, each side insisting on the methodological benefits of their approach.

Each style of interpretation has its virtues. Continentalists present a Nietzsche who is playful, destructive, poetic, wildly imaginative, meta-phorical and a great stylist of the German language. All of these elements are to be found in Nietzsche. He is a very clever writer, and his work is full of puns, plays on words and jokes. He is, by his own accounts, a "vivisectionist" of culture and takes pride in his destructive accomplishments. His writing is so imagistic, active and alive that it is often close to poetry. And no one can seriously deny that Nietzsche is one of the most, if not the most, imaginative philosophical writers ever.

If we read Nietzsche looking for the wild man of philosophy, we shall find attractive some of the interpretations of his work influenced by Michel Foucault, Jacques Derrida and like-minded others. However, those most influenced by developments in French philosophy during the 1960s and 1970s also make some of the most serious philosophical claims on behalf of Nietzsche about rejecting determinate semantic meaning, for affirming the perspectivity of knowledge, truth and morals, for denying that there is a subject who can be the owner of actions, and for a view of the world that makes of it an indeterminate plenum that lacks any structure in itself. These are substantive philosophical theses, and the argumentation adduced in support of them – both the textual support from Nietzsche and the original argumentation derived from those texts – is usually quite interesting.

Analytic interpreters of Nietzsche tend to find in Nietzsche a philosopher who is concerned less with the rejection of determinate meaning than

11

with unpacking the inherent complexities of meaning; a philosopher who is less insistent to pronounce that the subject is dead than to explore the implications of the death of the Cartesian subject; and a philosopher who is not confident that the world has no structure whatsoever but is confident that it does not have the structure imputed to it by past philosophers. Analytic interpreters of Nietzsche are also more likely than their continentalist counterparts to try to place Nietzsche *within* the philosophical tradition rather than to try to place him as the final modernist philosopher or, perhaps, as the first postmodern philosopher.

Some oppose the continentalist style of interpretation on the grounds that it is bad scholarship, and some oppose the analytic style of interpretation on the grounds that it puts a straitjacket on Nietzsche. I find this squabble a bore. The scholarship in continentalist interpretation is, as far as I can see, no worse on the whole than that found in analytic interpretation. I will also report that, as far as I can see, some of the most suffocating interpretations come from slavish adherents to Derrida and Foucault. It is safer to say that there are good books on Nietzsche and bad books on Nietzsche. Some of the best come from the continentalist side and some of the worst come from the analytic side. What makes a book on Nietzsche a good book on Nietzsche varies in part with its purpose, but all the books on Nietzsche that I think are good are clear and argumentatively rigorous and sensitive to Nietzsche's vacillations, weird dead ends and illustrative asides. They at least try to convey Nietzsche's remarkable intellectual range and make coherent sense of his various claims, and they try to understand some of the contexts in which he is writing.

## Method and coverage of this book

I have focused in this book on a cluster of problems and issues that Nietzsche addresses. I do not focus on all of them; as noted in the first paragraph, no book shorter than several thousand pages could do that. I have been guided in my selection of topics to include those that Nietzsche's philosophical predecessors took up and those that have continued to be philosophical topics since Nietzsche's death. They are among the so-called "perennial problems" in philosophy: morality, religion, nihilism, metaphysics, necessity, truth, logic, knowledge, consciousness and personal identity. And the subtopics that I cover within these chapters are among the issues regularly discussed by philosophers when they take these topics up. For instance, when I discuss Nietzsche's criticisms of metaphysics, I discuss his criticisms of necessity and ontology, and, within those topics, I discuss different assessments of necessity and different components of ontological views, such as substance, soul, consciousness and identity. Likewise, when I discuss his epistemological perspectivism, I do so in the framework of the distinction between sceptical and anti-sceptical views, knowledge of things (*de re* knowledge) and knowledge of statements (*de dicto* knowledge) and the role of science in the generation of knowledge.

This is, admittedly, only one kind of interpretive scheme of Nietzsche's work and a pretty conservative one at that. It has the virtue of at least placing Nietzsche in the continuing conversation of philosophy that has been going on for about 2500 years in the West and longer in India and China. It also has the virtue of underwriting a particular structure to the book. In the first three chapters, I consider ways in which Nietzsche speaks out directly against the philosophical tradition. In the next three chapters, I consider ways in which Nietzsche engages the great philosophers from the Western tradition (and some Buddhists and Hindus as well). And in the final three chapters, I suggest how his views go well beyond the philosophical tradition he inherited and how those views are still germane despite another hundred years of philosophizing.

The limitations of this approach are obvious. Because I focus on those aspects of Nietzsche's thought that are parts of the tradition of *Western* philosophy, I cannot address in any detail the fascinating things he says about philosophers from other traditions. And because I focus on those aspects of his thought that are parts of the tradition of Western *philosophy*, I cannot address in any detail the wealth of observations and arguments he makes that are outside my scope of coverage. The second is a particularly serious problem. I readily admit that many of Nietzsche's most interesting engagements with the Western philosophical tradition are embedded in cultural arguments that are, for him, more important than the narrowly construed philosophical problem he is considering. This problem is reflected not only in the way I carve some problems off from the cultural context in which they occur in Nietzsche's texts, but also in my failure to cover his aesthetic reflections at all. Unfortunately, not every book on Nietzsche can cover every interesting philosophical topic, and I have decided, for better or worse, not to include discussions of Nietzsche's aesthetics.

Despite the artificiality of carving these philosophical problems off from the cultural context in which they emerge, it would be just as artificial to reduce the philosophical problems Nietzsche investigates to the cultural context from which they emerge. Culture and philosophy coexist; ignoring the former to focus on the latter and reducing the latter to the former are equally wrong-headed. I have tried, especially in

Chapters 1–3, to show how many of Nietzsche's philosophical concerns emerge as parts of his overall criticism of European culture. Other books do this better because their authors are trained differently from me (I recommend some of these books in the bibliography). This theme is less pronounced in the second part of the book, because I move to detailed assessment of Nietzsche's arguments with the philosophical tradition. By the end of the third section, however, I re-establish the connection between some of the more arcane reaches of philosophy with the social and cultural contexts that Nietzsche hopes to create by recommending the cultivation of particular types of individuals. There is, then, some recognition in the overall structure of the book that we start from within our culture and return to it. Of course, retreating from existing social and cultural contexts to engage philosophically with their presuppositions guarantees that when we return after philosophizing we shall be changed, and our change will, in turn, change those cultural contexts, sometimes for the better. That is, I think, Nietzsche's hope.

The reader will notice that Chapters 1–3 contain considerably more long selections from Nietzsche's work than do Chapters 4–9. There are two reasons for this. First, there is no point in reading a book of this sort if it does not provoke the reader into reading more Nietzsche, and there is no better way to do that than to quote Nietzsche at the height of his powers, as he is on the issues covered in these chapters: morality, religion and nihilism. Secondly, these topics are those on which his reputation as a culturally dangerous iconoclast rests, so it is appropriate to get a feeling for the tone of Nietzsche's engagement with his culture. It is against morality, religion and nihilism in particular that the most prolonged war must be fought.

In Chapters 1–3, we shall investigate Nietzsche's engagement with morality and religion and his self-professed nihilism. In Chapter 4, we look at his criticisms of Western metaphysics; in Chapter 5, his criticisms of truth; and, in Chapter 6, his criticisms of the tradition's obsequiousness to knowledge. In the last part of the book, we turn, in Chapters 7–9, to Nietzsche's psychology, his doctrine of the will to power and his views about the flourishing life. Here, Nietzsche goes well beyond the tradition he inherited, and, in my opinion, well beyond much of the philosophizing that has occurred in the hundred years since his death.

# CHAPTER 1
# Morality

Morality is that branch of philosophy that studies what is good and what is right. It immediately divides into two sub-disciplines: meta-ethics and normative ethics. Meta-ethics is concerned with analysing moral concepts and claims, and normative ethics is concerned with identifying and explaining moral values. Nietzsche is primarily concerned with meta-ethical issues, although some of his most amazing claims against morality are directed to substantive, normative claims of morality. Nietzsche is probably the most trenchant critic of morality in the philosophical tradition (the only close competitor is the French existentialist Jean-Paul Sartre). The following passage from *Twilight of the Idols* is entirely representative of his assessment of morality: "Moral judgment belongs, as does religious judgment, to a level of ignorance at which even the concept of the real, the distinction between the real and imaginary is lacking" (*TI* VII 1). Nietzsche has no truck with any moral views that precede his own, except in so far as they are exemplars of wrong-headedness, stupidity, blindness and viciousness. He thinks that every moral system hitherto developed is hopelessly naive, as in the case of English utilitarianism, a boneheaded misreading of human psychology, as in the case of Stoicism, malicious slavery, as in the case of Christianity, or foggy and grey, as in the case of Kant.

For those of us who are steadfast in our adherence to universalizable moral codes, reading Nietzsche can be a brutally disruptive experience, as we find cherished assumptions repeatedly laid on the table and smashed to bits. For those of us who are already sceptical about morality, on the other hand, reading Nietzsche's tirades will only confirm much of what we already suspect. But his criticisms should be famous for more than their malevolence, for they are in turns infuriating, psychologically and sociologically astute and, in many ways, depressing. And although his criticisms sometimes miss their mark, the impression we are left with after

15

understanding his views is that he is probably right about many of the issues he takes on.

In this chapter, we shall investigate Nietzsche's criticisms of moral systems by outlining what he variously calls "herd" or "slave" morality. We shall seek to understand what Nietzsche thinks the herd is, show how morality uses the fears of the herd to motivate the real world–apparent world distinction, and discuss the selling points for particular moral views used by the morality salesmen once that distinction is made. According to Nietzsche, the edifice of morality is nothing but a shell game: moralists offer arcane and esoteric explanations for the discrepancy between the way things are in this world and the way things are in their "real world" and thus prop themselves up as protectors of that real world.

## The Genealogy of Morals

Morality presumes to provide us with a guide to how to live. Nietzsche agrees that this is the proper function of morality. However, he is convinced that what we have inherited from our moral thinkers is a catastrophically wrong-headed guide. In fact, in morality values are inverted so that what is called morally good is not really good and what is called morally evil is not really bad. Nietzsche lays the blame for this inversion of values squarely on the shoulders of a particular social class, the weak, and their compatriots, the religious. Thus begins his lifelong war with morality and Christianity.

Nietzsche discussed morality in every book he wrote, but his most extended discussions of it occur in *Beyond Good and Evil* and *The Genealogy of Morals*. In *Beyond Good and Evil* he discusses but does not explain in any detail the slave revolt in morality, a claim about the origins of moral values and moral thinking that is uniquely Nietzschean and that forms the core of his critique of morality. Contemporary European moral thinking is, he thinks, debased and poisoned by the influence of society's weakest and most ignoble elements, the herd. This claim is explained in detail in *The Genealogy of Morals*. It is a remarkable argument.

*The Genealogy of Morals* is Nietzsche's most recognizably philosophical book. Composed in 1887, near the end of his productive life, and intended as a sequel to *Beyond Good and Evil* (published the previous year), *The Genealogy of Morals* is an extended argument in defence of a clear thesis. That thesis is that a critique of moral values will reveal that their value lies almost exclusively in the support they provide for the herd or slave elements of a society and not, as is claimed on their behalf, the ethical guidance they provide for all of us. As a consequence, it is a mistake to think that moral values are disinterested or not self-interested and it is another mistake to think that they are universally binding. They are, instead, thoroughly self-interested and are binding only on those for whom they promise to provide some relief from the suffering of life.

He begins soberly enough in the preface with the acknowledgement that what will follow may not be pleasant, but he suggests that truth's ugliness is of no concern to the philosopher. Here, Nietzsche is anything but anti-rational, as some have suggested. He is proposing a critique of moral values, that is, a rational assessment of the value of moral values. He will show that, despite their puffed up self-importance, moral values are only one kind of ethical evaluation possible. (Note the distinction between morality and ethics that we draw here. We shall say that *ethics* is the study of right and wrong behaviour and that *morality* is one way of establishing what is right and wrong. As artificial as this distinction may be, we want to make some such distinction because Nietzsche nowhere abandons ethical evaluation; it is an issue found in every one of his books. By distinguishing morality from ethics, we can reserve the former for the object of his scorn while allowing him the logical space within which to develop his alternative views.)

The body of *The Genealogy of Morals* is divided into three essays, each with its own topic. In the first essay, Nietzsche investigates the history of moral values by contrasting the distinction between good and bad, on the one hand, and good and evil, on the other. In the second essay, he analyses the emergence of the psychological capacity for guilt and bad conscience, a cornerstone for the development of modern moral values. And in the third essay, he investigates the implications of the ascetic moral values of chastity, humility and poverty. Let us look at the argument in greater detail.

## Essay I

The question of Essay I is this: how did herd morality become the dominant form of ethical evaluation, so dominant that we do not even recognize that it is a perspective of a particular class of people rather than something that is universal in scope? Genealogy is designed to answer this question. Genealogy is a uniquely Nietzschean enterprise, a peculiar kind of history, but, at its simplest, a quite familiar form of reasoning. With certain contemporary phenomena as its objects of explanation, genealogy devises hypotheses about the causal antecedents of those phenomena and then tries to confirm the hypotheses. In this, genealogy is not markedly different from other kinds of history. What makes it peculiar in comparison with most other history is fourfold. First, genealogy denies that contemporary practices represent an improvement over what caused them. Secondly, genealogy does not think that contemporary practices can always be read back into the distant past or be found intact in their current form at the point of their original emergence. Thirdly, genealogy denies that the inception of ethical evaluation has much in common with its contemporary descendant. Fourthly, genealogy is unabashedly perspectival and engaged in a way that typical histories pretend not to be. Nietzsche is quite happy to allow that his is not an objective history of moral values. He does not think there can be such a thing.

The second and third aspects of genealogy are interesting divergences from typical histories. With these differences, Nietzsche distinguishes himself from anyone who uses our contemporary social practices to explain the inception and development of the chain of social practices that culminates in these social practices. Nietzsche actually avails himself of two equally significant methodological points. First, from the contemporary social value of some characteristic we cannot infer that that characteristic had that value when it first developed. Secondly, from the archaic social value of some characteristic we cannot infer that that characteristic has that value now. He uses the first point against the so-called "historians of morality"; the second he deploys against those who would uncritically endorse any version of the noble savage model of human flourishing.

We do not question the value of morality because we assume that moral values are valuable for everyone. Nietzsche rejects this assumption. Far from being universal, moral values are, he thinks, valuable only for some. Far from being immutable, moral values are an historical product, contingent creations of particular groups of people, designed to serve their interests. Far from being intrinsically valuable, moral values are, where they are valuable at all, valuable instrumentally. Genealogy also shows that their emergence is explained not, as moral defenders would have it, as our recognition of some universally held "moral sense" whose dimensions and structure are delineated by moral concepts but, rather, as the result of a struggle between the herd and the nobility, a struggle that the herd – the slaves – have won.

Typical histories of morality begin with the present and read it back into time. In the first section of Essay I, Nietzsche has a good laugh at the expense of English moral historians who, convinced of the truth of utilitarianism and social Darwinism, read them back into history and place them at the embryonic stages of moral development. Utilitarianism was the dominant form of moral theory in the nineteenth century and, in its contemporary guise as decision theory, it remains the moral theory most frequently discussed by philosophers. According to utilitarianism, the moral *good* is maximal net happiness or pleasure. Maximal net happiness or pleasure is what we aim at when we make ethical decisions and is that which serves as the criterion of goodness of our actions. Given two actions, that with the maximal net happiness is the better of the two, and so it is the morally *right* thing to do. Social Darwinism is the claim that evolutionary development guarantees both that only those individuals who are best adapted to their social environment will live long enough to pass on their genes and that, as a result, those gene lineages that have survived the longest and are most widely distributed are the best adapted. (This sort of thinking is, whatever Nietzsche thinks about it, independently a ridiculous misreading of Darwin, for whom evolutionary explanation restricted itself to only some kinds of properties, and for whom there were a variety of causal forces at play in evolutionary development, some of which had little, if anything, to do directly with survival to mating age.)

The moral historians alluded to here in the preface and first essay of the *The Genealogy of Morals* are accused of thinking that we moderns are the cream of the evolutionary crop and that, since maximal net happiness is what the utilitarian's moral theory claims is morally good, it must be that when moral values first developed they did so as the result of a similar line of reflection. Nietzsche finds both claims preposterous. There is, he thinks, absolutely no reason to think that the modern European is the best that evolution can muster. On the contrary, he thinks that the modern European is mediocre and vicious. And, being a well-trained classical philologist, he is in a peculiarly well-qualified position to counter the utilitarian potted history of morality. He thinks that, at the beginnings of evaluation, there was nothing like nineteenth-century utilitarian considerations in the reflections that resulted in the creation of moral values. His explanation of the origin of moral values is quite different: there are two senses of "good", to each of which there is an opposing term. In the first sense of "good", call it "noble good", the opposing term is "bad". In the second sense of "good", call it "moral good", the opposing term is "evil".

Nietzsche thinks that the evaluative distinction between good and bad originated within the noble classes of a society. Those who were blessed by birth or by attainment to be members of the highest castes of society – that is, those with the greatest privileges and the noblest spirits – called themselves good and those lower in social rank bad (*GM* I 2). Nietzsche offers etymological evidence for this hypothesis: "*schlecht*", the German word for "bad", is related to "*shlicht*", the German word for "plain" (*GM* I 4). We might trace a similar history with the English words "bad" and "base". Nietzsche hypothesizes that the nobility, who in earliest days were identical with what he calls the masters, first designated themselves as good and the rest as bad.

The masters are truthful among themselves (*GM* I 5), spontaneous, open and trusting, unable to take injuries seriously, self-controlled (*GM* I 10), delicate, loyal, prideful, and friendly (*GM* I 11). But when they are not among themselves they are little better than animals:

> There they savor a freedom from all social constraints, they compensate themselves in the wilderness for the tension engendered by protracted confinement and enclosure within the peace of society, they go *back* to the innocent conscience of the beast of prey, as triumphant monsters who perhaps emerge from a disgusting procession of murder, arson, rape, and torture, exhilarated and undisturbed of soul, as if it were no more than a students' prank, convinced they have provided the poets with a lot more material for song and praise. One cannot fail to see at the bottom of all these noble races the beast of prey, the splendid *blond beast* prowling about avidly in search of spoil and victory; this hidden core needs to erupt from time to time, the animal has to get out again and go back to the wilderness: the Roman, Arabian, Germanic, Japanese nobility, the Homeric heroes, the Scandinavian Vikings – they all shared this need.          (*GM* I 11)

This is one of the most notorious passages in Nietzsche's writing, for the reference to the blond beast was used by the German Nazis to justify their eugenic project of creating a master race of Aryans. They should have read Nietzsche more closely: the blond beast of prey does not refer to Germans or blond Europeans at all but to the lion, and the lion in noble humans. It is glaringly obvious that he does not mean to be identifying the blond beast of prey with the blond Germans; after all, he includes Arabs and Japanese among the blonds.

The contrary value of the noble sense of good is bad. Bad consists in the denial of noble values and bad people are those who exemplify such ignoble values. The ignoble slaves are dishonest, strategic, distrustful, resentful, uncontrolled, crude, disloyal, humble and unfriendly. They are common, base, weak, sycophantic and greasy people.

It would be a mistake to think that, simply in virtue of their being the best their society has to offer, the masters of *The Genealogy of Morals* have an unlimited supply of value or that they exemplify the best *any* society has to offer. Nietzsche thinks to the contrary that the masters are irredeemably limited by their intellectual dullness and their inability to see beyond their own self-glorification. It is a great temptation to read Essay I of *The Genealogy of Morals* as valorizing the masters as ideals for all historical epochs and for all cultures. This is a mistake. The masters are one, extremely crude, example of a kind of human that justifies humanity, but they lack all psychological depth and are not in the least bit interesting (*GM* I 6). To think that the masters of Essay I provide a contemporary ideal is to ignore what two thousand years of Christianity has bred in us – psychological depth and character – and to try to revert back to an early phase of our development. Any contemporary attempt to "rediscover" the blond beast within us is doomed to fail. Our image of what that life could be were we only a master is hopelessly distorted by selectivity, biased representation and a longing to escape the tedium of contemporary life. We might find *something* by roaming wild places, looking for blood and honour, tanning deer hides to make our own clothes, drinking bad wine, banging drums, dancing and attacking people. However, the conditions that made the masters exemplars of their time – poorly developed technology, an ineffective economic system, primitive psychology – make the attempt to revert now to their example little more than a wrong-headed anachronism. It is also likely to get us arrested, which just makes the point: we are no longer who they were.

On the one hand, then, we have a contrast between good and bad, that is, a contrast between the nobility and the wretched masses. However, there is another contrast: that between moral good and evil. Moral good is the product of the slave elements of society. Moral good emerges when those who are bad according to the noble valuation – the base and common – view themselves as good and the denial of their characteristics as evil. The slaves present a fairly straightforward reversal of noble valuations. Noble valuations are autonomous and made independently of any comparison with the common, the base. Slave valuations, on the other hand, are the product of individuals who are self-reflective and whose thoughts about themselves are mediated by their knowledge that they are weak (*GM* I 10). Their action is fundamentally *reaction* and their values are fundamentally *reactive* values, reactions against the perceived threat posed by the powerful to their survival (*GM* I 13). The slaves are passion-less, pale and meek. They denigrate their bodies, express pity, practise charity, believe in other worlds where their fortunes are reversed and hope that they can achieve that world. And evil for them is that which they fear, namely, power.

The agents of the slave revolt in moral evaluation are, of course, the weak and the ignoble. But Nietzsche makes it clear in Essay I that the slave revolt would never have been successful were it not for the recruitment of the slave's case by organized religion, and by Christianity in particular. We shall look at this in greater detail in Chapter 2. Here, let us simply say that Christianity provides the slaves with a worldview wholly consonant with their hopes to find a reason for their suffering and to undermine the powerful. Christianity provides the argumentative ammunition the slaves take into battle with the powerful: an arsenal of metaphysical claims, psychological explanations, promises, threats, social institutions and justifications for their aggressive reaction against those whom they loathe because they are better. The slave revolt in morality is successful because Christianity above every other social institution has enlisted the rancour and seething resentment of the masses.

The proof of the success of Christianity's involvement in the slave revolt in morality is in the moral authority of the church, as Nietzsche notes:

> The two *opposing* values "good and bad," "good and evil" have been engaged in a fearful struggle on earth for thousands of years …. The symbol of this struggle, inscribed in letters legible across all human history, is "Rome against Judea, Judea against Rome": – there has hitherto been no greater event than *this* struggle, *this* question, *this* deadly contradiction.
>
> Which of them has won *for the present*, Rome or Judea? But there can be no doubt: consider to whom one bows down in Rome today, as if they were the epitome of all the highest values – and not only in Rome but over almost half the earth, everywhere that man has become tame or desires to become tame.      (GM I 16)

One curious twist to Nietzsche's condemnation of morality is that, for all the acid he pours on it, Nietzsche actually identifies himself with those for whom these values are values (although his reasons for valuing these values are different). In *Ecce Homo* he identifies himself with the decadent product of two thousand years of the slave revolt (*EH* "Why I am So Wise"). Why does he do this? The answer is that he recognizes that saying "no" to the slave revolt in morality, to resentment, to Christianity, is to say "no" to ourselves, and that is incompatible with loving our fate, a requirement for flourishing that Nietzsche makes repeatedly, especially towards the end of his sane life. While it is tempting to think that we can simply turn away entirely from our personal and cultural pasts through an act of free will and head off bravely in a new direction, such a negation is no more possible than the wilful reversion to the masters. Both are romantic delusions. Loving our fate (*amor fati*) requires that we become who we are, and it is self-deception to think that we are nothing to begin with and can become whatever we want to be. We return to this matter in the final two chapters of this book.

## Essay II

Essay II is most surprising. After the first essay, one might expect Nietzsche to advocate a return to the evaluative system of the masters or at least a wholesale repudiation of the slaves. However, Nietzsche refuses both temptations. Instead, he offers another genealogical account of the development of another pair of phenomena: guilt and responsibility. Why? Nietzsche thinks these two capacities are essential for understanding ourselves as moderns and essential for understanding how we moderns might flourish. To overcome who we are and to express our power we must first understand who we are. Essay I offered part of an answer; Essay II offers another part by tracing the development of our modern sense of guilt and responsibility. Nietzsche's thesis is that the necessary conditions for guilt are also necessary conditions for the best and noblest things we can do with ourselves now. In short, realizing human excellence now entails the development of some of the very personality characteristics that morality implanted in human beings. The first two are self-identity at a time (synchronic identity) and self-identity over time (diachronic identity). Both of these are necessary for a sense of responsibility for the actions we perform. After all, in order to be responsible for what we do now, we have to know that who we are now is the same as who we were ten minutes ago and who we shall be in ten minutes' time. Responsibility is, in turn, necessary for bad conscience and guilt, which in turn are necessary for the highest forms of autonomy, self-creativity and nobility. So without all of them – synchronic and diachronic identity, responsibility and bad conscience (guilt) – the highest forms of human excellence available to us now cannot obtain. What is needed, then, is a genealogy of responsibility and the bad conscience. Here, punishment is relevant, because it explains the first appearance of responsibility.

Nietzsche's genealogy reveals that responsibility was developed through a mutilating, bloody and deadly regime of techniques designed to ingrain through punishment a sense of identity at and over time. The original purpose of punishment is unknown – perhaps it was the enjoyment of inflicting pain on others – but one initial consequence of punishment is that memory is ingrained in humans. As Nietzsche notes, only that which is most painful will be burned into memory. Since memory entails continuity over time, that is, diachronic identity, it is to the mechanisms of memory inducement that Nietzsche calls attention. So he provides a list of mechanisms that, over the course of history, have been used for this purpose. The sadistic catalogue includes

> stoning ... breaking on the wheel ... piercing with stakes, tearing apart or trampling by horses ("quartering"), boiling of the

criminal in oil or wine … the popular flaying alive … cutting flesh
from the chest, and also the practice of smearing the wrongdoer
with honey and leaving him in the blazing sun for the flies.

(*GM* II 5)

That is *our* history: a history of using pain to communicate to victims that
they are now the same person as the person who earlier committed a
transgression. So even if we do not know what the original purpose of
punishment was, we can hazard a guess that the first social consequence
achieved by punishment was to instil a sense of diachronic identity and
with that a sense of prudential responsibility in debtors who promise to
repay what they cannot repay. As Nietzsche notes, the "actual *effect* of
punishment must beyond question be sought above all in a heightening of
prudence, in an extending of the memory, in a will henceforth to go to
work more cautiously, … in a kind of improvement in self-criticism" (*GM*
II 15).

Once the appropriate sense of prudential responsibility was ingrained –
once prudence was accomplished – punishment should have reached the
end of its utility. Yet punishment did not evaporate just because its original
consequence was satisfied. How do we explain this? Nietzsche's answer is
not kind. The occurrence of punishment is underdetermined by any single
social function and it continues after prudential responsibility is established because it is repeatedly endowed with new functions. For example,
punishment makes not just the debtor, but also the creditor, more predictable and humane, for it prevents arbitrary rampaging by unpaid creditors.
Woven through all these various functions of punishment is the public
display of punishment, the *festivity* of inflicting pain on others. One of the
constants in European, indeed, most, societies is the spectacle of publicly
imposing pain:

> To see others suffer does one good, to make others suffer even
> more: this is a hard saying but an ancient, mighty, human, all-too-
> human principle to which even the apes might subscribe; for it has
> been said that in devising bizarre cruelties they anticipate man and
> are, as it were, his "prelude." Without cruelty there is no festival:
> thus the longest and most ancient part of human history teaches –
> and in punishment there is so much that is *festive*!      (*GM* II 6)

Such elements are not absent even today. Every time a convicted murderer
is executed anywhere in the United States, people gather at the prison
walls to celebrate the announcement of the death. As painful as it may
be to admit to ourselves, there is an element of truth to Nietzsche's

fundamental point, that all the stated humanitarian and political goals of punishment are secondary to the spectacle of inflicting pain.

For all our viciousness, Nietzsche is prepared to admit that over the past two thousand years the spectacle of cruelty has moderated somewhat. For, as we become tamer – more predictable, less prone to outrageous rampages, refined, guilty, "spiritualized" – so too does the need for flaunting pain become less salient. The spiritualization of cruelty culminates for Nietzsche in the eventual overcoming of punishment altogether in mercy:

> It is not unthinkable that a society might attain such a *consciousness of power* that it could allow itself the noblest luxury possible to it – letting those who harm it go *unpunished*. "What are my parasites to me?" it might say. "May they live and prosper: I am strong enough for that!"
>
> The justice which began with, "Everything is dischargeable, everything must be discharged," ends by winking and letting those incapable of discharging their debt go free: it ends, as does every good thing on earth, by *overcoming itself*. This self-overcoming of justice: one knows the beautiful name it has given itself – *mercy*; it goes without saying that mercy remains the privilege of the most powerful man, or better, his – beyond the law. (GM II 10)

Here, Nietzsche mentions power and the role that it plays in distinguishing the best elements of a society from its worst. We shall see throughout this book that these mentions of power are representative of one of Nietzsche's most cherished ideas, that life is a struggle for power.

There is a problem with Nietzsche's explanation of punishment. The kind of responsibility it instils is prudential, not moral. The debtor knows that his actions are his, and so knows that if he does not repay the debt he is likely to forfeit some part of his body, his spouse or his life. But moral responsibility and a sense of guilt are deeper than prudential responsibility, for they are internally imposed states of mind and not just prudent responses to external threats. So we need to add to the explanation of prudential responsibility some additional resource to explain moral responsibility and the bad conscience. Nietzsche thinks this additional resource is the "internalization of man" (GM II 16), the psychological revolution attending our enculturation in which outwardly directed drives are turned inwards.

When we become civilized we lose the primitive vent for our instincts in war and dancing and turn those instincts for mastery over others and things inwards on ourselves in cruelty to ourselves. While this internal laceration is, at least initially, sick and leads to self-mutilation, it also deepens our psychology and makes possible entirely new forms of self-overcoming hitherto unknown. The following description of the transition is justly famous:

> The man who, from lack of external enemies and resistances and forcibly confined to the oppressive narrowness and punctiliousness of custom, impatiently lacerated, persecuted, gnawed at, assaulted, and maltreated himself; this animal that rubbed itself raw against the bars of its cage as one tried to "tame" it; this deprived creature, racked with homesickness for the wild, who had to turn himself into an adventure, a torture chamber, an uncertain and dangerous wilderness – this fool, this yearning and desperate prisoner became the inventor of the "bad conscience."
>
> Let us add at once that, on the other hand, the existence on earth of an animal soul turned against itself, taking sides against itself, was something so new, profound, unheard of, enigmatic, contradictory, *and pregnant with a future* that the aspect of the earth was essentially altered. Indeed, divine spectators were needed to do justice to the spectacle that thus began and the end of which is not yet in sight – a spectacle too subtle, too marvelous, too paradoxical to be played senselessly unobserved on some ludicrous planet! From now on, man is *included* among the most unexpected and exciting lucky throws in the dice game of Heraclitus' "great child," be he called Zeus or change; he gives rise to an interest, a tension, a hope, almost a certainty, as if with him something were announcing and preparing itself, as if man were not a goal but only a way, an episode, a bridge, a great promise.
>
> (*GM* II 16)

Among many other claims made here, the most relevant for our purposes is that Nietzsche causally links the emergence of the bad conscience with the internalization of what were once outwardly directed drives. This is a little mysterious. Why should internalizing cruelty lead to the emergence of the bad conscience, the sense of guilt?

Nietzsche has an answer to this question, and it is at least plausible. Nietzsche abstracts away from all the observable acts of cruelty against others to a drive to impose form (*GM* II 17). The mark of crude power is, he thinks, not observable bits of behaviour such as impaling a deer, but the drive behind those bits of behaviour: the drive to command, to impose oneself on others. Nietzsche insists that this drive is an instance of the drive of giving form to the world. Once our outwardly directed drives are thwarted, as they are in society, they take as their object not others but ourselves. The internalized drive to impose form then takes not others but the self as its raw material and demands that it be stamped with direction, structure, discipline and control. As Nietzsche puts it:

> This *instinct for freedom* forcibly made latent – we have seen it already – this instinct for freedom pushed back and repressed, incarcerated within and finally able to discharge and vent itself only on itself: that, and that alone, is what the *bad conscience* is in its beginnings. (*GM* II 17)

Note that he does not say that the instinct for freedom turned inwards is *all* that the bad conscience is, but it is the primordial drive from which variants of the bad conscience develop. There are, in principle, many interesting developments of this primordial form of the bad conscience. Nietzsche focuses on two. The first is what Nietzsche calls "active bad conscience" (*GM* II 18), which is the soil from which everything beautiful and worthwhile grows. We shall return to this matter again in our discussion of Essay III and in subsequent chapters. But we must confront the other form of bad conscience, for it is this second form that has become, through Christianity, the most familiar form of guilt.

Nietzsche's explanation of the moral sense of guilt – the moral bad conscience – is that the debt primitive peoples feel to their ancestors for their very existence continuously grows as the power of the tribe itself increases until the most powerful tribes convert their ancestors into gods. Since gods are transcendent beings, the debt owed to these gods becomes increasingly difficult to repay. Finally, with the Christian God, which, as Nietzsche notes, is the "maximum god attained so far" (*GM* II 20), the sense of debt becomes maximal, that is, unpayable in principle, and religious guilt is formulated. Religious guilt is the logical precursor to moral guilt. Moral guilt precipitates out of religious guilt the phenomenon of inflicting pain upon ourselves and the belief that we have fallen so far away from God that our debt to him for our existence is "irredeemable" (*GM* II 21). We cannot redeem the debt because our sin in the face of God is original, final and infinite. This will to find ourselves guilty "to a degree that can never be atoned for" (*GM* II 22) is moral guilt. Given his view of the matter, Nietzsche's despairing conclusion to the essay seems the only possible one: "Oh this insane and pathetic beast – man! What ideas he has, what unnaturalness, what paroxysms of nonsense, what *bestiality of thought* as soon as he is prevented just a little from being a *beast in deed*!" (*GM* II 22).

## Essay III

Essay III is the most complex of the three essays composing *The Genealogy of Morals*, in part because it addresses what looks like a paradox. That paradox flows from the topic of the essay: the attraction of what Nietzsche calls "ascetic" values. These ascetic values – poverty, chastity and humility – form the core of the moral outlook resulting from the slave revolt in morality. They are typically used by the slave elements of society as a kind of anaesthetic against suffering, but, amazingly, they can also be used by others, such as philosophers, artists and other exemplars of human flourishing, for the noblest and most far-reaching experiments with life. The paradox that flows from the investigation is this: how can self-abnegation be an expression of *power* both for the worst exemplars of humanity and for some of its best? Another way of putting the point is this: it looks as though ascetic ideals are both systematically against life and yet necessary for some of the highest forms of life. We can even put the paradox as the conclusion of a simple argument:

Premise 1:    Morality as it has been practised and promulgated in the past two thousand years professes to lead us to a good life.
Premise 2:    Morality is decadent and against life.
Premise 3:    Morality's decadence must be a function of life.
Conclusion:  Morality is both against life and a function of life.

That conclusion certainly looks like a self-contradiction. Nietzsche's response, as we shall see, is that the paradox is only apparent.

Let us set the scene for Essay III by summarizing the results of the first two essays. According to Essay I, there has been a revolution in ethical evaluation, the slave revolt. The result of the slave revolt is to invert noble forms of ethical evaluation. Moral evaluation makes the ideals of the slaves binding on all, the best and worst alike. Why then did the masters of Essay I succumb to the slaves' evaluation? Part of the answer comes in Essay II. The slave revolt in morality accompanies the development of the bad conscience, which, in turn, is a result of our enculturation. With an alternative system of evaluation and the bad conscience both in place, the morality salesmen prop up the slaves by justifying their existence and start to eat away at the nobility's sense of self-worth, difference and distance, eroding its confidence that what applies to the masses does not apply to it. Slowly, over the centuries, the moralists spread their infection through the masses, giving them a reason to live, and, eventually, they poison the noble classes as well, contaminating them with guilt about their well-being.

Still, for all the historical detail of Essays I and II, neither essay completely answers some fundamental questions. First, Essay I does not answer the question, *why* was the slave revolt successful? Essay I *describes* what happened, but it does not *explain* why the nobles did not simply turn their backs on the slaves and the morality salesmen and go their own way. And, secondly, why, of all the ways the bad conscience can be dealt with, does Christianity and its prescriptions for the alleviation of suffering come to dominate all others? Again, Essay II *describes* the development of diachronic identity, responsibility and guilt, which are necessary for morality, but it does not *explain* how morality, Christian morality in particular, capitalized on them to become the pre-eminent mode of evaluation. So it is up to Essay III to answer these questions.

The first eleven sections of Essay III describe the ways in which ascetic ideals are used by artists and philosophers. Nietzsche discusses artists in the first six sections and philosophers in the next five. Let us focus on the manner in which philosophers use ascetic ideals. The philosopher uses chastity, humility and poverty as bridges to independence from contemporary culture:

> What, then, is the meaning of the ascetic ideal in the case of a philosopher? My answer is – you will have guessed it long ago: the philosopher sees in it an optimum condition for the highest and boldest spirituality and smiles – he does *not* deny "existence," he rather affirms *his* existence and *only* his existence, and this perhaps to the point at which he is not far from harboring the impious wish *pereat mundus, fiat philosophia, fiat philosophus,* **fiam!** (Let the world perish, but let there be philosophy, let there be the philosopher, *me!*). (GM III 7)

For the philosopher, adoption of chastity, humility, and poverty is prudential. It is by their cultivation that the philosophical animal "achieves its maximal feeling of power" (*GM* III 7). Otherwise put, they are a means to augment will to power. Since what is true of philosophers is true of other "great, fruitful, inventive spirits" (*GM* III 8), many truly great individuals have licence to practise them as well, for by their cultivation we also cultivate discipline and self-overcoming. Philosophers see the ascetic ideals as means of expressing their own power and of becoming and overcoming who they are. Of course, they do not thereby condemn those who deny the value of ascetic ideals. Philosophers recognize that their life is one of a number of distinct kinds of life.

Moral asceticism is a rather different story. Moral ascetics make a blanket judgement against all of life. That is one of the things that sets moral ascetics apart from philosophers, who restrict use of the ascetic ideals to their own lives:

> The ascetic treats life as a wrong road on which one must finally walk back to the point where it begins, or as a mistake that is put right by deeds – that we *ought* to put right: for he *demands* that one go along with him; where he can he compels acceptance of *his* evaluation of existence. (*GM* III 11)

So unlike philosophers who use ascetic ideals as instrumental values to enhance their peculiar kind of life, as a means to the end of philosophical insight, moral ascetics affirm ascetic ideals as an intrinsic end, as the highest goal of *every* life. Moral ascetics reject life and compel others to agree with their disgust. Nietzsche makes the point evocatively by imagining another species investigating us from afar:

> Read from a distant star, the majuscule script of our earthly existence would perhaps lead to the conclusion that the earth was the distinctively *ascetic planet*, a nook of disgruntled, arrogant, and offensive creatures filled with a profound disgust at themselves, at the earth, at all life, who inflict as much pain on themselves as they possibly can out of pleasure of inflicting pain – which is probably their only pleasure. (*GM* III 11)

All those who seriously believe that ascetic ideals have any but limited instrumental use are included in this description and that, Nietzsche thinks, is everyone who thinks that moral values are universally binding, for moral values are nothing more than the popularized expression of ascetic ideals.

This sorry state of affairs is the end product of the slave revolt in morality. The ascetic, disgusted with life and resentful of those who are not, parades his self-loathing ideals and insists that they apply to everyone, and apply in particular to those who think contrary to him. Those who are otherwise healthy succumb to this presentation because they share with the ascetic a sense of responsibility and guilt, the cognitive nodes to which the ascetic ideals attach like leeches. Once attached, those ideals suck the life-enhancing drives out of their host, leaving even the healthiest and most interesting nothing but desiccated shells of their former selves.

We now face the paradox fully. The moral ascetic's ideals drain all the life-enhancing drives and yet he offers those ideals as a way to enhance our life. The only resolution to the paradox is to admit that the kind of life actually enhanced by ascetic ideals must already be so debased that only denying the conditions that make life possible in general make this particular kind of life endurable. It is only a sick, decadent and declining life, a life shot through with self-loathing, that could find the prospect of denying drives and strong affects altogether a tonic, a possible prescription for health. Nietzsche puts the matter as follows:

> Where does one not encounter that veiled glance which burdens one with a profound sadness, that inward-turned glance of the born failure which betrays how such a man speaks to himself – that glance which is a sigh! "If only I were someone else," sighs this glance: "but there is no hope of that. I am who I am: how could I ever get free of myself? And yet – I *am sick of myself!*"
>
> It is on such soil, on swampy ground, that every weed, every poisonous plant grows, always so small, so hidden, so false, so saccharine. Here the worms of vengefulness and rancor swarm; here the air stinks of secrets and concealment; here the web of the most malicious of all conspiracies is being spun constantly – the conspiracy of the suffering against the well-constituted and victorious, here the aspect of the victorious is *hated*. ... What do they really want? At least to *represent* justice, love, wisdom, superiority – that is the ambition of the "lowest," the sick. And how skillful such an ambition makes them! Admire above all the forger's skill with which the stamp of virtue, even the ring, the golden-sounding ring of virtue, is here counterfeited. They monopolize virtue, these weak, hopelessly sick people, there is no doubt of it: "we alone are the good and just," they say, "we alone are *hominess bonae voluntatis* (men of good will)". (GM III 14)

The psychology outlined here is at the core of Nietzsche's thinking about morality. All of us seek to be powerful individuals – strong, intelligent, goal-directed, creative, disciplined, rich in contradictions – but only a few ever achieve it, for it is difficult and causes a considerable amount of suffering. The rest of us are failures, know it and are miserable as a result. We hate ourselves for our weakness, uselessness and redundancy, and we hate those who are demonstrably better. So we latch on to any evaluation scheme on which we, *qua* failures, are exemplars, especially if that also means laying low the powerful.

Enter the priest. The priest offers an explanation of our suffering, an explanation of its causes and a cure. According to morality, the source of suffering is not our self-hatred, unrealized dreams and envy of the powerful, but our being power-desiring creatures at all. The priest's recommended cure for our suffering is to extirpate drives and passions altogether, a solution that

Nietzsche sees through: "To *exterminate* the passions and desires merely in order to do away with their folly and its unpleasant consequences – this itself seems to us today merely an acute form of folly" (*TI* "Morality as Anti-Nature" I). Power itself and the desire for it are, for the Christian priest, the great sins. We who desire power are sinners and are therefore responsible for our own suffering (*GM* III 15). The priest offers the ascetic values as a strategy to deaden the suffering caused by unrealizable desires for power. This is a classic consolation strategy: extirpate passion and drive and the desires that follow from them and suffering will cease. Succeeding at this game is of course decadent, but the genius of Christianity and morality is that they offer evaluative systems that permit the failures in life to succeed at *something*, even if what they succeed at is confounding the conditions of a healthy life. Life's failures become themselves by undoing the very conditions that make their life possible.

This is how the paradox is dissolved. The ascetic ideals are contrary to most *healthy* lives but consolations to *sickly* and *unhealthy* lives. So although they are, at best, instrumentally useful to some kinds of mental health, they are necessary to avoid a nihilistic collapse in the unhealthy. How then can Nietzsche criticize the moral ascetic? In the end, what Nietzsche objects to is the ascetic's universalization to everyone of what applies only to him. Morality inverts the natural order of values and thereby provides a reason for life's failures to feel good about themselves, but accomplishing that reversal requires disguising forever its own perspectivity. Christianity and ascetic morality lie about their own perspectivity, denying altogether that they serve the interests only of a group. They pretend to be something they are not and pretend not to be something they are. We shall return to the more rococo extremes of religion in Chapter 2.

Nietzsche adds an extended discussion of science toward the end of Essay III, whose relevance becomes clear only when we realize that he is warning against an all too familiar temptation that emerges once religion has been exposed as an enslaving tyrant. Most people think that *science* can liberate us from and be an alternative to religion and morality. Nietzsche is not most people. To think that he recommends replacing religion with science is not to understand Nietzsche, and anyone who thinks Nietzsche is a staunch defender of science is mistaken. The great hope of the Enlightenment, a hope that is, if anything, more pronounced now than it was during Nietzsche's life, has always been to replace the superstition and myth of folk religion with the clarity and reason of scientific method and scientific truth. We see the consequences of this hope every day, in creationism/evolution debates, abortion debates, debates about insanity and mental illness, arguments about prayer in school, and many others. These debates are inevitable given the assumption that science opposes myth and faith and given the expectation that the findings of science can and should replace religion.

Nietzsche rejects the Enlightenment's optimism in science. He is willing to allow that science can be deployed against Christianity and the absurdities of extra-sensory worlds, altruism and higher beings. However, science itself is nothing more than a secularized expression of exactly what it criticizes: asceticism stripped of metaphysical and moral excess. As such, science is, Nietzsche thinks, the *best* ally moral asceticism can have. After all, both still rely on truth:

> This pair, science and the ascetic ideal, both rest on the same foundation – I have already indicated it: on the same over-estimation of truth (more exactly: on the same belief that truth is inestimable and cannot be criticized). Therefore they are *necessarily* allies, so that if they are to be fought they can only be fought and called in question together. (GM III 25)

If true, the claim that science overestimates the value of truth no less than moral asceticism undermines any view that would have Nietzsche unqualifiedly defending science. On the contrary, he thinks that science, every bit as much as religion, *depends* upon the assumption that there is an objective world beyond all interpretation (even if it is no longer a heavenly realm) that licenses absolute truths that are equally binding on everyone. Likewise, science counsels abstraction from one's own life in order to view the world objectively, an intellectually twisted expression of the moral ascetic's adherence to chastity.

Nietzsche goes further than simply assimilating science to asceticism. He understands that science and asceticism are both attempts to stave off nihilism but are, for all that, nihilistic to the core. For, as he speculates:

> Man, the bravest of animals and the one most accustomed to suffering, does *not* repudiate suffering as such; he *desires* it, he even seeks it out, provided he is shown a *meaning* for it, a *purpose* of suffering. The meaninglessness of suffering, *not* suffering itself, was the curse that lay over mankind so far – *and the ascetic ideal offered man meaning!* It was the only meaning offered so far; any meaning is better than none at all ... In it, suffering was *interpreted*; the tremendous void seemed to have been filled; the door was closed to any kind of suicidal nihilism. (GM III 28)

Nihilism here refers to the collapse of all values and the despair that results from such a collapse. Nietzsche is explicit in his judgement about the salvific function of ascetic ideals. By making the nihilistic ascetic values binding on all, pointless suffering of the masses is replaced with suffering for a reason, namely, our infinite guilt. In a slogan, the ascetic's suffering on behalf of his nihilistic ideals saves him from the nihilism of meaningless suffering.

That, believe it or not, is the conclusion of *The Genealogy of Morals*. The book may seem unrelentingly negative and critical, especially of Christianity (as we shall see in Chapter 2, although Nietzsche is even *more* critical of Christianity in *The Anti-Christ*). Still, for all of his condemnation of Christianity and morality, we have to remember that Nietzsche nowhere excludes himself from the criticism. He is relating his own history because he is discussing modern European history. Let us note here, then, that in so far as Nietzsche allows that consciousness, guilt and a sense of responsibility are required for self-control and self-discipline, and in so far as ascetic ideals are still instrumentally viable, the debts we owe to herd thinking in general and Christianity in particular are enormous. It was, after all, in the herd – the weak, the decadent and the resentful – that such reflection and self-awareness first developed as a force for change. It was the herd that, in their response to the rapacious masters described in Essay I, turned their inevitably frustrated attempts to augment power against others inwards. In that way, they claimed a direct victory over themselves. They became those who have control of themselves and who overcome themselves in exhibitions of self-directed cruelty. And they also accomplished an indirect victory over the strong, but unreflective, masters. They burrowed into the mind of the master and have been watching it rot for a millennium.

No doubt the masters were a little mystified when the herd reacted against them by labelling them evil. After all, they were no more capable of being other than they were than a predator was. But the herd of slaves was different; their misery prompted them into brooding about things, reflecting on things and on themselves. They wanted *explanations* of their misery and *solutions* to it. In this process, they became interesting and devastatingly effective. In some ways, the slaves were like poisonous insects, coming in droning swarms, poisoning the masters by infecting them with slave values and slave ways of thinking until the masters turned against themselves. The masters hobbled around in a stupor of domestication and civility, humbled not by any physical violence done against them, but by their own poisoned psyches.

A necessary condition for the slave revolt's success is that the masters had to be able to reflect on themselves. Otherwise, how would the self-doubt that the slaves infected them with ever find purchase? And that is the second crucial reversal introduced by the slave revolt and the second great debt we all owe to the herd. In the herd, conscious awareness and guilt first developed, and from them they spread into the masters. The development of consciousness and its attendant bad conscience fundamentally changed the human psyche and the future of humanity. As Nietzsche notes, consciousness and the bad conscience were "so new, profound, unheard of, enigmatic, contradictory, and pregnant with a future that the aspect of the earth was essentially altered" (*GM* II 16).

What had happened was nothing less than a Copernican revolution in psychology and morality. Copernicus reoriented astronomy, cosmology and theology by rejecting the view that the Earth was the centre of the universe, replacing it with the heliocentric model with which we are all familiar. The slave revolt in morality was, at least if Nietzsche is right, of comparable significance. Where before reflection was a rare and sporadic episode quickly dismissed as a voice of the gods, now reflection became an everyday occurrence without otherworldly explanation. Where power in the masters had been exercised against the flesh of the weak and against enemies, in the herd, power was internalized. Where the masters had once been the exemplification of a good life, now they became pitiful and barbaric residues of a bygone era. Where the slaves had once been the pawns of the masters, they now became the exemplars of a new regime of power, one focused inwards rather than outwards, a regime bent on power enhancement by self-improvement rather than by acts of violence against others. Refocusing our drive for power within our own bodies and psyches opened up worlds of refinement undreamt of by the uni-dimensional masters, who were no more capable of becoming a Beethoven than a beetroot might be, no more capable of thinking about mathematics than a dog. And this Copernican revolution of our interior life was premised on the discovery and cultivation of reflective consciousness and guilt. It succeeded, of course, but more importantly it sowed the seeds for the extraordinary accomplishments of the past two thousand years.

The highly condensed discussions in the latter part of Essay III are, it is to be admitted, depressing. But they also reveal the awful virtuosity of Nietzsche's intellect. Especially towards the end of this essay, claim after incredible claim flows out of Nietzsche's pen at a dizzying rate, as if he could not capture in writing all that he was thinking. Indeed, Essay III introduces in one way or another all the topics we shall cover in the remainder of this book. We have already postponed until Chapter 2 a detailed discussion of the role of the priest in promulgating decadence and resentment. We must now postpone until Chapter 3 discussion of the nihilistic consequences of asceticism introduced in Essay III, sections 27 and 28. It will take another entire chapter, Chapter 4, to unpack the metaphysical issues Nietzsche raises about science in section 26. We shall dedicate two more chapters, Chapters 5 and 6, to the epistemological and logical issues introduced in sections 25 and 27. Chapter 7 tries to understand the psychology that lies behind Nietzsche's assimilation of the scientific spirit to the ascetic ideal discussed in sections 25 and 26. Only then shall we be able to understand what Nietzsche is talking about in section 27 when he introduces the law of life and self-overcoming. We shall address that topic in Chapter 8, where we discuss the will to power. With that in hand, we shall finally be able to broach, in Chapter 9, the topic of law-giving, mentioned only in passing in section 27, which Nietzsche thinks is central to a flourishing life.

# CHAPTER 2
# Religion

Nietzsche is the most notorious philosopher because he is alleged to be an anti-Semite, a proto-Fascist and an anti-Christian. He is neither anti-Semite nor proto-Fascist, but he is anti-Christian. Nietzsche announces that God is dead in *The Gay Science* and spells out the reasons in his searing attack on Christianity in *The Anti-Christ*. This book in particular has made Nietzsche a target of vilification by most Christians and political conservatives. Unlike the other two sources of infamy, however, Nietzsche's notoriety on *this* score is accurately attributed and entirely deserved. He despises most religions and Christianity in particular. Consider:

> In Christianity neither morality nor religion come into contact with reality at any point. Nothing but imaginary *causes* ("God", "soul", "ego", "spirit", "free will", – or "unfree will"); nothing but imaginary *effects* ("sin", "redemption", "grace", "punishment", "forgiveness of sins"). A traffic between imaginary *beings* ("God", "spirits", "souls"); an imaginary *natural* science (anthropocentric; complete lack of the concept of natural causes); an imaginary *psychology* (nothing but self-misunderstandings, interpretations of pleasant or unpleasant general feelings, for example the condition of the *nervus sympatheticus*, with the aid of the sign-language of religio-moral idiosyncrasy – "repentance", "sting of conscience", "temptation by the Devil", "the proximity of God"); an imaginary *teleology* ("the kingdom of God", "the Last Judgment", "eternal life"). (*AC* 15)

Christianity is a fraud on every level imaginable: psychological, teleological, ethical, cosmological and scientific. It is, from start to finish, nothing but lies motivated by the vile aspiration to destroy what is best in humanity. The conclusion of *The Anti-Christ* is explicit: "I call Christianity the *one* great curse, the *one* great intrinsic depravity, the *one* great instinct for revenge for which no expedient is sufficiently poisonous, secret, subterranean, *petty* – I call it the *one* mortal blemish of mankind" (*AC* 62).

Still, for all the venom he spits at Christianity, we have also to remember that there are religions Nietzsche is rather fond of and gods that Nietzsche openly admires. Moreover, he is well aware, and discusses in some detail, that were it not for Christianity humanity would have remained in the doldrums of an uncouth and unconscious social world dominated by the brutish masters described in Essay 1 of *The Genealogy of Morals*. He is even prepared to admit that without Christianity we would not be in the position we now find ourselves in: disillusioned but presented with a new world of possibility opened up only by the revelation that Christianity was an error.

Some try to dismiss Nietzsche's criticism of religion as the output of a deranged mind. True enough, the book in which his most sustained attacks of Christianity, *The Anti-Christ*, is his last published work; true too, it is more fragmentary and hyperbolic than any of his other published works. The final paragraphs in particular are rather shrill. Nonetheless, *The Anti-Christ* is also among Nietzsche's most accessible books, and its polemical style, designed to enrage, is, because it is far less subtle than others of his works, far easier to understand. Indeed, Nietzsche's original intention was to have *The Anti-Christ* serve as an introduction to his planned but never completed *Will to Power*.

Nietzsche thinks the good Christian, someone whose altruism camouflages a hidden nihilism and hatred of life, is pathetic. For the bad Christian, someone who mouths Christian slogans but acts from resentment, revenge and oppressive power-lust, Nietzsche's loathing knows no boundaries. Yet Nietzsche also openly admires Jesus as one of the noblest men ever to have lived, and he thinks that there is a great deal to be learnt from Jesus, even if, in the final analysis, what is to be learnt is contrary to what he thinks is crucial for a flourishing human life. Likewise, although Buddhism is decadent to the core, Nietzsche praises it for being "a hundred times more realistic that Christianity" (*AC* 20) and for being the first positivistic (that is, scientific) religion. Here, as in so much that has to do with Nietzsche, his subtlety is entirely lost on those who rush to condemn him. So in this chapter, we shall investigate his criticism of religion. We begin with Christianity and then discuss Buddhism.

## Christianity

Surprisingly, Nietzsche's rejection of God does not play a central role in any of his attacks on Christianity. Since he believes that there is no God as

Christians think of God – divine, transcendent, omnipotent, omniscient, omnibenevolent – he sees no point in criticizing Christians on the grounds that they think God exists. Nietzsche believes that wherever they develop, gods are always and only projections of their host culture's self-image. On the basis of this assumption, Nietzsche ranks gods on being projections of the best or worst a culture has to offer. The Greek gods, which exemplify the strengths of the Greeks, those characteristics that made them unique, proud, a group to be reckoned with and held in awe, are much more admirable than the Christian God because the Christian God is so ridiculous a god that even were he to have existed, he would have no right to exist.

With that sarcastic assertion in mind, consider the famous passages from *The Gay Science* and *The Anti-Christ* that assert that God is dead:

> After Buddha was dead, his shadow was still shown for centuries in a cave – a tremendous, gruesome shadow. God is dead; but given the way of men, there may still be caves for thousands of years in which his shadow will be shown. – And we – we still have to vanquish his shadow, too.　　　　　　　　(GS 108)

> Have you not heard of that madman who lit a lantern in the bright morning hours, ran to the market place, and cried incessantly: "I seek God! I seek God!" – As many of those who did not believe in God were standing around just then, he provoked much laughter. Has he got lost? Asked one. Did he lose his way like a child? Asked another. Or is he hiding? Is he afraid of us? Has he gone on a voyage? Emigrated? – Thus they yelled and laughed.
>
> The madman jumped into their midst and pierced them with his eyes. "Whither is God?" he cried; "I will tell you. *We have killed him* – you and I. All of us are his murderers. ... God is dead. God remains dead. And we have killed him.　　　　　　(GS 125)

> What sets *us* apart is not that we recognize no God, either in history or in nature or behind nature – but that we find that which has been reverenced as God not "godlike" but pitiable, absurd, harmful, not merely an error but a *crime against life* ... We deny God as God ... If this God of the Christians were *proved* to us to exist, we should know even less how to believe in him. – In a formula: *Deus, qualem Paulus creavit, dei negatio* (God, as Paul created him, is a denial of God).　　　　　(AC 47)

The first passage raises the spectre of nihilism, a topic to which we shall return in Chapter 3. God's shadow lurks everywhere, and the vapours of his existence will continue to pervade European culture for a long time, most notably in the felt loss of established moral value and metaphysical stability. In the second passage, Nietzsche asserts that we are responsible for God's death, which suggests not only that there once was a God, but, amazingly, that he has been put out of his misery because he has outlived his usefulness. On Nietzsche's view, God did not get bored or disgusted with us and change the channel; rather, God has lost whatever function he once had because of the actions taken by those who believed in him. Likewise, the final passage does not deny that there might be a valuable god, but claims instead that God is so absurd that he could not be believed in even if he were to exist.

What Nietzsche finds most objectionable about the Christian God is that he has been fashioned after the needs of the weak. The Christian God, a personal God, has nothing of the awe-inspiring dreadfulness of great gods. Having been modelled after the herd, the Christian God is mediocre in comparison:

> Possessing even the tiniest bit of piety in the body, we should find a god who cures a cold at the right time or who bids us enter a coach at the very moment when a violent rainstorm begins, such an absurd god that we should have to abolish him if he existed. A god as servant, as mailman, as calendar man – at bottom, a word for the most stupid of all accidents. Divine providence of the kind in which approximately every third person in educated Germany still believes would be an objection to God so strong that one simply could not imagine a stronger one. And in any case, it is an objection to the Germans! (AC 52)

The last crack should be kept in mind whenever anyone tries to suggest that Nietzsche was a proto-German nationalist. This remark, along with dozens of others, makes it abundantly clear that Nietzsche was embarrassed by Germany and embarrassed to be a German.

Without the divinity of God to prop Christianity up, Nietzsche turns his attention instead to the figure of Jesus and the historical institution of Christianity. Nietzsche is fascinated by Jesus and repulsed by the institution. As an exemplar, as a symbolist, as a psychological type, Nietzsche thinks Jesus has *no* equal in *all* human history. In fact, Nietzsche's opinion of Jesus is so high that he is willing to consider him an example of a type of individual that he frequently praises: the free spirit. So whatever criticisms Nietzsche levels against typical Christian doctrines and Christian psychological profiles completely miss their mark when applied to Jesus, whom Nietzsche recognizes as unique. As he notes: "In reality there has been only one Christian, and he died on the Cross. The 'Evangel' died on the Cross. What was called

'Evangel' from this moment onwards was already the opposite of what *he* had lived: '*bad* tidings,' a *dysangel*" (*AC* 39). And, a little later in the same section: "*In fact there have been no Christians at all*. The 'Christian', that which has been called Christian for two millenia, is merely a psychological misunder-standing." Hence, the only Christian to have lived, the Evangel Jesus, is distinct from the community that took shape upon his death, the dysangelic Christians.

This distinction is grounded in the differences between Jesus's exem-plary life and extraordinary psychology, on the one hand, and Christian doctrine and the herd psychology of Christians on the other. Although he disavows Jesus's glad tidings as nasty bits of decadence, the *example* Jesus sets as a person who lives on earth as if he were already in heaven is something that Nietzsche finds unrivalled:

> One could, with some freedom of expression, call Jesus a "free spirit" – he cares nothing for what is fixed: the word *killeth*, everything fixed *killeth*. The concept, the *experience* "life" in the only form he knows it is opposed to any kind of word, formula, law, faith, dogma. He speaks only of the inmost thing: "life" or "truth" or "light" is his expression for the inmost thing – everything else, the whole of reality, the whole of nature, language itself, possesses for him merely the value of a sign, a metaphor . . . [S]uch a symbolist *par excellence* stands outside of all religion, all conceptions of divine worship, all history, all natural science, all experience of the world, all acquirements, all politics, all psychology, all books, all art – his "knowledge" is precisely the *pure folly* of the fact *that* anything of this kind exists.                                   (*AC* 32)

Again, Nietzsche praises Jesus because:

> This bringer of glad tidings died as he had lived, as he had taught – *not* to redeem men but to show how one must live. What he bequeathed to mankind is his *practice*: his bearing before the judges, before the guards, before the accusers and every kind of calumny and mockery – his bearing on the *Cross*. He does not resist, he does not defend his rights, he takes no steps to avert the worst that can happen to him – more, he *provokes* it. . . . *Not* to defend oneself, *not* to grow angry, *not* to make responsible . . . But not to resist even the evil man – to *love* him . . ..          (*AC* 35)

In both passages, Nietzsche lauds Jesus because in him there can be found no rancour, no *ressentiment*, no hatred, and because he, more than anyone before or since, lives as if there were no difference between heaven and earth. Jesus is beyond all petty human emotions because he has convinced himself that he is nothing more than a conduit for God's will. By the time of the Passion, there is nothing left of Jesus – he has emptied himself out and become a vessel through which God acts on earth. For Nietzsche, this is nothing short of uncanny: *why* would anyone do this and *how* could it ever be successful? He is baffled by Jesus's example and makes no pretence to fully understand it.

Despite Jesus's exemplary life, the content of Jesus's teaching is decadent, in Nietzsche's sense of the term, by which we understand being against life (*AC* 6). Jesus's teaching counselled internal peace by submission of all of one's intentions to those of God. On Nietzsche's view, Jesus's glad tidings are that "True life, eternal life is found – it is not promised, it is here, it is *within you*: as life lived in love, in love without deduction or exclusion, without distance" (*AC* 29). *Agape* – impersonal, non-erotic, love – is, Nietzsche is prepared to admit, so completely embodied in the person of Jesus that, were we only able to believe that *agape* is a virtue, he would be well worth following. Unfortunately, draining ourselves of passions and drives – prerequisites of *agape* love (love "without deduction or exclusion" as Nietzsche puts it) – is anything but a Nietzschean virtue. Eliminating our internal war is antithetical to Nietzsche's whole moral psychology because it requires eradicating the emotions that enhance the feeling for life. So although Nietzsche admires Jesus as someone whose practice of a kind of life is exemplary, Nietzsche rejects the life so exemplified.

Matters are not as ambivalent with the historical institution of Christianity, for which Nietzsche shows almost nothing but contempt. Nietzsche has four primary complaints against Christianity: it perverts Jesus's message; it is decadent; it is a causal consequence of, and reinforcing agent for, *ressentiment*; and it is irrational. Take the charges in order.

According to Nietzsche, Jesus bequeathed to his followers his practice, a way of life in which doctrine was mere symbolism and belief superfluous. It is in part because this is all that Jesus taught that his life is exemplary. Jesus rejects intellectual sophistication altogether and suggests that what leads to a flourishing life is abandonment of all intention so as to permit God's will to be one's own. Now, rejection of intellectual sophistication and abandonment of intention are utterly foreign to Nietzsche, but one result of Jesus's practical teaching is not entirely dissimilar to some of what Nietzsche advocates on behalf of philosophers and other free spirits. Living as Nietzsche's Jesus did directly entails rejection of whatever culture we find ourselves inhabiting. If our passions and intentions are replaced *in toto* by God's, then no other moral authority, including our own or that of our culture, may be permitted to speak. As we shall see in Chapter 3, rejecting contemporary culture is superficially similar to Nietzsche's nihilism and revaluation of values. Of course, the similarities are only superficial. The stance Jesus and Nietzsche take against contemporary culture are outcomes of diametrically opposed attitudes toward life and in each that stance has divergent consequences as well.

One of Nietzsche's primary tasks is to explain how Jesus's teaching – how to become, quite literally, a *child* of God – changed to having as its emphasis belief in a set of doctrines and creeds. There must, he thinks, be a reason why Jesus's teachings were ignored almost immediately by his followers. Nietzsche is not shy in suggesting it. Those who followed Jesus were less interested in what he taught than in initiating a social movement with him as their mythical leader and themselves as his representatives and figures of authority for the movement. In the central sections of *The Anti-Christ* (*AC* 39–46), Nietzsche offers a genealogy of Christianity to support his contention. The main villain in this history is St Paul. Nietzsche attributes to Paul and the other Apostles the intention to begin a cult. Accomplishing this task entailed regimentation of the little band of followers, and that was accomplished by creating, first, a myth about their spiritual leader's death that galvanized support within and for the group; secondly, an explanation of their leader's death that identified guilty parties; thirdly, a myth about Jesus's return; and, finally, a set of doctrines belief in which became a condition of membership in the group. These were of course utterly foreign to the teachings of Jesus, who taught only a change in one's state of being. However, those responsible for the change no longer had Jesus to oppose their designs.

Whether Nietzsche's history of early Christianity is accurate is a matter of debate. Stripped of its rhetorical excesses, his story of early Christianity is fairly close to what some contemporary scholars of Christianity affirm. Other scholars also mark a distinction between Jesus's unique life and non-doctrinal example, on the one hand, and Paul's role in fixing the doctrinal content and binding myths that forged the community of Christians in a hostile Roman world.* What is more salient for our purposes is Nietzsche's claim that the early fathers of Christianity were fueled by decadence, *ressentiment* and ambition. Now, attributing to the early Christians decadence, *ressentiment* and ambitious intentions is not supported by any biblical text, but that is not conclusive disconfirmation of Nietzsche's claims. For it is readily apparent that intentions can be camouflaged by noble-sounding rhetoric and that a proposition that might be true and

---

* See, for example, W. Meeks, *The First Urban Christians*, 2nd edn (New Haven, CT: Yale University Press, 2003) and T. Sheehan, *The First Coming* (New York: Vintage, 1988).

warranted can be used to engender beliefs that are quite inconsistent with the claim; politicians of all kinds rely on this capacity of language. So it is at least plausible that early Christian leaders used the teachings strategically to advance their own ambitions. Nor is it implausible to suppose that establishing Christian doctrine was accomplished by drawing from Jesus's teachings implications that did not in fact follow from them but that were compatible with the interests of early Christianity. Attributing such strategies to individuals with whom he disagrees is a favourite ploy of Nietzsche's. Of course, Nietzsche's criticism of Christianity is convincing only to the degree that his attribution of decadence, *ressentiment* and ambition is convincing. At least this much is clear: *ressentiment* and ambition are opposed to what Jesus taught. By Nietzsche's own admission, Jesus was free of *ressentiment*, as *The Anti-Christ* makes clear: "the little community did not understand the main point, the exemplary character of his kind of death, the freedom, the superiority over any feeling of *ressentiment*" (AC 40).

Christian decadence is a fuller and more lavish development of Jesus's own decadence. As argued above, Jesus was a decadent because he simply renounced his own intentions and passions and replaced them with God's commandment to love everyone without exception. Christianity takes Jesus's example and, by codifying it, both loses everything unique and compelling about Jesus and erects a structure of decadent doctrines and institutions around their leader that have nothing to do with his exemplary life. Christianity takes Jesus's practice of decadence and turns it into an entire edifice of decadence, every room of which has some new decadent surprise hidden in it. From the myth of Jesus's resurrection to the promise of his return, from the two-world metaphysics that Christianity cannot survive without to the fictional psychological explanations that metaphysical view imposes, from the inversion of ethical values in the slave revolt to the elevation of the priest as a moral example, from the promise of eternal blessedness in heaven to the condemnation of this life, Christianity is, for Nietzsche, a work of decadent genius.

Pity is a prime example of decadence. Pity is only one of a number of types of concern for another's suffering, others being empathy, sympathy, compassion and mercy. What distinguishes pity from these others is that pity conserves suffering and multiplies it. Pity is occasioned by another's suffering but is conjoined with a disposition to keep that suffering alive and salient as a symptom of our deep understanding of the despair that this earthly life engenders. That is the *conserving* part of pity. Secondly, when we pity another person's suffering we add our own suffering to that of others. That is the *multiplying* part of pity. Finally, pitying convinces us that such suffering is inevitable and that, as a result, it actually has moral value. Our suffering becomes a criterion of our faith and right thinking.

Nietzsche thinks this is madness. He does not deny that there is suffering; indeed, he believes that there is a lot of it, and he acknowledges that the worst thing about it is not its existence but its pointlessness (we shall return to these issues in Chapter 3). The point here is that pity provides those who have no other explanation of their suffering a wholly *fictitious* explanation of it. As any institutional representative of Christianity is happy to point out, we disobeyed God and were cast out of Eden in order to suffer. It is the *human lot* to suffer. Pity serves as a tactic for revealing the ubiquity and appropriateness of suffering and our culpability in it. Nietzsche puts it this way in *The Genealogy of Morals*:

> "I suffer: someone must be to blame for it" – thus thinks every sickly sheep. But his shepherd, the ascetic priest, tells him: "Quite so, my sheep! Someone must be to blame for it: but you yourself are this someone, you alone are to blame for it – *you alone are to blame for yourself*!" (GM III 15)

Once we are convinced that pity is the suitable response to suffering, the game is up. Upon the epiphany prompted by pity, the Christian priest jumps in not only with his explanation of our suffering and our guilt, but with a cure for it as well: have faith in God, subject yourself to the Church as God's earthly representative, and prepare yourself for heaven by doing what the Church tells you to do. It is a wonderful package deal. The Christian makes us sick and then offers his potions as the cure for that sickness.

These accusations, if true, are among the most thoroughgoing denunciations of Christianity ever broached. Nietzsche is saying more than that Christianity is an opium of the people, a way of deadening pain, as Karl Marx famously suggested. Nietzsche thinks that Christians are not just junkies using religion to anaesthetize their suffering; he thinks they are their own pushers. After all, Christianity *invents* most of the pain it pretends to cure, parades that invention around as if it were a *discovery* about the human condition, *prescribes* a cure for it and then *supplies* everything necessary to induce dependence. This analysis explains Nietzsche's otherwise incredible claim that in Christian-influenced moralities all values are not just wrong but inverted and reversed, that all utterances of Christians are lies and falsehoods, and that Christians are a negative criterion of truth:

> Every word in the mouth of a "first Christian" is a lie, every act he performs an instinctive falsehood – all his values, all his aims are harmful, but *whomever* he hates, *whatever* he hates, *has value* ...

> The Christian, the priestly Christian especially, is a *criterion of values*.                                                        (AC 46)

This judgement is warranted, Nietzsche thinks, because the Christian priest starts from decadence, so every claim he makes will be coloured by that decadence. It is completely predictable that Christians conclude that this life is worthless and only a preparation for heaven: after all, it is their most deeply held assumption. Any argument of the form *p*; therefore *p*, is ironclad.

Consider *ressentiment* next. *Ressentiment* is a technical term in Nietzsche's work, one that he borrows from French. *Ressentiment* refers to a set of psychological dispositions and character traits that are reactive states against insult and injury. *Ressentimentful* states are found in those whose direct attempts to respond to insult and injury would entail further insult and injury. We might say the following: A psychological state is a *ressentimentful* state if and only if: (i) it is a state of anger or frustration; (ii) its cause is insult or injury by another or recognition of one's ill-constitutedness; and (iii) direct reprisal against an agent of insult or injury is known to have as a likely consequence further insult and injury. Clause (i) distinguishes *ressentimentful* states from other states an ill-constituted person might have. Clause (ii) identifies the state as a causal result of certain actions of others or ourselves and so distinguishes *ressentimentful* anger or frustration from other kinds of frustration and anger (such as frustration about our incapacity for tolerating opera). Clause (iii) distinguishes *ressentimentful* states from other reactive states that we might consider were we confident of success, such as reprisal. It is only humans who are properly capable of *ressentiment* because only humans are conscious and sufficiently complex to recognize consciously their own weakness, to plot and to strategize. Some paradigm examples of *ressentimentful* states are, of course, resentment, revenge, corrupt desires for insulting others, envy, self-pity and other-directed pity, and desires for retribution. Some examples of products of *ressentiment* are strategies to weaken the agents of insults and consolation strategies to make ourselves feel better.

Pity is, for Nietzsche, also a *ressentimentful* state. In pity we respond to another's suffering, but the other's suffering is also the occasion for calibrating our minimally better lot *vis-à-vis* the other at that time. This comparison reveals pity's unexpressed but presupposed *ressentiment*, for such calibration is possible only if we antecedently equate ourselves with the sufferer and his weakness, and therefore only if we antecedently are frustrated with our own ill-constitutedness. This anger and frustration is, as we have already seen, constitutive of *ressentiment*.

It is hard to overemphasize the importance that *ressentiment* plays in Nietzsche's assessment of the Christian psychological profile. Nietzsche believes that contemporary Europe is dominated by *ressentimentful* evaluative codes, even to the extent that those who should, by rights, be exempt from their reach feel themselves bound by them and even to the extent that those who fight against them tend only to add further twists to those codes without understanding that their reaction against them is determined by them. This is, after all, why the slave revolt in morality has been victorious. When even the most powerful are constrained by herd values in voicing their opposition to them, the slave revolt has clearly won, for it sets the agenda for any opposition to itself. Those who oppose herd values now start their opposition so deeply influenced by those values that any reversion to the masters is anachronistic foolishness and any wilful assertion of independence from them empty rhetoric. For better or worse, those of us who want to oppose Christian values have to start by admitting that we too uphold them and are thoroughly stained by them.

*Ressentiment* is often affiliated with decadence, but the two are distinct. Jesus and Buddha, for example, are both decadents but neither are agents of *ressentiment*. The difference between *ressentiment* and decadence is that decadent states of being, although the causal result of being ill-constituted, do not, as do *ressentimentful* states, take the downfall or elimination of the well-constituted as a goal. Decadence expresses itself as moral codes that value what is contrary to life, but they do not, as do *ressentimentful* moral codes, prescribe active strategies for undermining the powerful. *Ressentiment* is not the *only* or *best* reaction to self-loathing, but it is a most *creative* reaction to that self-loathing, for it redirects loathing away from ourselves and on to the powerful.

That we can redirect our hatred on to another is, of course, why Jesus remains such a magnetically attractive model to those who suffer but cannot on their own overcome their narcissism to renounce blaming others for their suffering. He presents to decadent Christians an exemplar of a life free of *ressentiment* to which even they can aspire. Of course, his model can be realized only if they completely transcend themselves and their inevitably frustrated desires, and that will never happen, since Christians, no less than all other human beings, are *nothing but* passions and desires (we investigate this startling psychology in Chapter 7). But at least they have the good company of their congregation helping them along the impossible path.

Nietzsche's disclosure of *ressentiment* in the depths of the Christian psychological profile is one of his most enduring contributions to our self-understanding as Westerners. When it comes right down to it, he is profoundly *concerned* about all of us, even Christians. This is *his* "love of man" (*AC* 2). And, at its core, his concern is the sorrowful and compassionate admission that we have done this to ourselves. He looks around himself and sees pervasive resentment, decadence and suffering. He thinks that he has found a key to understanding this sickness: it is a self-created and self-imposed regime of self- and other-directed hatred, in part explanatory, in part prescriptive, that shows the fantastic lengths we shall go to in an effort to avoid emptiness. We would rather consume ourselves with orgies of *ressentiment* and daily inject ourselves with decadence than admit that we cannot confront a world without the meaning God provides. That is astonishing, perverse and, because it is in the end unnecessary, heartbreaking.

Finally, Nietzsche claims that Christianity is irrational, its irrationality expressed in a hatred of science and a reliance on faith. He is no doubt right that Christianity is anti-science. From Luther's insistence that we should tear out the eye of reason to contemporary creationism debates, Christianity has a long and embarrassing tradition of rejecting science and reason. The explanation is straightforward: faith in God and his hierarchy of earthly representatives requires a lack of knowledge. That much follows directly from the story of Eden, according to which Eve tempts Adam into tasting from the tree of knowledge of good and evil. By acting on our will to knowledge we become godlike, for knowledge is a form of power. The Christian God abhors our presumption to be equal to him:

> The old God was seized with hellish fear. Man himself had turned out to be his *greatest* mistake; he had created a rival for himself; science makes godlike – it is all over with priests and gods when man becomes scientific. Moral: science is the forbidden as such – it alone is forbidden. Science is the *first* sin, the seed of all sin, the *original* sin. *This alone is morality.* "Thou shalt not know" – the rest follows. (*AC* 48)

From this argument, Nietzsche draws a remarkable conclusion: that sin was invented to *ensure* suffering. "Sin, to repeat it once more, this form of man's self-violation par excellence, was invented to make science, culture, every elevation and nobility of man, impossible; the priest rules the invention of sin" (*AC* 49). This looks like a *non sequitur*: how could sin have been invented to make us suffer? Suffering is, according to Christianity, the *result* of sin, not its *cause*. The Nietzschean answer is that Christianity gets the direction of causality backwards. The entire psychological economy of sin, guilt, punishment, grace, redemption and forgiveness is a lie, a lie driven by the need to "assassinate cause and effect" (*AC* 49).

With the observation that Christian views represent nothing less than a reversal of the natural direction of causality, Nietzsche ridicules the entire doctrinal structure of Christianity as one mistake heaped upon another. It is abundantly clear from Nietzsche's criticism that he believes that there is an alternative view of things that respects natural causality, is scientific and lacks the deleterious psychological consequences of Christianity. In *The Anti-Christ*, this alternative is only alluded to in passing. Nowhere in this work does Nietzsche explain in any detail that preferred alternative; he leaves that task to *Beyond Good and Evil*, *Twilight of the Idols* and *The Gay Science*. But an observation is in order here. The success of his criticism of Christianity depends in no small measure on the plausibility of his alternative views on causality, truth, human psychology and science. His critique of Christianity is that it is anti-natural, reverses the direction of causality, is shot through with bogus explanations and demonstrably false claims and is hostile to science. If his own developed views are no more natural, no more respectful of the natural direction of causality, no more tolerant of science than Christianity's, his criticism of Christianity is weakened considerably. We shall have to look at his alternatives carefully in the subsequent chapters to make sure that his reasons for attacking Christianity do not boomerang back on his own views.

## Buddhism

Nietzsche is much kinder to Buddhism than he is to Christianity. Although Buddhism is decadent, not only is the Buddha free of *ressentiment* but so too is the social institution of Buddhism. Buddhism escapes *ressentiment* for a number of reasons, and they are worth examining, for they show both how decadence can exist without God as its symbol and how perilously close to nihilism we come when we embrace decadent moral values.

It might strike us as a little unusual for a philosopher so deeply engrained within the Western philosophical tradition to say anything about Buddhism. However, this is one of those places where Nietzsche's wide range of interests reveals itself. Nietzsche was, at least early in his career, deeply influenced by the work of Arthur Schopenhauer, and Schopenhauer was, in turn, deeply influenced by Eastern thought, especially the thought of Hinduism and Buddhism. As we saw in the Introduction, Nietzsche read Schopenhauer's *The World as Will and Representation* when he was still in his twenties, and was so impressed with it that Schopenhauer always remained for him his single most important teacher. In *The World as Will and Representation*, Schopenhauer argued that life would never provide permanent happiness, that it was shot through with dissatisfaction and suffering, and that the solution was to eradicate the will to live. This argument came straight out of the Buddhist tradition. Nietzsche also read three other books on Buddhism by German religious scholars. So his knowledge of Buddhism derives completely from Schopenhauer's appropriation of it and from scholarly texts written by German intellectuals rather than from any first-hand experience with Buddhism as it was practiced in the nineteenth century. This helps to explain his apparent complete ignorance of folk Buddhism, a motley of doctrines, liturgical practices, daily routines, and mythologies that is as bizarre and pettifogging as the folk Christianity he ridicules in *The Anti-Christ*. At least part of the difference Nietzsche detects between Buddhism and Christianity and his preference for Buddhism are functions of nothing more than his daily familiarity with the worst excesses of folk Christianity and his unfamiliarity with the deification of Buddha by peasants everywhere Buddhism is practised. He saw Christianity at its worst in Germany, but never had the chance to see Buddhism at anything but its best as depicted by sympathetic scholars.

Be that as it may, there are real philosophical differences between Christianity and Buddhism. The first is that Buddhism does away with God, so it has no need for the fictitious psychologies of souls and miraculous causes, no need for moral mystifications such as sin, redemption and grace, no need for realms wholly separate from this world. Furthermore, without God and heaven, there is in Buddhism no need for jealousy between it and other religions, no need for prayer, no need for displays of faith, and no desire to spread misery as though it were a gift. Buddhism starts not with sin, which is a particular interpretation of suffering, but with suffering itself. This alone makes Buddhism a much more interesting religion to Nietzsche. First, starting with suffering is more scientific than starting with sin, and for this reason Nietzsche is willing to call Buddhism the first "positivistic" religion (*AC* 20) and the first "objective" religion (*AC* 23). Secondly, without the built-in guilt from sin, Buddhism is already beyond the moral evaluative system of the slaves, beyond herd morality, or, as Nietzsche puts it, echoing the title of one of his own books, "beyond good and evil" (*AC* 20). Thirdly, by recommending that we ease our suffering by practising moderation, benevolence and tranquility, Buddhism defuses the circuits of comparison, hatred and scheming that are constitutive of *ressentiment*.

Primarily because Buddhism arises in a mature culture in which the barbarous passions have already long since been re-channelled, Nietzsche thinks that Buddhism is a much more mature religion than Christianity. Contrary to Christianity, which postulates transcendent beings as overseers and which tries to gain control over the rancour and bitterness of the failures of life, Buddhism calmly accepts the unavoidability of suffering without trying to lay blame for its occurrence on anyone. This is already a considerable advance over Christianity and one of the reasons why Nietzsche thinks that, once we Europeans finally shake Christianity off, we may go through a period of Buddhistic nihilism (*WP* 132).

Suffering is, according to the Buddha, endemic to the human condition. With that Nietzsche agrees and he commends Buddhism for refraining from interpreting suffering as guilt and sin. Yet, despite its accuracy in assessing the prevalence of suffering, Buddhism goes wrong in its prescription for the alleviation of suffering. For Buddhism, suffering is caused by desire (or thirst) for things, for experiences, for self-improve-ment, for other people, that must inevitably go unsatisfied. Buddhism suggests that there is a cure for the suffering resulting from desire. We should, it suggests, eliminate desire altogether, since desiring is both necessary and sufficient for suffering. That is, without desire, there will be no suffering, and, given desire, there will be suffering. The practice of Buddhism is a regimen of mental and physical activities for eradicating desire. The Buddhist argument is quite simple, really (in fact, drained of specific cultural content, it is every decadent's argument). First, we observe that there is suffering. Secondly, we claim that suffering is bad. Thirdly, we locate the source of suffering in our psychological capacity to desire. Fourthly, we make the obvious claim that if something is bad, then we should work to eliminate it. Fifthly, we recommend eliminating desire as the cure for our suffering. We conclude with the injunction to strive to cut out our desires.

There is, Nietzsche admits, something compelling about this analysis of suffering. He agrees that suffering is an ineliminable aspect of human existence, that it is caused by desire and that we could eliminate suffering if we could turn ourselves into passionless blobs. In a number of other significant ways as well, Buddhism anticipates Nietzsche's own critical assessments of such philosophical concepts as the self, two-world meta-physics, causality and *ressentiment*. For example, with Nietzsche, Buddhism denies outright that there is anything like a soul, that is, a self-substance that remains identical over time and is separable from us at death and God-given. Instead, Buddhism analyses away the self by, first, distinguishing between the *experience* of a self and the *existence* of a self and, secondly, by *reducing* the existence of a self to the experience of a self, and then showing that experience of a self does not require a permanent, transcendent entity. Likewise, neither Buddhism nor Nietzsche have any patience for views of the world according to which there are substances that are self-sufficient and separable from the properties they have and enter into determinate causal relations. In fact, Buddhism's view that the world is composed of entities standing in relations of co-dependent co-origination, according to which everything is dependent upon everything else, mirrors exactly some of Nietzsche's own reflections on causation, as we shall see in Chapters 4 and 8.

Still, for all the points of contact with Buddhism, Nietzsche concludes that it is fundamentally wrong-headed. The reason for his disagreement should by now be apparent. Buddhism counsels elimination of the passions as a cure for the suffering they invariably cause. Nietzsche thinks this is folly. As he snidely notes, "we no longer admire dentists who *pull out* teeth to stop them hurting" (*TI* V 1). Buddhism's decadence, like Christianity's, follows directly from its commitment to a regime of self-abnegation, a regime that is anathema to Nietzsche. Moreover, not only is it simple-minded and crude to want to eliminate desire just because it sometimes leads us astray, but it is impossible to do so. We are, Nietzsche thinks, constitutionally desiring animals, so to endeavour to overcome desire entirely is to try to do something that will spell the end of our kind of existence.

## Religion and human flourishing

Despite his considerable hostility to various religions, Nietzsche is not completely averse to the promises that religions make to improve us. Take Christianity as an example. His attack on Christianity works hand in hand with his assessment of the slave revolt in morality. As we have already pointed out in Chapter 1, Nietzsche thinks that Christianity is the single most important cultural force responsible for the slave's victory. His tone is vitriolic in part because the potential for celebrating what is great in humanity and for cultivating our potential is squandered in Christianity in the service of its ambition to celebrate what is mediocre and cultivate the worst in us. That fills Nietzsche with weary disgust. However, Christianity has so fundamentally altered our psychology that, without it, we would not even know how to go about cultivating our virtues. As he remarks in *The Genealogy of Morals* regarding the bad conscience, in an observation that is equally applicable to psychologies bred by Christianity and other decadent religions: "the bad conscience is an illness, there is no doubt about that, but an illness as pregnancy is an illness" (*GM* II 19). Having helped to cultivate the bad conscience in us, Christianity then developed it in a particular, albeit mistaken, manner. And, even if we cannot slough off the bad conscience, there are alternative evaluative schemes presupposing it still available. We shall investigate some of these alternatives in Chapter 9.

One unexpected consequence of Nietzsche's acknowledgement of the value of religion is that he actually endorses many of its *practices*, so long as they are given a different context. An illuminating example of this is a note from the *Nachlass*, in which he catalogues activities, rituals and existential data that have been corrupted by the Christian church but that are redeemable even now. Included in his catalogue are asceticism, fasting, monastic practice, feasts, morality and even death. As examples, consider what he says about monastic practice and feasting:

> The "monastery": temporary isolation, accompanied by strict refusal, e.g., of letters; a kind of most profound self-reflection and self-recovery that desires to avoid, not "temptations," but "duties": an escape from the daily round; a detachment from the tyranny of stimuli and influences that condemns us to spend strength in nothing but reactions and does not permit their accumulation to the point of *spontaneous activity* (one should observe our scholars from close up: they think only *reactively*; i.e. they have to read before they can think). (WP 916)

What is clear about a passage such as this one is that Nietzsche admires the presumption of religions to elevate humanity and that he endorses some of the practices, even some of the ideals, recommended in the religious attempt to elevate us. But things go terribly wrong, in part because religions cannot seem to avoid affiliating themselves with the most banal elements of humanity, in part because religions invariably twist those practices and ideals into something that prevents us from elevating ourselves, and in part because religion attaches those practices and ideals to pre-existing psychological capacities and evaluative practices that undercut any hope of using the former to undo the latter. While there are occasional insights bouncing around the halls of religion, they continually collide with everything else in religion that is wrong-headed.

Certain elements of Nietzsche's work are themselves religious in at least a couple of senses. The first is the shadow of God's death. Philosophers who write about Nietzsche frequently underplay the importance of Nietzsche's own intellectual history. But one of the signal events in his life was his rejection of Christianity. The impact of abandoning Christianity lingers in Nietzsche's work in his acute sensitivity to the loss of certainty and confidence that flows from God's existence, in his ability to uncover new expressions of the desire for such certainty and confidence in science and metaphysics, and in his acknowledgement that scientists are ascetics and that the advances of science are often nihilistic. As he himself recognizes, he is a barometer for the psychological impact of the death of God – educated to enter the clergy, he is an exemplar of the psychological perturbations of the disillusioned religious personality. That is one reason why his bitter attack on Christianity is as powerful as it is. He is both revisiting his own fall from the Church, and, after having survived, indeed flourished, for twenty years without religion, trying to provoke recognition in others that the fall is not fatal.

Moreover, in all Nietzsche's mature work we find repeated references to the highest spirituality, the boldest spirituality and the spiritualization of power. These are not idle slips of the pen. Nietzsche was deeply impressed with the human ability to sublimate drives and passions and convinced that the greatest humans were so precisely because they could redirect their drives away from boorish displays of power over others and towards experiments with themselves. In this will to outdo even ourselves, the religious ascetic, artist and philosopher stand "at the end of the ladder" (*D* 113) for they, more than anyone else, have recognized the feeling of power that results from the joy of giving form to themselves, of giving style to their character (*GS* 290). This joy is not utterly alien to those elevated psychological states aimed at by virtually all religions. Of course, Nietzsche separates himself from religions by insisting that the boldest spirituality neither has its source in anything extra-worldly nor is an intimation of worlds beyond this one. For all that, however, it remains the case that the ascetic and the saint remain compelling figures for Nietzsche.

Nietzsche's conviction that we are capable of becoming earthly saints is, no doubt, one reason why so many people find in his work, and in *Thus Spoke Zarathustra* in particular, the reflections of a mystical sage with secret teachings. Nietzsche never wanted slavish followers, although he fully knew that his work would incite misinterpretation and attract epigones and disciples. In fact, Nietzsche knows precisely what he is doing when he exploits religious tactics to serve anti-religious ends. His style *encourages* the belief that really understanding him permits us to enter a secret club. Throughout his mature work we find passages in which Nietzsche is talking only to *his* readers, *his* followers, those lucky few who *understand him*, those free spirits who are, if not yet beyond good and evil, at least aware that such a place exists. This conspiratorial tone permeates much of *Beyond Good and Evil* and significant parts of *Twilight of the Idols* and *The Anti-Christ*. It is easy to feel that Nietzsche is luring us into a mysterious fraternity of free-spirited Dionysian new philosophers. This aspect of Nietzsche's work also has its religious grounding. He recognizes the attraction of mystery and ineffability as a fundamentally religious attraction to features of our existence that defy simple explanation, and he exploits them for his own purposes.

Yet, in the very act of tempting us with his "dangerous" knowledge, Nietzsche steps out from the shadows to reveal himself as a sarcastic buffoon. He uses the tactics of religion only to persuade the already sceptical but still latently religious away from their dependence on mysterious doctrines and esoteric rituals. Nietzsche's own attitude about having adherents, disciples and fans is abundantly clear. After having congratulated himself in *Ecce Homo* for his wisdom, cleverness and abilities as a writer, Nietzsche remarks that: "I *want* no 'believers'; I think I am too sarcastic *to* believe in myself; I never speak to masses. I have a terrible fear that one day I will be pronounced *holy*: You will guess why I publish this book *before*; it shall prevent people from doing mischief" (*EH* IV 1). Nietzsche's self-directed irony underscores his delight in puncturing his own balloon. In the end, all his various styles, different kinds of arguments, cajoling, winking asides, cultural broadsides, absurd comparisons and hyperbolic blasts are cultivated to get us to recognize the pervasiveness of religious decadence, in us and in our culture, and to get us to acknowledge that it is possible not just to survive but to flourish without it. That too has its religious contours, for it is Nietzsche's counter to religious claims to enlighten us. Nietzsche presents himself as a liberator, but a liberator whose promise requires denouncing all liberators.

# CHAPTER 3
# Nihilism

Nietzsche is a self-professed nihilist, although, if we are to believe him, it took him until 1887 to admit it (he makes the admission in a *Nachlass* note from that year). No philosopher's nihilism is more radical than Nietzsche's and only Kierkegaard's and Sartre's are as radical. Nietzsche's nihilism is certainly more radical than the theatrical nihilisms paraded around for public consumption by the terminally hip. Compared to Nietzsche, such nihilists are flimsy poseurs. Although they may espouse a morose detachment from bourgeois society and flaunt their anxiety about political and moral legitimacy, and although they may recognize that moral values are shot through with inconsistency and hypocrisy, none of them understand, as does Nietzsche, the conceptual connections between various components of the Western tradition and nihilism, and none of them undertake to analyse the philosophical assumptions of their detachment and anxiety. Nietzsche's nihilism, on the other hand, is thorough and existentially committing; he rejects as meaningless most Western philosophical and theological traditions and condemns European culture as decadent and devoid of content. Surprisingly, however, we look in vain in his work for despair in the face of the loss of meaning; in fact, Nietzsche celebrates it. It will take us the remainder of this book to unpack his reasons for doing so.

Nietzsche's nihilism is complicated by the fact that it is double-edged, even triple-edged. Not only does he think that the Western philosophical tradition, science, religion generally and Christianity in particular are wrong, but he also accuses them of being *internally* nihilistic. In addition, he is a nihilist *about* these and other cultural idols of the Western tradition. Finally, he is a nihilist not just about other things but about *himself* as well. So we are faced with a bit of a quandary. If Nietzsche thinks the Western tradition is nihilistic and he is nihilistic about it and he is also nihilistic about himself, then, since Nietzsche's position can be generalized, we might reasonably wonder whether it is possible for anyone to evade nihilism. After all, it appears that both those who espouse the values of the Western tradition and those who oppose those values most vehemently are alike nihilists.

Nietzsche agrees with this assessment. Nihilism is unavoidable for anyone who upholds a worldview that makes a distinction between the real world and the apparent world, that commits itself to the existence of absolute truths, that promises to provide foundations to knowledge, or that assumes that logic or mathematics directly apply to the world. The vast majority of philosophical and religious worldviews do commit themselves to the first two claims, and science commits itself to the latter two. Except for the pre-Socratic Heraclitus, in fact, every form of Western philosophy is nihilistic and science is the inheritor of those nihilistic tendencies. It follows that everyone has to confront nihilism, and that includes Nietzsche himself. There is a way out, however. Upon revealing the decadence and *ressentiment* of Christian morality, he exposes in the latter part of *The Genealogy of Morals* the strands of nihilism threading through virtually every region of the Western philosophical tradition. He takes it as his intellectual duty to bring those nihilistic presuppositions into the light of day and cut them, one by one, until they are annihilated and he is liberated. As we shall see in this chapter, cutting through the strands of nihilism is an arduous task, for some of those threads are our most cherished and confident beliefs.

## Varieties of nihilism

"Nihilism" comes from the Latin *nihil*, which means nothing or what does not exist. The verb "annihilate" – the activity befitting a nihilist – describes the activity of destroying something until there is literally nothing left. Nihilism found its first self-conscious expression in European intellectual circles in 1862, when Ivan Turgenev published *Fathers and Sons*, a novel in which one of the characters is described as a nihilist. Turgenev's novel galvanized a social nihilism movement in Russia, a movement that lasted until the Bolsheviks overthrew the Tsarist regimes in 1917. The Russian nihilists, exemplified by Mikhael Bakunin, rejected the religious authority of the Orthodox Church, the political authority of the state and the social authority of the family and argued instead that only those social and political institutions that could rationally justify themselves by providing material benefits to all were legitimate. One of the remarkable facets of Nietzsche's nihilism is that it takes the promise held out by the Russian nihilists to rationally ground social and political institutions, exposes *its* inherent nihilism and cuts it up, thereby out-annihilating the nihilists.

Nietzsche enjoys providing annihilating critiques of the central planks of the Western tradition's presuppositions. In a *Nachlass* note from 1885, he goes so far as to predict that the next two hundred years of Western philosophizing will be the nihilistic age of philosophy and that its nihilism will become more pervasive as time goes on. It will, like acid, corrode everything it touches, leaving us dazed, mutilated, terrified and alone:

> What I relate is the history of the next two centuries. I describe what is coming, what can no longer come differently: *the advent of nihilism*. ... For some time now our whole European culture has been moving as toward a catastrophe, with a tortured tension that is growing from decade to decade: restlessly, violently, headlong, like a river that wants to reach the end, that no longer reflects, that is afraid to reflect.
>
> A movement ... in some future will take the place of this perfect nihilism – but [this movement] presupposes [nihilism], logically and psychologically, and certainly can come only after and out of it. For why has the advent of nihilism become *necessary*? Because the values we have had hitherto thus draw their final consequence; because nihilism represents the ultimate logical conclusion of our great values and ideals – because we must experience nihilism before we can find out what value these "values" really had.
>
> (WP Preface)

We are, Nietzsche thinks, heading for an inevitable, even necessary, catastrophe. Well, that is not quite right. We are not *heading* towards catastrophe; we are *living through* it *now*, as these pages are written. It is easy to cite evidence to support Nietzsche's contention: participation in religions is low; moral standards are falling; relativism is rampant; science is predominant; and the list could go on. But, in the end, citing evidence for nihilism is unhelpful, for Nietzsche's nihilism is the result of philosophical reflection on the conceptual bases of culture. Let us then explain those reflections.

Nihilism can be regional or global, and where it is regional it often goes under other names. Epistemological nihilists, for instance, are also known as epistemological sceptics. (We may note in passing that sceptics are not relativists and that epistemological relativism is not a nihilistic position, but just a step on the road to nihilism. Epistemological relativism indexes truth and justification to something – culture, perspectives, societies – but this is, unlike scepticism, a positive position about truth and justification. Epistemological nihilism is the entirely negative claim that there either is no truth or no justification, or that there is neither truth nor justification.) Political nihilism, also known as anarchism, is the denial that there are any justified political principles. Moral nihilism, or immoralism, is the denial that there is any moral value. Nietzsche is a nihilist in each of these senses and in others as well. For example, Nietzsche is also a metaphysical nihilist, for he denies that there is a real world as described by metaphysicians. There is no objective, perspective-free, structure to the world. And he is, finally, a logical nihilist or irrationalist, for he denies that logic or mathematics come into contact with reality. Global nihilism is the recognition that all of these regional nihilisms are conceptually connected and that there are entailments from one region of nihilism to another. Once those entailments are uncovered we can start to dismantle them. We could start anywhere, with any of the components of the Western tradition, but since we have already begun the investigation of morality and Christianity, it is easiest to start there.

## Moral and religious nihilism

Herd morality, Christianity and Buddhism are, as we have seen, decadent. They are decadent because they are against life, and they are against life because they recommend elimination of the drives that give life meaning. Of course, herd morality and religion have their reasons for counselling us to deaden and eliminate our passions. Both are convinced that passions and drives are so chaotic and that we have so little chance to organize them that it is better to recommend their extirpation than their discipline. However, once we start down the path of eliminating our drives and passions because of the silliness and suffering they can cause, we eventually end up in a place where causes and effects get reversed, and imaginary causes are taken for real ones, a psychological mirror world in which everything is upside-down and backwards.

Nietzsche is convinced that the explanatory categories and the explanatory powers found in religious psychology in general but Christianity in particular are gross falsifications. We have already seen in the past two chapters that the decadent reverse the moral evaluation of the old masters and that Christianity is the decadent's greatest ally, but here Nietzsche makes another, more fundamental, accusation: religious decadents fabricate an entire world of things and powers to serve as the theoretical superstructure for a psychology that does not "come into contact with reality at any point" (AC 15). This fictitious psychology starts with souls and a personal God, neither of which exist. It then constructs a set of fictitious causes, such as souls and free will, and a set of fictitious effects, such as sin, redemption, grace and forgiveness. Of course, none of these exist either, but that does not stop the Christian from deploying them across our entire existence. The Christian priest and believer interpret all our drives, passions, pleasures, pains, sufferings, hopes, desires, fears and thoughts in light of this fictitious psychology.

Nietzsche has an explanation for the development of the religious psychology. He thinks that feelings of power are so disturbing and strange that a person in the grip of such feelings posits an external cause for it:

> When a man is suddenly and overwhelmingly suffused with the *feeling of power* – and this is what happens with all great affects – it raises in him a doubt about his own person: he does not dare to think himself the cause of this astonishing feeling – and so he posits a stronger person, a divinity, to account for it. (WP 135)

Once granted existence and causal power, the divinity must of course find something in the human realm with whom to communicate, upon which to act and that mirrors its causal efficacy. That something is the soul, an extra-mundane agent of causal influence separate from but capable of acting in the world. In a note from the *Nachlass* entitled "*Rudimentary psychology of the religious man*", Nietzsche provides an outline of the inverted psychology that results from the dissonance that feelings of power provoke: "All changes are effects; all effects are effects of will (– the concept 'nature,' 'law of nature' is lacking); all effects suppose an agent. Rudimentary psychology: one is a cause oneself only when one knows that one has performed an act of will" (WP 136). In brief, our feelings of power confuse and frighten us so we posit another entity as their cause; we then turn around and model our own psyche on that of the projected entity we created.

We thus come to think of ourselves as agents who have the same kinds of purposes for our actions as God has for his and who, like God, produce consequences that are immediately and best interpreted spiritually, that is, supernaturally. Entirely natural activities such as showing concern for others get reinterpreted as doing God's will on earth or spreading the gospel. Over procreation we pour an interpretation of religious blessedness. We devise rituals of being born again in the spirit to signify our repudiation of our natural life. And, of course, we construct the causes and effects of sin, redemption, and grace to explain why our will fails to comport to God's and how God can, given our self-abasement, effect his forgiveness on earth. Once in place in rudimentary form, religious psychology is free to blossom unfettered into the ornate marvel it has become. Feelings of power are reinterpreted as arrogance, the essence of sin. Self-abasement and the intoxicating fear of relinquishing control before another are reinterpreted as humility before God and the essential act of contrition that leads to redemption. Our routine ability to forgive and forget is reinterpreted as God's miraculous gift of grace, necessary as a counterweight to our selfish and sinful nature and miraculous because it is inexplicable otherwise given our sin. There is in principle no end to the psychological phenomena that can be reinterpreted religiously because in principle religious psychology knows no explanatory constraints. It is like an enormous sail kept aloft by its sheer size; it only gets more buoyant as it gets larger.

For all the reversals, inversions, mystifications and lies that the religious psychologist can muster, two in particular gnaw at Nietzsche. The first is the myth of free will, which we shall examine in greater detail in later chapters. The second is the way that the priest – who is, after all, religion's clinical practitioner – has convinced us that deadening our passions and drives is the best solution to the suffering they sometimes cause. The priest should acknowledge instead that some suffering is ineliminable, some is harmful and some beneficial. Moralists and priests routinely either pass over or intentionally mislead us by not admitting that the suffering caused by foolish passion is the result only of its foolishness and that the suffering caused by unrealized or frustrated passions and drives is inevitable and often good for us. And, above all, they fail to acknowledge that the only kind of suffering that could ever be undone by excising the passions and drives is the suffering that they, the moralist and the priest, have instilled in us in the first place: the drive not to have drives.

At some level religion and morality recognize their shell game with passions and drives, for both have liturgical rituals for re-engaging the passions in their sterilized settings. Christianity, for instance, has created flamboyant rituals for confessing sin and guilt in front of others, rituals for sharing guilt, rituals for unburdening ourselves to those we have wronged and a whole host of celebration rituals. Moral guilt spawns entire industries devoted to celebrating our inability to discipline ourselves and devoted to helping us deaden the passions so that we can at last be free from them. For Nietzsche, these rituals, rites and practices are healthy displays of passionate drives, admirably sublimated drives and passions, but put to the thoroughly decadent end of defusing those very drives and passions. None of these techniques and mechanisms will ever work for the goal they purport to be serving, not simply because they mistake symptom for cause, not simply because they get causality altogether backwards, but more importantly because they prescribe cures where there is no sickness to begin with. As we have already noted, herd morality and religion make us sick and then addict us to narcotic anaesthetizing balms that, in their anaesthetizing effects, only make us sicker. Nietzsche puts the point directly: "The supposed remedies of degeneration are ... mere palliatives against some of its effects: the 'cured' are merely one type of the degenerates" (*WP* 42).

The mirror psychology of herd morality and religion and their accompanying prescriptions are, in the end, nothing but practical nihilism: nihilism in action and deed. Nietzsche notes in the *Nachlass* that, "nihilism is no cause but merely the logical result of decadence" (*WP* 43). We might be tempted to think to the contrary that, by being nihilistic, we provoke decadence. This is certainly a widespread response to the public libertinism practised by decadent pop cultural figures: "Ooh! Just look at him!" the prude will say, "What a nihilist – no wonder he takes those drugs and does those lewd things!" For Nietzsche, this response gets things exactly backwards. It is not the libertine's alleged nihilism that causes his decadence, but his alleged decadence that causes his nihilism.

In point of fact, Nietzsche agrees with the prudish response that libertines are decadents. However, libertines are reactive decadents rather than, as are prudes, direct decadents. Nietzsche will criticize a life of nothing but sex, drugs and rock and roll, not because sex, drugs and rock and roll are morally evil, as the prude claims, but because such a life too easily ends up being excessive, undisciplined, full of ennui and misery, self-destructive, uncaring and hurtful to others. But it is at least a life that does not annihilate the passions. The prudish response to such a life is directly decadent because it does try to annihilate the passions and condemns any life that does not so try. Still, even the libertine is an indirect or reactive decadent because he rebels against prudery and thereby discloses that he initially agrees with the prude's decadent psychology. Certainly, libertinism is a creative response to that decadent psychology, in much the same way that *ressentiment* is a creative response to weakness, but its celebration of passionate anarchy is only marginally more interesting than direct decadence, and, since it shares the inverted psychology of the direct decadent to begin with, whatever its benefits may be, they are certain to be transient.

The incessant swinging between prudish and libertine decadence convinces us that the pendulum reflects an accurate and ineliminable tendency in the human psyche that religion and morality have and must counter. Nietzsche thinks this is a sham that will eventually result in complete exhaustion and collapse. As the swings of the pendulum become more extreme, other alternatives simply vanish. In such a poisoned and topsy-turvy psychological environment, once God's death is announced, the cures that religion and herd morality introduce to eliminate the vacillations of decadent psychology become impotent and the whole thing comes down like a house of cards:

> Extreme positions are not succeeded by moderate ones but by extreme positions of the opposite kind. Thus the belief in the absolute immorality of nature, in aim- and meaninglessness, is the psychologically necessary affect once the belief in God and an essentially moral order becomes untenable. Nihilism appears at that point, not that the displeasure at existence has become greater than before but because one has come to mistrust any "meaning" in suffering, indeed in existence. One interpretation has collapsed; but because it was considered *the* interpretation, it now seems as if there were no meaning at all in existence, as if everything were in vain. (WP 55)

If they acknowledge God's death, prudish decadents will just collapse in exhaustion and misery; libertine decadents will go on lewd rampages of self-gratification, either destroying themselves and those around them or, like the prudes, exhausting themselves because in them too there is nothing but a "multitude and disgregation of impulses" (WP 46) left by the decadent psychology of the weak, each of which impulses insists on instantaneous satisfaction. Either way, the end result is the same: "hopeless despair" (WP 55). No wonder Nietzsche thinks that announcing God's death is always premature. Those who believe in God are so thoroughly poisoned by that belief that a life without it is agony, and they would rather continue to believe in something that does not exist than believe in everything that does. Even those who mouth their denial of God's existence carry in themselves the psychological residue of a belief in God, and even they will be unable to outrun nihilism.

It is easy, 120 years after Nietzsche's announcement that God is dead, to assume a jaded attitude about his self-congratulation at revealing the inversions of religious psychology and about his ominous tone in predicting nihilism. When we disillusioned Christians review his vivi-section of Christianity we may be tempted to think that we are above and beyond its commitment to sins, redemptions, souls and the like. We may also be tempted to think that the past century of psychological science has purged our self-understanding of past mistakes. We would be mistaken. Even if all of the explicitly religious elements were flushed out of psychology, our faith in psychology to discern the contours of human nature remains. With the advent of cognitive neuro-psychology and the increasing audacity of evolutionary psychology, that faith is, if anything, undergoing renewal. Every year, we are treated to dozens of treatises that pronounce that another mystery of the human psyche has at last been solved or is being solved or will be solved in the near future. In so far as we continue to believe that we can discover anything more than the most banal truths of human nature, we continue to act as if God were still around, for faith in a natural order of things is, in Nietzsche's opinion, nothing more than the secular sediment of our faith in God. Let us see why he thinks this is true.

## Darwin, evolution, and cultural nihilism

Nietzsche does not restrict nihilism to the consequences of assuming a decadent psychology, its buttressing by the moral order vouchsafed by believing in God, and the collapse that attends God's death. Once the tendrils of nihilism start to spread outwards from our disillusionment in God and into the secular and the political realms, he thinks that *everything* will be up for grabs. And we shall, Nietzsche predicts, start grabbing at every straw we can find. The first things we shall grab on to are our social and political institutions, but they will fail to provide the order we hope for. Next, we shall grab on to science, but that too will fail. We shall then grab on to metaphysics, but that will lead us right back to nihilism. Then, and only then, shall we be ready to listen to Nietzsche's proposal for emerging from nihilism.

The easiest response to religiously based nihilism, hence the first we shall think of, is to hope that our economic, social and political organizations and structures will provide the order and meaning necessary to prop our confidence up again once we admit that the social order and meaning provided by God are no longer warranted. Nietzsche thinks this will fail. After all, democracies and socialisms are as decadent as their creators, and people who are decadent to the core, whether socialist or capitalist, populate all the Western democracies:

> The time has come when we have to pay for having been Christians for two thousand years: we are losing the center of gravity by virtue of which we lived; we are lost for a while.
> One attempts a kind of this-worldly solution, but in the same sense – that of the eventual triumph of truth, love, and justice.
>
> (*WP* 30)

Democracy and egalitarianism are no salves for nihilism because they only generalize the decadence of their citizens as the criterion of political legitimacy; as a result, democracy and egalitarianism both "enhance weakness of the will" (*WP* 132). Socialism is just as bad, for it is the "logical conclusion of the *tyranny* of the least and the dumbest, i.e. those who are superficial, envious, and three-quarters actors" (*WP* 125).

We might instead turn to science to rediscover the order that we can no longer find in religion or our social institutions, but again we shall be disappointed. The social sciences of psychology, sociology and economics are immediate non-starters because they just recapitulate and puff up as "fact" all the facets of our antecedent decadence. What then of the natural sciences: physics, chemistry and biology, for example? In Chapter 6 we shall investigate Nietzsche's philosophical criticisms of science in greater detail. Here, we shall focus on the way that the promise of one natural science, evolutionary theory, postpones recognition of its inherently nihilistic content.

By the mid-1870s, Charles Darwin's evolutionary theory had found a large audience and wide acceptance, especially by those who, already sceptical about God, turned to naturalistic explanations of our psychological and social characteristics. With evolutionary theory these disaffected Christians hoped to provide some stability to our kind of life. Nietzsche is highly critical of such attempts, for he thinks both that Darwin gets things wrong and that the nature of Darwin's mistake entails that his evolutionary theory is nihilistic.

We do not know how much Darwin, if any, Nietzsche actually read. He did read, and admired, Friedrich Lange's *The History of Materialism*, which contains an entire chapter devoted to Darwin. More important to his thinking about Darwin and evolution than Lange, however, is the thinking of two anti-Darwinian biologists of the time, William Roux and William Rolph. Roux's *Der Kampf der Theile im Organismus* (*The Struggle of the Parts of the Organism*) and Rolph's *Biologische Probleme* (*Biological Problems*) had a lasting and deep effect on Nietzsche's interpretation of Darwin and evolutionary theory and on the development of his own views on the will to power.* Roux's work on temporary equilibria in biological systems and Rolph's rejection of an instinct of self-preservation in favour of self-expansion are central to Nietzsche's willingness to use the will to power as a basic explanatory category. We investigate these matters in Chapters 8 and 9.

Beginning with *Untimely Meditations* and extending through the rest of his work, there are more than fifty citations to Darwin in Nietzsche's work

---

* F. Lange, *History of Materialism*, 2nd edn, 3 vols, E. C. Thomas (trans.) (London: Trübner, 1877–1881); W. Roux, *Der Kampf der Theile im Organismus* (Leipzig: Wilhelm Engelmann, 1881); W. Rolph, *Biologische Probleme* (Leipzig: Wilhelm Engelmann, 1884).

and hundreds of passages that mention or use evolutionary explanations. Correlatively, Nietzsche's work has often been cited as one of the most unforgiving forms of social Darwinism ever proposed. The latter attribution is unforgivable; Nietzsche is not a social Darwinist. In fact, he believes that understanding the implications of Darwinian evolution results in nihilism. After all, the two aspects of Darwin's work that come in for Nietzsche's strongest criticism are the struggle for survival and, as just noted, the assumption that there is an instinct for self-preservation. As the following passage from *The Gay Science* makes clear, he thinks both are false:

> The wish to preserve oneself is the symptom of a condition of distress, of a limitation of the really fundamental instinct of life which aims at the *expansion of power* and, wishing for that, frequently risks and even sacrifices self-preservation ... in nature it is not conditions of distress that are *dominant* but overflow and squandering, even to the point of absurdity. The struggle for existence is only an *exception*, a temporary restriction of the life-will. The great and small struggle always revolves around superiority, around growth and expansion, around power – in accordance with the will to power which is the will to life. (*GS* 349)

In this passage, Nietzsche rejects both Darwinian assumptions. The instinct for self-preservation is, he claims, a special case of the instinct for the expansion of power, and the struggle for existence is an exceptional case in a world that is better characterized as profligate, wasteful and excessive to absurdity.

It is, however, with another aspect of Darwin's work that Nietzsche disagrees most strongly. Darwin had an undying optimism in science's ability to uncover the truth and in its promise to liberate us from the mystifications of religion. This optimism is, in Nietzsche's opinion, nothing but the embers of religious hope. Witness this passage from *On the Origin Of Species*:

> As all the living forms of life are the lineal descendants of those which lived long before the Silurian epoch, we may feel certain that the ordinary succession by generation has never once been broken, and that no cataclysm has desolated the whole world. Hence we may look with some confidence to a secure future of equally inappreciable length. And as natural selection works solely by and for the good of each being, all corporeal and mental endowments will tend to progress towards perfection.*

---

* C. Darwin, *On The Origin of Species* (Cambridge, MA: Harvard University Press, 1975), 489.

Here, in the very text that has done so much to undo the creationist's divine explanation of human development, we still find a faith in "progress towards perfection". For Nietzsche, this faith exposes not only Darwin's residual optimism that the world is an orderly and meaningful place, but his inability to fully commit himself to the consequences of his own theory.

Evolutionary theory is, in its rejection of final causes and divine explanations of development, systematically deflationary about humans. Nietzsche notes in *Daybreak* that: "Formerly one sought the feeling of grandeur of man by pointing to his divine *origin*: this has now become a forbidden way, for at its portal stands the ape, together with other gruesome beasts, grinning knowingly as if to say: no further in this direction!" (*D* 49). Evolutionary theory punctures the optimism of the religious, but then Darwin of all people comes along to proclaim that "the way mankind is *going* shall serve as proof of his grandeur and kinship with God" (*D* 49). Witness this passage from *The Descent of Man*:

> Looking to future generations, there is no cause to fear that the social instincts will grow weaker, and we may expect that virtuous habits will grow stronger, becoming perhaps fixed by inheritance. In this case the struggle between our higher and lower impulses will be less severe, and virtue will be triumphant.*

Nietzsche sees right through this as a redirected, but equally delusional, optimism: "Alas, this, too, is vain" (*D* 49). The real consequence of Darwinian evolutionary theory is that it entails "that man has emerged from the ape and will return to the ape" (*HAH* 247). Evolution is nihilistic because, in the final analysis, it entails our dehumanization. For all its decadence, mistakes, inverted psychological explanations and imaginary causes, religion at least succeeded in getting us beyond the animal stupidity of the masters. Evolution would, if taken to its logical conclusion, leave us no other choice but their unreflective orgies of violence.

We may quibble with Nietzsche's assessment of Darwinian evolution. Evolutionary theory does not imply that there is no psychological progress whatsoever or that the progress there is must be nothing more than the last vapours of religious optimism. It does not imply the first because every mutation that results in enhanced genotype survival is *some* kind of progress, if only progressively better survivability. There is no reason that psychological changes cannot be instances of progress of that kind. That such progress is so colourless also explains why the second claimed

---

* C. Darwin, *The Descent of Man, and Selection in Relation to Sex*, 2nd edn, 2 vols (London: Murray, 1877), I, 124–5.

implication does not hold, for enhanced survivability is consistent with the complete absence of religious or any other kind of optimism. Nietzsche's characterization of Darwin is, thus, a caricature. Of course, salvaging evolutionary theory in this way only proves Nietzsche's general point, which can be stated as a dilemma: either evolutionary theory explains human progress as enhanced survivability, in which case it dehumanizes us, or it explains human progress as something more than enhanced survivability, in which case it presupposes religious optimism. In the first case, evolution retains internal theoretical consistency but loses the ability to explain interesting kinds of human progress; in the second, it retains the ability to explain interesting kinds of human progress, but internal theoretical consistency goes out the window.

Nietzsche's conviction that natural science is nihilistic generalizes to other claims of knowledge as well; thus some conclude that he is a sceptic. That which makes science nihilistic – its optimism that there is a "natural order" that we can discover – infects logic, mathematics, and any claimed knowledge forthcoming from philosophy. To the extent that logic, mathematics and philosophy affirm this optimism, they preserve the religious faith that God provides order to the world. But even scepticism is itself a specification of a more comprehensive nihilism that, Nietzsche thinks, affects every kind of theory that presumes that there is a real world of objects "out there" just waiting for us to discover and investigate. This presumption is, in the end, an article of faith no less decadent than belief in God. Indeed, belief in God and belief in the real world go hand in hand, for the latter is nothing more than the belief that our faith in God's omnibenevolence and omnipotency is confirmed in the congruence between the world as we experience and know it and the world as it is in itself. Nietzsche believes that the real world is "the greatest error that has ever been committed, the essential fatality of error on earth" (WP 584). Believing that there is a real world is nihilistic in itself, and realizing that it is fictional precipitates another, more pervasive, episode of nihilism.

In *Twilight of the Idols,* Nietzsche provides a history of the real world–apparent world distinction that clarifies why he thinks it is fundamentally a nihilistic distinction. He calls this history *"How the 'Real World' at Last Became a Myth."*

1. The real world, attainable to the wise, the pious, the virtuous man – he dwells in it, *he is it*.
(Oldest form of the idea, relatively sensible, simple, convincing. Transcription of the proposition "I, Plato, *am* the truth").
2. The real world, unattainable for the moment, but promised to the wise, the pious, the virtuous man ("to the sinner who repents").

THE PHILOSOPHY OF NIETZSCHE

(Progress of the idea: it grows more refined, more enticing, more incomprehensible – *it becomes a woman*, it becomes Christian ... )

3. The real world, unattainable, undemonstrable, cannot be promised, but even when merely thought of a consolation, a duty, and imperative.

   (Fundamentally the same old sun, but shining through mist and skepticism; the idea grown sublime, pale, northerly Könegs-bergian.)

4. The real world – unattainable? Unattained, at any rate. And if unattained also *unknown*. Consequently also no consolation, no redemption, no duty: how could we have a duty towards something unknown?

   (The gray of dawn. First yawnings of reason. Cock-crow of positivism.)

5. The "real world" – an idea no longer of any use, not even a duty any longer – an idea grown useless, superfluous, *consequently* a refuted idea: let us abolish it!

   (Broad daylight; breakfast; return to cheerfulness and *bon sens;* Plato blushes for shame; all free spirits run riot.)

6. We have abolished the real world: what is left? The apparent world perhaps? ... But no! *with the real world we have also abolished the apparent world!*

   (Midday; moment of the shortest shadow; end of the longest error; zenith of mankind; INCIPIT ZARATHUSTRA.)          (*TI* IV)

For all its terseness, this potted history is remarkably accurate. Plato famously argues that the world as we know it in sensory experience is populated by processes that are undergoing constant change. Since there is no stability in this flux of processes, there can, Plato insists, be no knowledge of the apparent world either. Whatever knowledge we have must instead be of the real world behind the world of appearance: a domain of stable entities that remain the same across change, whose properties are fixed and graspable by the mind. Because knowledge is internally related to moral goodness, those who know the real world also reside in it as moral exemplars of virtue; more, since they reside in the real world, they legislate for those whose virtue and knowledge does not match theirs.

With Christianity, the real world is no longer achieved by anyone in this life, as the second stage points out, but it does continue to be held out as the otherworldly reward for a virtuous life. This change is fundamental, both for philosophy and for religion. For philosophy, the real world's retreat behind the veil of death signals the severance of knowledge and moral virtue. To live a morally worthy life it is no longer sufficient that we live the life of knowledge, and our love of wisdom can no longer guarantee spiritual salvation. Here starts the unresolved and irresolvable tension between religion and knowledge.

The tension between philosophy and religion reaches its most sublime expression in Kant (who was from Königsberg). Kant simply concedes the real world to religion and morality and admits that the only world we can know is the world as it is presented in sensory experience. Still, for all its unknowability, Kant never loses his faith that the real world (in his terms, the domain of noumena or things-in-themselves) is an appropriate object of our deepest thought and most abiding faith. After all, the noumenal realm contains persons with free wills and rational powers, respect between and for whom grounds our moral imperatives, our duties. Although we cannot *know* that we are inhabitants of the noumenal realm, that we are such inhabitants is a presupposition of any morality and every form of Christianity.

Kant's concession of the real world to religion is the beginning of the end for the real world. By admitting that it is in principle unknowable, Kant opens the door for the sceptical challenge – a challenge Nietzsche delights in providing – that the real world plays no role in any human endeavour, that it is superfluous. Once we recognize the real world's superfluity, science (positivism) emerges as the only purveyor of knowledge.

Stages 5 and 6 of Nietzsche's history represent Nietzsche's own philosophizing. He is an "active" nihilist who abolishes the real world. Plato blushes at stage 5 because his advocacy of the real world is revealed to be a lie, a noble lie certainly, a lie that propelled us out of the archaic past and put us on a different, more promising trajectory, but a lie nevertheless. Now, after having spent two thousand years following the trajectory Plato first put us on, we can finally transcend him and his real world; with Nietzsche as guide, we can take up residence in the apparent world. Finally, if we follow our nihilism about the real world to its end, we shall find ourselves on the other side of the looking glass of the real world–apparent world dichotomy. We shall find ourselves in *the* world, a world finally ready for Nietzsche's Zarathustra.

## Nihilistic consequences of nihilism

We shall, in this critical project, expose the nihilistic elements of existing cultural idols and values, annihilate those elements, and, if we are strong enough, liberate ourselves. We should not suppose, however, that we shall be impervious to our annihilating, and we should not suppose that, just by engaging nihilism against our culture, we can thereby avoid it. In fact, we shall probably end up annihilating ourselves as we smash away at our culture. So he says in a *Nachlass* note:

> nihilism as a psychological state will have to be reached, first, when we have sought a "meaning" in all events that is not there: so the seeker eventually becomes discouraged. Nihilism, then, is the recognition of the long *waste* of strength, the agony of the "in vain," insecurity, the lack of any opportunity to recover and to regain composure – being ashamed of oneself, as if one had *deceived* oneself all too long. Now one realizes that becoming aims at *nothing and achieves nothing.*

With the recognition that the world aims at nothing and achieves nothing we also lose the hope that there is some underlying order to the world, and with the loss of that hope nihilism takes over:

> nihilism as a psychological state is reached, secondly, when one has posited a totality, a systematization, indeed any organization in all events, and underneath all events, and a soul that longs to admire and revere has wallowed in the idea of some supreme form of administration. Some sort of unity: this faith suffices to give man a deep feeling of standing in the context of, and being dependent on, some whole that is infinitely superior to him. But behold there is no such universal! At bottom, man has lost the faith in his own value when no infinitely valuable whole works through him; i.e. he conceived such a whole in order *to be able to believe in his own value.*

Finally, granted that we recognize the aimlessness and disunity of the empirical world, we may attempt, as in Christianity, to generate a distinct realm that is the antithesis of this world of becoming – a true world of logical relations and stable beings – from which perspective we may pass judgement on this world and reject it altogether. But of course, this other-worldly world is motivated by a psychological need for stability and nothing else, so the admission that it does not exist will provoke despair:

> What has happened, at bottom? The feeling of valuelessness was reached with the realization that the overall character of existence may not be interpreted by means of the concept of "aim," the concept of "unity," or the concept of "truth." Existence has no

goal or end; any comprehensive unity in the plurality of events is lacking: the character of existence is not "true," is false. Briefly: the categories "aim," "unity," "being" which we used to project some value into the world – we *pull out* again; so the world looks *valueless.* (WP 55)

The psychological development culminates in this last form of nihilism, in which we recognize that *all* order is imposed upon the world. For anyone committed to the assumption that the world has some order (and who among us is not such a person?) this is bound to lead to a crisis of intellectual, emotional and existential confidence. This is the moment of deepest nihilism.

Admitting that order is imposed on, rather than found in, the world prompts despair because the depth of our self-deception and the extent of the world's anarchy are utterly pervasive. It goes well beyond rejecting the philosopher's daydream of a real world and its quaint inhabitants, such as substances, properties, selves, souls, logic, necessity and absolute truth, to include causality and explanation as well. Broaching the possibility that there are no causal relations between events even in the world that we can know undercuts the pretension of any science, any logic, and any mathematics to explain anything. As he points out in *Beyond Good and Evil*, "it is perhaps just dawning on five or six minds that physics, too, is only an interpretation and exegesis of the world ... and *not* a world-explanation" (*BGE* 14). We can see the nihilistic consequences immediately: if every level of our theoretical activity from physics upwards provides interpretations and descriptions of the world rather than causal explanations of its events, that will eventually include *us* and *our* interpretations and descriptions of *ourselves*. We shall become a mystery to ourselves, and those of us who are most driven to know ourselves will become the most enigmatic.

Nietzsche is not confident that he can accurately predict the shape of the nihilism that he knows is coming. In stronger individuals it may take the form of "active nihilism" (*WP* 23), a "violent force of destruction" (*WP* 24) that clears the decks of outmoded explanations and celebrates destruction:

Indeed, we philosophers and "free spirits" feel, when we hear the news that "the old God is dead," as if a new dawn shone on us; our heart overflows with gratitude, amazement, premonitions, expectation. At long last the horizon appears free to us again, even if it should not be bright; at long last our ships may venture out again, venture out to face any danger; all the daring of the lover of knowledge is permitted again; the sea, *our* sea, lies open again; perhaps there has never been such an "open sea".　　(*GS* 343)

On the other hand, passive nihilism, the nihilism manifested by the weak, will probably be characterized by collapse, despair, exhaustion and meaninglessness, as described above. We may even, he thinks, enter a period of "European Buddhism" (*WP* 55), during which time, the psyche will disintegrate, loosen and as a result become subject to the attraction of "whatever refreshes, calms, numbs" (*WP* 23). Then dissolving the drives and passions will make sense as a prescription, since, with the exhaustion definitive of passive nihilism, it will already have occurred.

Nietzsche offers to direct any of us who do not collapse in passive nihilism through the destructive phase of nihilism and even to provide some alternatives to the smashed philosophical, religious and scientific idols. Let us turn to this part of Nietzsche's project.

CHAPTER 4

# Metaphysics

Metaphysics studies the basic elements of existence. The field of metaphysics immediately divides into two sub-fields: *ontology*, which studies the basic categories of existence; and *modality*, which studies the nature of necessity and possibility. Nietzsche has a lot to say about both ontology and modality, and what he has to say about each is fascinating albeit in the end incomplete and fragmentary. As we should expect, Nietzsche has no patience for the views of most metaphysicians. He calls himself a "godless anti metaphysician" (*GS* 344), and for good reason; as far as he is concerned, the history of metaphysics is a heritage of bogus explanations, fictitious entities and erroneous causes. This is not to say that Nietzsche thinks that metaphysical explanations of phenomena are not seductive. The worldwide success of religion attests to the contrary that they are. Nietzsche's assessment of that attraction is twofold. First, he thinks that metaphysics is a juvenile pastime indulged because it makes "meaningful ... things that [one] found unpleasant or contemptible" (*HAH* I 17). But this jejune interest is, eventually, discarded and replaced with history and science. The second reason is more general and more pernicious. Nietzsche thinks that many of us share a set of assumptions that force us into compliance with metaphysical claims. These assumptions are "in the last resort the spell of *physiological* value judgements" (*BGE* 20) that life is not worth living and they work together to form the "theological instinct" or the philosophical "idiosyncrasy" (*TI* III 1) of being fundamentally queasy with transience, change, power, life and suffering. This nausea with life is, of course, decadence. Since so many of us are decadent, the metaphysicians have a faithful audience for their pronouncements. Admittedly, this criticism smacks of the *ad hominem*, but, remember, it is an explanation for the affective attraction of metaphysics, not his philosophical criticism of metaphysics.

In this chapter, we discuss Nietzsche's philosophical criticisms of metaphysics. Nietzsche attacks the real world–apparent world distinction,

substance–attribute metaphysics, the relation of identity, the soul, causation and necessity with sophisticated philosophical arguments. Among the
more interesting arguments he unleashes are a semantic criticism of
substance–attribute metaphysics, a naturalist argument against the implications of substance–attribute metaphysics, an epistemological argument
against the tenability of things-in-themselves, an ethical argument against
the decadent moral consequences of substance–attribute metaphysics and a
conceptual argument against causal laws.

## Against the real world–apparent world distinction

Nietzsche's favourite target of criticism is the real world–apparent world
distinction, a distinction that he claims is "the greatest error that has ever
been committed, the essential fatality of error on earth" (*WP* 584). The
distinction comes in many forms, in varying degrees of plausibility, but all of
them agree that the apparent world presented through sensory experience
is not the only world. Somewhere behind the veil of appearance lies
another domain of things, the so-called "real" world. This "real" world is
invariably thought to be of greater moral and existential value than the
apparent world, so it is to the real world that we are invited to direct our
hopes, leaving the apparent world behind as nothing more than illusion.
The real world–apparent world distinction is pervasive in philosophy and
religion. Consider just a few examples. Plato famously argues that the
transitoriness of the apparent world requires the durable world of the non-
sensible Forms to provide stability and explanation. Christianity and Islam
both build entirely distinct realms – heaven – where God and His "honour-
roll" reside. Every variant of Hinduism claims that sensory experience is a
veil of illusion and ignorance and that behind it lies a true world. We find
variants of the real world–apparent world distinction in Spinoza, Leibniz,
Descartes, Kant and Schopenhauer, among many others.

Nietzsche takes on most versions of the real world–apparent world
distinction at some point in his corpus. His basic argument against them is the
same: the real world is premised on the belief that there must be something
fixed over time in nature; but its entities are fictitious projections from a belief
in the soul; and belief in the soul and in diachronic identity are bogus. His
starting point is the metaphysician's objection to this world's transitoriness
and lack of diachronic identity. The metaphysician argues from that
transitoriness to the existence of a real world in which unity and permanence
arc upheld. This is, according to Nietzsche, a fallacy: we have no epistemological justification for making the inference, and the domain of entities

established by metaphysical argument are demonstrably fictions. (Of course, Nietzsche has a ready genealogical explanation of these temptations to hand. The metaphysician is a decadent, unhappy and unsuccessful in this world of becoming. Inhabiting this energetic world is harmful to the metaphysician's life, so he fabricates another one where he is more at home: a world composed of souls, egos, substances and things, each identical over time, each with identifiable sets of properties, and all standing in precise and perspective independent relations of causality and meaning to one another.)

Nietzsche thinks it is only proper to reveal the real world's fraudulence. He begins by arguing that the entities fabricated by the metaphysician are frequently the result of nothing more than a mistake implicit in the subject–predicate structure of language:

> It is *this* which sees everywhere deed and doer; this which believes in will as cause in general; this which believes in the "ego", in the ego as being, in the ego as substance, and which *projects* its belief in the ego substance on to all things – only thus does it *create* the concept "thing" ... Being is everywhere thought in, *foisted upon*, as cause; it is only from the conception "ego" that there follows, derivatively, the concept "being".                    (*TI* III 5)

The point here is that European languages separate singular terms, such as proper names like "Winston Churchill", class names like "whales", demonstratives like "it" and "that", and other referring devices from predicates, such as "is hot", "never follow sharks", "is raining" and "is way too high". There is a tendency, then, to think of the entity referred to by a singular term as distinct from the properties it has as expressed by the predicate. But this is, Nietzsche thinks, blatant projection.

The argument presented in this passage from *Twilight of the Idols* is augmented by a similar, more generalized, argument in *Beyond Good and Evil*:

> The strange family resemblance of all Indian, Greek, and German philosophizing is explained easily enough. Where there is affinity of languages, it cannot fail, owing to the common philosophy of grammar – I mean, owing to the unconscious domination and guidance by similar grammatical functions – that everything is prepared at the outset for a similar development and sequence of philosophical systems ...                    (*BGE* 20)

Take the category of substance, for instance. Nietzsche thinks that the abstract concept of substance is the result not of abstraction from experience, as, for example, the British empiricists claim, but of a shared grammar across natural languages. It is because the languages of Greece, India and Germany all contain singular terms that we believe there are things in the world – substances – to which those singular terms refer. This point can be further generalized. Philosophical concepts in general "grow up in connection and relationship with each other", so in the end they "belong just as much to a system as all the members of the fauna of a continent" (*BGE* 20). And, to the extent that they are all members of a system, they are subject to Nietzsche's semantic deflation.

This sort of semantic argument may work against some philosophers, but certainly not against Immanuel Kant, Nietzsche's favourite target. Kant's version of the real world–apparent world distinction is the distinction between a phenomenon (how a thing appears) and thing-in-itself (the *ding-an-sich*). Kant's arguments for the distinction as presented in his monumental *Critique of Pure Reason* nowhere rely on obviously semantic premises. They rely instead on a supposed implication from the existence of phenomena in sensory experience to the existence of a domain of entities stripped of all sensory properties. Kant's general idea – an idea shared by a large number of philosophers – is that colour, mass, dimension, texture and other sensory properties cannot be known to be the properties that a thing has independent of sensory experience and so cannot be known to be essential to the thing that has them. So Kant and other philosophers argue that there must be something logically anterior to, and metaphysically more basic than, sensory things. There is, then, an entire realm of these metaphysically more basic entities. In Kant's hands, this domain is the realm of things-in-themselves.

Nietzsche counters in *Human, All too Human* that since it is bereft of all sensory properties, the thing-in-itself can have no connection whatsoever to the world of phenomena and that we can have no knowledge of it. Of course, Kant agrees with these claims, up to a point. What sets Kant apart from the other philosophers who thought they could establish the existence of substances is that he argues that, although the thing-in-itself must be posited, we can have no knowledge of any kind of it, since it is beyond all experience. Still, Kant routinely utilizes the thing-in-itself for various philosophical purposes, and Nietzsche thinks this is philosophically irresponsible. For Nietzsche, that the thing-in-itself is entirely beyond our experience and knowledge makes it worthy of a "Homeric laugh" (*HAH* I 16), and not, as for Kant, worthy of the most far-reaching thought of which we are capable.

By the mid-1880s, Nietzsche became convinced not only that the thing-in-itself is unknowable, but that its existence is an absurdity. This view receives succinct formulation in a note from the *Nachlass*: "The properties of a thing are effects on other 'things': if one removes other 'things', then a thing has no properties, i.e., there is no thing without other things, i.e., there is no 'thing in itself'" (*WP* 557). Although the thing-in-itself is absurd, belief in it is magnetically attractive. Nietzsche's explanation is that such belief is a displaced and projected belief in the subject atom (the soul, the subject, the ego). For example, a note in the *Nachlass* observes that the "psychological derivation of the belief in things forbids us to speak of 'things in themselves'" (*WP* 473), and another notes that once we see "that the subject is a fiction", then "at last the 'thing in itself' also disappears, because this is fundamentally the conception of a 'subject in itself'" (*WP* 552).

Nietzsche thinks that Kant's strongest defense of the existence of a domain of things-in-themselves actually rests on another premise, one that is a variation of our faith in the subject. Since, for Kant, the domain of human freedom is outside the phenomenal realm, he argues that there must be *something* there in that realm of which freedom is a property and for which freedom is essential. Kant draws two conclusions from this supposed necessity: first, there is a realm distinct from the realm of phenomena; and, secondly, one of the denizens of that other realm is the transcendental ego. Note the structure of this argument. In it Kant derives the necessity of certain ontological categories from a moral requirement. This is an instance of Nietzsche's methodological hunch, voiced in *Beyond Good and Evil* (*BGE* 6), that behind every metaphysical system there lies a morality. In Kant's case, the domain of moral freedom cannot be the same as the domain of experienced things since the latter is governed by causal law. Hence, there must be some other domain entirely distinct from that of phenomena. Hence, there must be transcendental egos and things-in-themselves. Nietzsche's counter-argument is just as straightforward. There are neither transcendental egos nor things-in-themselves. Hence, there is no domain behind the domain of phenomena. Hence, there is neither causal law nor moral freedom. We shall unpack these claims presently.

## Against substance and identity

The philosophical tradition has, since Aristotle, formulated its commitment to the real world by arguing that beneath the veil of appearance there is a world of stable entities – substances – each of which is self-identical at a time and over time. Philosophers spell out substance ontology in various ways, but every version of substance ontology shares certain features, among them the claim that substance is what is really real, that it is the bearer of properties and relations, that it is self-identical at a time (synchronic identity) and over time (diachronic identity), and that it is what remains identical across change. Nietzsche denies all these characteristics of substance. He does not think that substance is really real; he occasionally denies that there is anything that is self-identical at a time; he generally denies that there is anything that is self-identical over time; and he denies that there is anything that stays the same across change.

Nietzsche's view is that things are collections of properties (he also has an alternative view – that things are collections of power quanta – which we investigate in Chapter 8). So, for example, ordinary everyday things such as cups are bundles of properties, such as being of a particular shape, being composed of a certain number of molecules, being a certain colour, being a certain mass, having a handle and so on. In none of this is there any logical need to posit the existence of an additional thing of which those properties are properties: a bare nub that holds those properties together. This "thing", this substance, this hard little kernel to which all the properties of a thing stick, is, he thinks, a fabrication: "the 'thing' in which we believe was only invented as a foundation for the various attributes" (WP 561). To the extent that we are seduced into thinking that there must be substances by the referential devices in ordinary language, the mistake reappears in every similarly structured language.

Nietzsche understands quite clearly that if there are no substances, in the tradition's sense of the term, then, arguably, there is nothing that is self-identical either at a time or over time. As hard as it may be to believe, Nietzsche actually flirts with the idea that there is nothing self-identical at a time. Consider this passage:

> Supposing there were no self-identical "A", such as is presupposed by every proposition of logic (and of mathematics), and the "A" were already mere appearance, then logic would have a merely apparent world as its condition ... the "A" of logic is, like the atom, a reconstruction of the thing.                    (WP 516)

That looks rather odd: why countenance denying that $A = A$ at a time? Nietzsche countenances it because his claim is that whatever is self-identical is an appearance, not a substance. That is, synchronic identity is a property of the world we experience, not of the world behind experience. Just as there is no thing-in-itself, so too there is no identity-in-itself.

From Nietzsche's position that a thing is a bundle of properties, it also follows almost immediately that there is no diachronic identity. If a thing is identified as a bundle of properties, then, given standard assumptions about sets and their members, every property $P$ is essential to the identity of the thing of which $P$ is a constituent. Thus, no thing $a$ can change even one of its properties without *a* going out of existence. Suppose we have some bundle thing *a* composed of three properties, *P*, *Q* and *R*. Then *a* = <*P*, *Q*, *R*>. Take away one property, say *P*, and *a* does not exist, for *a* = <*P*, *Q*, *R*> and <*P*, *Q*, *R*> ≠ <*Q*, *R*>. That is just to say that *a* cannot add or lose any properties and remain *a*. So there is no identity across time wherever there is a change of properties. And there will always be a change of properties across time. After all, *a* at time $t_1$ has the property of existing at $t_1$; at the next instant, whatever exists then exists at $t_2$ and has the property of existing at $t_2$ rather than at $t_1$. Hence, nothing endures across change, or, put another way, nothing changes, or put still another way, there is nothing but change. Nietzsche recognizes this consequence and, amazingly enough, accepts it, at least on occasion. Since bundle things are formed via perspectives, and since these perspectives can revise the bundles, things are constantly going out of existence and coming into existence as perspectives change. Thus there is no genuine diachronic identity *anywhere*. The duration of a bundle thing is as permanent or as fleeting as the perspectives taken on them. Identity through time is a convenience, but there is no real, no substantial, persistence.

## Against the soul

Nietzsche explicitly denies the existence of souls, egos and conscious selves. In his various works, he argues directly against the Cartesian ego, the Kantian transcendental ego and the Schopenhaurian subject, among others. In each case, some philosopher claims to discover an entity altogether separate from its actions, an autonomous, usually conscious, subject whose identity is fixed at a time and over time. According to Nietzsche, the self is not a thing at all, is not a conscious thing in particular and is not identical over time. For instance, in *Beyond Good and Evil* he writes that "it is a falsification of the facts of the case to say that the subject 'I' is the condition of the predicate 'think'" (*BGE* 17). And in *Twilight of the Idols* he claims it is a "rude fetishism" that "believes in the 'ego', in the ego as being, in the ego as substance" (*TI* III 5).

Nietzsche's thought on this particular topic is complex. A revealing clue to that complexity can be found in a passage from *Beyond Good and Evil*. In this passage, he begins by characterizing belief in the soul as, at bottom, a religious belief, and connecting such religious beliefs with grammar. So he writes: "formerly, one believed in 'the soul' as one believed in grammar and the grammatical subject: one said, 'I' is the condition, 'think' is the predicate and conditioned-thinking is an activity to which thought *must* supply a subject as cause". But he then suggests that modern philosophy has a subterranean anti-Christian thrust that finds expression in its whittling away at the subject. As he points out:

> Then one tried with admirable perseverance and cunning to get out of this net – and asked whether the opposite might not be the case: "think" the condition, "I" the conditioned; "I" in that case only a synthesis which is *made* by thinking. At bottom, *Kant* wanted to prove that, starting from the subject, the subject could not be proved – nor could the object: the possibility of a *merely apparent existence* of the subject, "the soul" in other words, may not always have remained strange to him – that thought which as Vedanta philosophy existed once before on this earth and exercised tremendous power. (*BGE* 54)

(The reference to Vedanta philosophy in this passage is a reference to Buddhism. Recall from Chapter 2 that Buddhism also argues that subject-substances do not exist.) This passage is as good a précis of Nietzsche's views on the soul or philosophical subject as is to be found.

Philosophers such as Descartes argue that, since I think, I can conclude that I exist. Furthermore, Descartes claims that this "I" that exists is without parts, is simple and is identical over time. Nietzsche thinks there is a covert agenda at work here to establish the causal, and from this the metaphysical, dependence of thinking upon the subject. In typical versions, we find philosophers arguing from the admitted existence of thinking to the metaphysical necessity of a subject of thought. Descartes's *cogito ergo sum* – I think, therefore I am – is a straightforward instance of this argument form. Nietzsche denies the validity of all such arguments. He points out that, beginning with David Hume, an eighteenth-century British empiricist, and extending to Kant, philosophers exhibit doubts about the argument. Hume points out that when he looks inside himself he does *not* find any subject of thought. Hume's point is generalizable: even where we admit that there is thought, it does not follow from that fact alone that there is a *subject* of thought. Kant took Hume's scepticism about the thinking subject to heart. As we shall see in the next section, he simply concedes to Hume the impossibility of ever establishing the *empirical* existence of a subject of thought and makes a philosophically sophisticated attempt to establish a *transcendental* subject of thought. This Kantian theme is what Nietzsche is alluding to when he says that the subject of thought is the result, not the cause, of the thinking: the subject emerges from the synthesizing activity of thought rather than being its necessary precondition.

We shall investigate Kant's views on the conscious subject in greater detail in the next section, but here we can note the following about Kant's argument and Nietzsche's interpretation of it. In his *Critique of Pure Reason*, Kant argues that we can never know anything about the subject of thought because the subject of thought can never get outside itself far enough to look back at itself as an object of knowledge. But he does not argue, as Nietzsche suggests here, that, beginning with the subject, we cannot prove the existence of the subject. The whole point of this section of the *Critique* is to establish the transcendental necessity of, and to admit the impossibility of empirically proving the existence of, the subject of thought. So Nietzsche gets that part of Kant wrong. However, in another way, Nietzsche is right. Beginning with the activity of thought, Kant does admit that we cannot prove the *empirical* existence of the thinking subject. His argument for the *transcendental* necessity of the thinking subject presupposes that every proof for the empirical existence of the subject must fail. Nietzsche is also right that Kant's argument entails that we can never know anything about the transcendental subject of thought, for, as transcendental, the subject of thought is beyond all knowledge. So Nietzsche is right that, so far as our knowledge is concerned, starting with the lack of knowledge of the empirical subject entails proving that there is no knowledge of the transcendental subject.

## Against the conscious self

The philosophical tradition has had a long love affair with consciousness. This infatuation usually focuses on the uniqueness of consciousness, the impossibility of providing a naturalistic explanation for its emergence, and its status as a gift from God. Among other things, this infatuation requires believing that consciousness "constitutes the *kernel* of man; what is abiding, eternal, ultimate, and most original in him. One takes consciousness for a determinate magnitude. One denies its growth and its intermittences. One takes it for the 'unity of the organism'" (*GS* 11). The last sentence is pretty obviously a crack at Kant, whose transcendental unity of apperception is the highest expression to date of the tradition's love affair with consciousness. Nietzsche is convinced that such views are false from beginning to end. He thinks, to the contrary, that consciousness is "the last and latest development of the organic and hence also what is most unfinished and unstrong" (*GS* 11), that consciousness is an "idea of an idea" (*WP* 476) and that it is "a second derivative of that false introspection which believes in 'thinking'" (*WP* 477).

The word "consciousness" is notoriously hard to define, so we begin by trying to circumscribe it. In his work, Nietzsche focuses primarily on transitive consciousness, in which a subject is aware of something, either something in the mind, such as another thought, or something outside of the mind, such as a rock. Transitive consciousness is divisible into at least four kinds. The first is *access consciousness*, in which the content of a psychological event is immediately available for subsequent reasoning, emotional response and control of action. This is the most pervasive kind of transitive consciousness, for it is nothing more than being awake with ongoing mental states. Examples include my enjoyment of ice cream and my hope that I will get to go to Brimstone Gulch next year. The second is *phenomenal consciousness*, in which there is a way that things are for us when some event occurs. Examples of phenomenal consciousness are the way ice cream tastes and the pleasure that thinking about going to Brimstone Gulch causes. The third is *reflective consciousness*, in which one psychological event is the object of another. Examples of reflective consciousness are my thinking to myself that I am eating ice cream and thinking that hoping that I get to go to Brimstone Gulch is only wishful thinking. Finally, there is *self-consciousness*, in which we have the concept of our self as the content of the event. An example of self-consciousness is the recognition I have of myself when I think to myself that I am eating ice cream.

Although he denies outright that there is self-consciousness, Nietzsche uses the words "conscious" and "consciousness" to describe phenomena that belong to the first three kinds of transitive consciousness. For example, some passages suggest that what he has in mind is phenomenal consciousness:

> That a sort of adequate relationship subsists between subject and object, that the object is something that if seen from within would be a subject, is a well-meant invention which, I think, has had its day ... how could this nook-perspective of consciousness permit us to assert anything of "subject" and "object" that touched reality! (WP 474)

In *The Gay Science* he suggests a kind of access consciousness:

> Before knowledge is possible, each of these instincts must first have presented its one-sided view of the thing or event; after this comes the fight of these one-sided views, and occasionally this results in a mean, one grows calm, one finds all three sides right, and there is a kind of justice and a contract .... Since only the last scenes of reconciliation and the final accounting at the end of this long process rise to our consciousness, we suppose that *intelligere* must be something conciliatory, just, and good ... (GS 333)

And he also suggests reflective consciousness:

> Man, like every living being, thinks continually without knowing it; the thinking that rises to *consciousness* is only the smallest part of all this – the most superficial and worst part – for only this conscious thinking *takes the form of words, which is to say signs of communication* ...                                    (GS 354)

Most of the time, Nietzsche appears to mean this reflective kind of consciousness. I am the first to admit that attributing to Nietzsche the claim that it is reflective consciousness that he usually means when he talks about consciousness is debatable. The preponderance of evidence points in that direction, but he never bothers to define "consciousness", so we cannot really be certain what he thinks consciousness is. Still, let us look at the available evidence.

In *Ecce Homo*, Nietzsche describes consciousness as a "surface" (*EH*, "Why I am So Clever" 9). In *The Gay Science* he claims that it is a "net" and that to be conscious of something is a kind of "mirror effect" (*GS* 354), a claim made also in *Daybreak* about the intellect as a whole (*D* 121). He also suggests in *Daybreak* that consciousness is "a more or less fantastic commentary on an unknown, perhaps unknowable, but felt text" (*D* 119). Together, these claims suggest that consciousness is a reflective and dependent phenomenon, reflective of and dependent upon some other kind or kinds of phenomena. That consciousness has these properties suggests that it is not simply being aware or having qualitative experience, that is, being access or phenomenal conscious of something. Nietzsche also claims that "the conscious world of feelings, intentions, and valuations is a small section" (*WP* 707) of our psychological life, and that "even ... our thinking, feeling, and willing life" (*GS* 354) frequently proceeds without consciousness's exegetical attachment. So consciousness attaches only to some psychological events and each of the psychological events to which it attaches can also exist without consciousness attaching to it. This also suggests reflective consciousness, for it is the only kind of consciousness without which our thinking, feeling and willing life could continue.

To these comments, we may add the historical observation that the concept of consciousness Nietzsche encounters in Leibniz and in Kant – apperception – is arguably a kind of reflective consciousness. Nietzsche endorses what he calls Leibniz's

> incomparable insight ... that consciousness is merely an *accidens* of experience and *not* its necessary and essential attribute; that, in other words, what we call consciousness constitutes only one state

of our spiritual and psychic world (perhaps a pathological state)
and *not by any means the whole of it.*                    (GS 357)

What Nietzsche is referring to here is apperception as Leibniz understood
it: a clear and distinct intellectual second-order perception of either a
sensation or a non-sensory perception. The crucial property of apperception in Leibniz's work is that apperceptions are episodic even while we
are awake.

Nietzsche's use of reflective consciousness fuels both his Kantian
objections to various views of the self as soul or substance and his anti-
Kantian objections to the transcendental unity of apperception. Let us
unpack these dense claims, and let us begin that process with Kant's
arguments in the *Critique of Pure Reason* for the transcendental unity of
apperception. These arguments may be familiar, but paying close attention
to them helps identify the Kantian points that Nietzsche uses in his
arguments against others and the Kantian claims from which Nietzsche
demurs. Kant appropriates Leibniz's use of "apperception" but the word
does not refer in Kant to the same psychological events as those referred to
when Leibniz uses the term. For Leibniz, apperceptions are intellectual
perceptions that acquaint us with non-apperceptive psychological events
as they are in themselves. Kant rejects Leibniz's commitment to this
property of apperception. For Kant, apperception acquaints us with non-
apperceptive psychological events only as they are already tinted with
certain features supplied by our minds. In its most general use,
apperception is for Kant a kind of psychological event in which the
intentional object of the event (the "intentional object" of a psychological
event is what we are thinking, or hoping, or fearing or whatever *about*) is
another psychological event as it is presented in space and time and as
categorized.

Kant distinguishes between empirical and transcendental apperception
in the *Critique of Pure Reason*. *Empirical* apperception is a psychological
event in which one psychological event is accompanied by a second-order
event that takes the first-order event as its intentional object. *The
transcendental unity* of apperception, on the other hand, is the possibility
of "I" accompanying all my psychological events. Kant's argument for the
necessity of the transcendental unity of apperception is one of the most
famous passages in philosophy. He argues that the constituents of sensory
experience are members of a set of presentations, the so-called "manifold
of presentation". However, that manifold of presentation is always a
manifold *for someone*, and for that manifold of presentation to be the
sensory experience of some such someone, say me, it must be unified,
which in turn requires that the members of the set of presentations

composing the manifold be synthesized as the thoughts of a synchronically and diachronically identical subject. In short, experience must be structured as being the experience of a unitary subject, and this requisite structure is the transcendental unity of apperception. The transcendental unity of apperception is, thus, that in virtue of which a continuous sequence of conscious psychological events is unified as *my* sequence of psychological events. Were it not to obtain, nobody would have unified experience of anything.

Hence, Kant acknowledges that the existence of the thinking subject is entailed by the nature of sensory experience. Still, he insists that *knowledge* of the thinking subject is impossible. Other than its being necessary for experience, we can know nothing of the transcendental unity of apperception. In particular, we cannot know that it is the activity of a thinking substance that is simple, synchronically unitary and diachronically identical. To think that we are so entitled is to follow the sloppy metaphysician, such as Descartes, into a trap. In order for the metaphysician to defend his claims that the subject is knowable, the transcendental unity of apperception would have to yield an empirical unified self of which knowledge is possible. But Kant argues (with Hume) that in empirical apperception we can find no such unified self. Those who think they can establish the existence of the ego or self-substance fallaciously turn the transcendental unity of apperception into an object of knowledge. The arguments of the first three Paralogisms in the *Critique of Pure Reason* expose the fallacies involved in such claims. Although the self is, and must be, represented as a simple, synchronically unitary and diachronically identical subject of experience, from this it does not follow either that the self *is* a simple, self-identical substance or that we can *know* that the self is a simple, self-identical substance. As Kant puts it: "as regards inner sense ... we intuit ourselves only as we are inwardly affected *by ourselves*; in other words, ... so far as inner intuition is concerned, we know our own subject only as appearance, not as it is in itself".*

Nietzsche sounds remarkably like Kant when he objects to the metaphysicians, Descartes being an exemplar. He concurs with Kant that those who make a thing of the self are mistaken. The following note is representative:

> "There is thinking: therefore there is something that thinks": this is the upshot of all Descartes' argumentation. But that means positing as "true *a priori*" our belief in the concept of substance –

---

* I. Kant, *Critique of Pure Reason*, N. Kemp Smith (trans.) (New York: St. Martin's Press, 1963), B 156.

that when there is thought there has to be something "that thinks" is simply a formulation of our grammatical custom that adds a doer to every deed. In short, this is not merely the substantiation of a fact but a logical-metaphysical postulate.          (WP 484)

With Kant, Nietzsche argues that any alleged knowledge of the self as a substance is fallaciously inferred from our need to believe that there is such a subject. Nietzsche's version adds the linguistic touch that the belief in the subject is a function of the grammatical requirement that there be a subject term in a statement. The argument in Kant's Second Paralogism against the simplicity of the subject also finds expression in Nietzsche's work at, among other places, this note: "No subject 'atoms.' The sphere of a subject constantly growing or decreasing, the center of the system constantly shifting; in cases where it cannot organize the appropriate mass, it breaks into two parts" (WP 488). Here, Nietzsche concurs with Kant that the subject cannot be known to be simple. Nietzsche drives the point home in another note that urges us to consider the possibility that there is "a multiplicity of subjects, whose interaction and struggle is the basis of our thought in consciousness" (WP 490). Nietzsche obviously goes beyond Kant's negative claim that we cannot know that the subject is simple, but the suggestion about the multiplicity of subjects presupposes that Kant is correct. Finally, Nietzsche concurs with Kant's argument, in the Third Paralogism, that the diachronic identity of the self cannot be known. Witness: "Duration, identity with itself, being are inherent neither in that which is called subject nor in that which is called object: they are complexes of events apparently durable in comparison with other complexes" (WP 552c). This point will become important in Chapter 7, where we discuss Nietzsche's views on personal identity.

To the extent that both argue against the reification of the thinking subject, Kant and Nietzsche agree. However, when it comes to the transcendental unity of apperception, Nietzsche and Kant go their separate ways. The transcendental unity of apperception is for Kant a prerequisite of any cognitive or sensory activity, but Nietzsche sees no reason why this *must* be the case. After all, the intermittency of reflective consciousness suggests to the contrary that there is no unified subject of thought. Nietzsche's counter-suggestion is, rather, that "we gain the correct idea of the nature of our subject-unity, namely as regents at the head of a communality" (WP 492) from the body, not consciousness. We shall also investigate this claim in greater detail in Chapter 7.

Let us note in passing that Nietzsche misses the mark with this criticism of Kant. Kant nowhere suggests that the empirical existence of a unified subject of thought follows from the necessity that there be such a subject of thought. Unfortunately, Nietzsche's criticism here attributes to Kant just this suggestion. Nietzsche argues that the intermittency of apperception entails that there is no unity of apperception over time. But that can only be an empirical unity of apperception, since it is an empirical claim about apperception that it is intermittent. With that Kant agrees. Kant's claim about the transcendental unity of apperception is, rather, a modal claim: it is necessarily the case that it is always possible that the manifold of sensory experience be unified as my manifold rather than someone else's. From that required possibility nothing whatsoever follows about any empirical unity of apperception, and Kant goes to great lengths to insist on that point.

## Against causality and necessity

We conclude our discussion of Nietzsche's criticisms of metaphysics by considering what he says about causality and necessity. Nietzsche's subtle criticisms of causality should not lead us to conclude that he recommends rejecting it altogether. Admittedly, some passages do appear to recommend a blanket elimination of causality. One of the most forceful is this note from *Beyond Good and Evil*:

> ... one should use "cause" and "effect" only as pure concepts, that is to say, as conventional fictions for the purpose of designation and communication – not for explanation. ... It is we alone who have devised cause, sequence, for each other, relativity, constraint, number, law, freedom, motive and purpose: and when we project and mix this symbol world into things as if it existed "in itself," we act once more as we have always acted – mythologically.
>
> (*BGE* 21)

Yet he also makes equally strong claims on behalf of causality. For example, one of the mistakes of morality and religion is that neither has the decency to respect natural causality:

> if we imagine ourselves back in the times when religious life was in fullest flower, we find a fundamental conviction we no longer share .... People in those times do not yet know anything of natural laws; neither for the earth nor for the heavens is there a "must". There is no concept of natural causality. ... There is nothing outside ourselves about which we are allowed to conclude

that it will become thus and so, must be thus and so: we ourselves
are what is more or less certain, calculable. Man is the rule, nature
without rule.                                                          (*HAH* 11)

In *The Anti-Christ* Nietzsche reiterates his contention that "In Christianity
neither morality nor religion come into contact with reality at any point.
Nothing but imaginary *causes*..., nothing but imaginary *effects*" (*AC* 15).

Given that Nietzsche appears both to discount and to endorse causality, we
really must proceed with caution. In fact, Nietzsche offers four direct
philosophical criticisms of causality: first, he claims that causes and effects are
not *things*; secondly, he argues that causes and effects are not *mechanistic*
things; thirdly, he thinks that causality is not a *nomological* relationship;
fourthly, he usually claims also that causality is not a *necessary relationship*.

## Causal things

One of Nietzsche's favourite points to make against causality is that neither
cause nor effect is a *thing*. Here is how he puts the matter in *The Gay Science*:

> "Cause" and "effect" is what one says; but we have merely
> perfected the image of becoming without reaching beyond the
> image or behind it. In every case the series of "causes" confronts us
> much more completely, and we infer: first, this and that has to
> precede in order that this or that may then follow – but this does
> not involve any comprehension. In every chemical process, for
> example, quality appears as a "miracle," as ever; else how could
> we possibly explain anything? We operate only with things that do
> not exist: lines, planes, atoms, divisible time spans, divisible
> spaces. How should explanations be at all possible when we first
> turn everything into an image, our image!                      (*GS* 112)

This passage makes two points that merit further discussion. First, our
scientific descriptions differ from other kinds of descriptions in identifying
entities as cause and effect. Secondly, science uses entities from mathematics and logic, entities that do not exist, so it does not achieve its goal of
providing explanations; instead, it offers a re-description.

It is the second criticism that is more important, for it leads us to his
criticism of cause and effect things. Later in the same passage, he expands:

> Cause and effect: such a duality probably never exists; in truth we are
> confronted by a continuum out of which we isolate a couple of

pieces, just as we perceive motion only as isolated points and then infer it without ever actually seeing it. . . . An intellect that could see cause and effect as a continuum and a flux and not, as we do, in terms of an arbitrary division and dismemberment, would repudiate the concept of cause and effect and deny all conditionality.   (GS 112)

According to this passage, it is a mistake to identify an entity with its role as a cause or as an effect. In fact, the identification is doubly mistaken. The first mistake is identifying an entity with its causal role. Having identified role and entity, it falls out readily that causes and effects are parts of a structure independent of interpreters, and this Nietzsche denies. Secondly, by identifying entities with causal roles, we facilitate the separation of doer from deed, a claim Nietzsche places considerable weight on in his criticism of the soul in *The Genealogy of Morals*. Having identified an entity with its causal role, we reify the role into a thing and distinguish the role from its causal effects. Hence, there are both causal activities (the deeds) and a "super added" cause thing (the doer) distinct from causal activities. This duplication of entities is, Nietzsche thinks, erroneous.

## Mechanistic causes

Nietzsche also rejects mechanistic theories of causality and mechanism in general. Mechanism is the general philosophical thesis that every kind of system that can be used in scientific explanation is a system for which a particular kind of analysis – a mechanistic analysis – can be provided. A mechanistic analysis is an analysis that makes no essential reference to biological structures or processes. Mechanism was rampant across scientific disciplines in the nineteenth century, not only in physics and the still relatively new science of chemistry, but also in biology and other higher-level sciences. Nietzsche is an unwavering opponent to mechanism. He says in a *Nachlass* note that, "'Mechanistic interpretation': desires nothing but quantities; but force is to be found in quality. Mechanistic theory can therefore only *describe* processes, not explain them" (WP 660). Mechanism describes phenomena only by falsifying them, so the explanations couched in terms of those descriptions also falsify those phenomena and do not really explain anything.

Mechanism falsifies the phenomena it purports to explain because it is nothing more than logic applied to space and time. In *The Gay Science*, for instance, Nietzsche argues that mechanistic science "permits counting, calculating, weighing, seeing, and touching, and nothing more" (GS 373). That restriction is the result of our decision to "operate only with things that do not exist: lines, planes, atoms, divisible time spans, divisible spaces" (*GS* 112). Since mechanism uses objects fabricated in mathematical and logical languages to make their formulae interpretable and manipulable in the first place, mechanistic descriptions never come into contact with reality. We shall return to this matter and discuss it at length in Chapter 6, where we discuss Nietzsche's anti-realism. It is enough to say here that Nietzsche is convinced that any scientific theory couched either in the language of mathematics or logic falsifies that to which its sentences purport to refer.

## Nomological causes

Nietzsche also argues that causality is not a lawlike, or nomological, relation. His central argument for this claim is that construing causality as a nomological relation presupposes a law-giver. The following passage from *The Gay Science* is a typical statement of this view:

> Let us beware of saying that there are laws in nature. There are only necessities: there is nobody who commands, nobody who obeys, nobody who trespasses. Once you know that there are no purposes, you also know that there is no accident; for it is only beside a world of purposes that the word "accident" has meaning.
> (*GS* 109)

Attributing a law-giver to explain the nomological causal relations between events in the non-human world certainly soothes us by encouraging us to believe that the non-human world is, even after God's death, still an orderly place and of a kindred sort because it is guided by the hand of nature.

The law-giver argument is not Nietzsche's only argument against causal nomologicality. With Hume, Nietzsche also argues that we routinely conflate regularity and nomologicality, taking experience of the former as evidence for the occurrence of the latter. For example, he notes in the *Nachlass* that:

> the unalterable sequence of certain phenomena demonstrates no "law" but a power relationship between two or more forces. To say "But this relationship itself remains constant" is to say no more than "One and the same force cannot also be another force." – It is a question, not of succession, but of interpenetration, a process in which the individual successive moments are not related to one another as cause and effect.
> (*WP* 631)

I have quoted Nietzsche at length here because, in addition to making the point that regularity does not entail nomologicality, he suggests something much more radical. He claims in the last sentence that relationships between events are a matter of interpenetration, not a matter of one event at a moment causing another event at a later moment. Here, he broaches one of the constituent claims of his proposal to replace causality with will to power. We shall return to this issue in Chapter 8.

## Necessity

Nietzsche usually criticizes attempts to construe causality as a relationship to which necessity attaches as well. Before going any further, let us make clear what we mean by the word "necessity". In so far as it refers only to the occurrence of causal relations between events, necessity is not a unique characteristic. However, the word "necessity" is usually taken to refer to something stronger, more metaphysical, than the occurrence of causal relations. When most philosophers use the word "necessity", they mean that, even if we inhabited a world with different natural laws and different causal laws, some events would still occur just as they occur in our world with its natural and causal laws. In fact, if an event is necessary, what most philosophers typically mean by that is that it will occur in any logically possible world or any metaphysically possible world. And what is true of events is true also of relations, properties, and other categories of existence to which necessity is thought to attach. For instance, the relation of identity, something we have discussed above, is often thought to be a necessary relationship. That is, if $A = A$, then necessarily $A = A$; that is, $A = A$ in all logically possible worlds. So, too, if there are any properties that are essential to, say, me – perhaps my genetic inheritance – then they are properties I have in every logically possible world in which I exist. Essential properties are necessary properties.

We are nit-picking with the property of necessity in part because we need to if we are to understand Nietzsche's various pronouncements on causal necessity, and in part because when we discuss, in Chapters 8 and 9, Nietzsche's notorious notions of eternal recurrence and *amor fati* (loving one's fate), we shall have need again for necessity. Here, let us focus on what Nietzsche says about causality and necessity. It is undeniable that Nietzsche occasionally affirms that necessity is a property not only of our human interpretations of the world but a constituent of the world itself. This passage from *The Gay Science* is perhaps the one most frequently cited as support:

> Let us beware of saying that there are laws in nature. There are only necessities: there is nobody who commands, nobody who

obeys, nobody who trespasses. Once you know that there are no purposes, you also know that there is no accident; for it is only beside a world of purposes that the word "accident" has meaning.

(*GS* 109)

In *Human, All to Human*, Nietzsche likewise notes that "when we see a waterfall, we think we see freedom of will and choice in the unnumerable turnings, windings, breakings of the waves; but everything is necessary; each movement can be calculated mathematically" (*HAH* 106). And in the next section of *Human, All too Human,* he suggests straightforwardly that "everything is necessity" (*HAH* 107).

These passages sanction attributing necessity to relations in the world independent of perspective. The problem is that Nietzsche also argues for the thesis that necessity is a matter of human interpretation and a function of our perspective. For instance, in *Beyond Good and Evil*, he insists that "In the 'in itself' there is nothing of 'causal connections,' of 'necessity,' or of 'psychological non-freedom'" (*BGE* 21). So too: "'Mechanical necessity' is not a fact: it is we who first intepreted it into events. We have interpreted the formulatable character of events as the consequence of a necessity that rules over events" (*WP* 552). These passages imply that necessity is not a component of some perspective-free world composed of things-in-themselves but is, rather, a function of particular perspectives taken on a world that is itself constitutionally perspectival. That looks like a flat-out inconsistency.

The inconsistency is only apparent. In the passages from the *Nachlass* and *Human, All Too Human*, Nietzsche connects necessity with calculability. In the *Nachlass* passage, for instance, he thinks that we have inferred the necessity of mechanistic explanations from the "formulatable character of events", and in *Human, All Too Human* (*HAH* 106), he claims that the necessity of natural events and phenomena consists in their being mathematically calculable. Resolving the apparent inconsistency is now easy. After all, it is our language, logic and mathematics that make events calculable in the first place. Necessity does not attach to things-in-themselves (not that there are any such anyway), but to our descriptions of events and things. Waterfalls, breaking waves and so forth may all be necessary but that is not because necessity attaches to events or phenomena antecedent to our descriptions of them but because our descriptions have made them calculable. In short, if we are willing to attribute necessity to events in the world, that attribution is consequent upon a logically antecedent attribution of calculability to events in the world. And that calculability is no more an intrinsic feature of the world stripped of perspectives taken upon it than the attribution to the world that flowers are an expression of God's joy.

So causality is not a relation between cause and effect things, is not a lawful relationship and is not a necessary relationship. Why, then, do we insist on making it thus? Here, again, Nietzsche suggests that we look to ourselves for an answer. Our beliefs about causality are repeatedly claimed to be the result of two factors. First, our faith in grammar and its requirement that there be a subject term leads us to accept that there must be a doer in addition to the deed. Secondly, our belief about ourselves that we are subjects, independent of all our actions, leads us to generalize the same subject–action structure to the non-human world.

About the first point, little needs to be added here to what has already been said. However, the point that our attachment to the belief that causes and effects are things is a result of our belief about ourselves that we are subjects, introduces a new wrinkle. Nietzsche holds that this affinity is the result not of seeing one event following another but of:

> our inability to interpret events otherwise than as events caused by intentions. It is belief in the living and thinking as the only effective force – in will, in intention – it is belief that every event is a deed, that every deed presupposes a doer, it is belief in the "subject". (WP 550)

This derivation is so pervasive and so pernicious that Nietzsche identifies it in *Twilight of the Idols* as one of the four great errors. Of it, he says:

> we had made a nice misuse of that "empiricism," we had *created* the world on the basis of it as a world of causes, as a world of will, as a world of spirit. The oldest and longest lived psychology was at work here – indeed it has done nothing else: every event was to it an action, every action the effect of a will, the world became for it a multiplicity of agents, an agent ("subject") foisted itself upon every event. (*TI* V 3)

We insert subjects and agents into the non-human world, and we do so because we buy into the theologian's (the priest's) interpretation of the world, an interpretation that requires causal agents in the human realm and therefore imputes them to the rest of the world. In the end, the attraction of causality is but another covert manifestation of decadence and *ressentiment*.

As we shall see in Chapter 8, one of the remarkable facets of Nietzsche's thinking about causality is that his proposed replacement for causality, will to power, seems on first reading to be an *exemplar* of the very mistake he warns against in *Twilight of the Idols* (*TI* V 3). After all, the will to power employs the category of *willing*, and willing is the philosophical tradition's chosen mechanism for human agency to engage with the non-human world. It is, at this point, an open question whether Nietzsche overcomes this fundamental inconsistency. In fact, we shall not really be ready to resolve the problem until we have worked through his views on truth, knowledge, willing in the human case and the will to power itself.

# CHAPTER 5

# Truth

More than most people, philosophers take truth *very* seriously, for they take as one of their primary tasks the investigation of the *nature* of truth. In many ways, this is a peculiar task: philosophers are not as interested in identifying true claims as they are in understanding what it means to say that a claim is true when it is true. Suppose we have some true statement. Here's one: "grass is green". Philosophers want to know what unique properties that statement has that make it true. For instance, they will ask: if a statement is true, is it true for everyone? Is it always true? Can a true statement ever be false? If so, when? In virtue of what is the statement true? Philosophers are also interested in the so-called "truths of reason", those logical, metaphysical and ethical statements that are routinely paraded about as absolutely true. Among these claims are: God exists; the world is/is not real; life is absurd; and happiness is the good. There are many others.

In this chapter, we investigate Nietzsche's criticisms of truth and his view of truth. We shall begin by canvassing Nietzsche's unwavering hostility to absolute truth. His criticisms of absolute truth range from semantic arguments about the function of the truth predicate in a language, through epistemological arguments that purport to show the impossibility of ever knowing that a statement is absolutely true, to practical arguments concerning the pernicious consequences of believing in absolute truths. We shall then try to clarify what Nietzsche means by claiming that truth is perspectival. It turns out that while perspectival truth is a defensible view, it has some strange consequences.

## Absolute truth

Truth perspectivism is intended by Nietzsche to serve as a counter to the pervasive absolutism about truth in the philosophical tradition. It is undeniable that philosophers have used their dialectical cleverness to try to establish absolute truths and, once established, have used them to bludgeon anyone who disagrees with them. Nietzsche is sceptical about absolute truths, and his scepticism is simply stated: why think there are *any* absolute truths of *any* kind? And if there are any, why think that the absolute truths offered by philosophers are among them?

To be clear on Nietzsche's answer to these questions, we should unpack "absolutism". Absolutism is the general view about truth that some statements are true in every perspective. Sometimes absolutism is taken to be the view that some statements are true outside any perspective (I shall make some comments on this version later in this chapter). Nietzsche denies both versions of absolute truth repeatedly, nowhere more famously than in this *Nachlass* note: "There are many kinds of eyes. Even the sphinx has eyes – and consequently there are many kinds of 'truths,' and consequently there is no truth" (*WP* 540). Even here, it is important to emphasize that Nietzsche does not deny that there are true statements. He thinks there are true statements, many kinds of them. Rather, it is the presumption that statements are absolutely true, true without being indexed to a perspective (to "eyes"), that he rejects.

In two millennia of thinking about truth, philosophers have proposed many varieties of truth: objective truth; absolute truth; contingent truth; universal truth; logical truth; necessary truth; scientific truth; personal truth; relative truth; pragmatic truth – the list goes on and on. But for all the ink that has been spilled defending this or that kind of truth, they are all easily distilled into two basic kinds: correspondence truth and coherence truth. There is one exception, and that one exception is Nietzsche.

The most widely defended variety of truth, and the one most people think of when they think about truth, is undoubtedly correspondence truth. Aristotle enunciated the correspondence theory of truth beautifully when he said that to say of what is that it is is true. Correspondence theories of truth affirm that there is a relation – the relation of correspondence – between two categories of things. On the one hand, we have sentences, propositions, statements, claims or beliefs. Since the differences between these kinds of entities are not germane to our purposes, let us choose a fairly neutral category, that of statements, as the first relatum of the correspondence relation. Statements are then taken to correspond to something else in the world. Various candidates for what these things in the world might be have been put forward, among them substances, things, states of affairs, facts and events. Again, the differences between the categories are irrelevant for our purposes.

To see how the correspondence theory of truth is supposed to work, consider a banal statement, say "Pikes Peak is 14,110 feet tall". The defender of correspondence truth will analyse the truth of this statement as follows. The statement:

Pikes Peak is 14,110 feet tall

is composed of a subject term – the name "Pikes Peak" – and a predicate expression – "is 14,110 feet tall". In the world there are, it is thought, corresponding entities: the mountain itself referred to by the name "Pikes Peak" and the property expressed by the predicate "is 14,110 feet tall". So the defender of the correspondence theory might say that the statement:

Pikes Peak is 14,110 feet tall

is true if and only if the thing referred to by the name "Pikes Peak" has the property expressed by the predicate "is 14,110 feet tall". Alternatively, the correspondence theorist might say that the statement is true if and only if it is a fact that Pikes Peak is 14,110 feet tall.

What is true for this banal claim can then be generalized for all the different kinds of truth we listed above. An *objective* truth is a statement that affirms that something is true of some objective state of affairs; an *absolute* truth affirms that something is true across all perspectives; a *contingent* truth affirms that something is true of some state of affairs that, given different states of affairs, would be false; a *universal* truth affirms something is true for everyone who utters it; a *logical* truth affirms that something is true that cannot, on pain of denying a truth of logic, be false; a *necessary* truth affirms that something is true that cannot, on pain of denying a truth of metaphysics, be false; a *scientific* truth affirms that something is true that has been discovered by science. All these kinds of truth can easily be parsed as varieties of correspondence truth, where the only variation (where it does occur – some deny that there is any distinction between logical and necessary truths, some that there is any distinction between universal and absolute truths) is in the nature of the entities that make the statement true.

Undoubtedly, there are many statements for which a correspondence analysis of truth is more than a little difficult to prosecute. Poetic and religious statements are obvious examples, but take the following statement:

Undoubtedly, there are many statements for which a correspondence analysis of truth is more than a little difficult to prosecute.

Is that sentence correspondence true? It is if the entities referred to by the subject term – "many statements" – have the property expressed by the predicate expression – "being such that a correspondence analysis of truth is more than a little difficult to prosecute". What kind of property is that? And how do we determine whether a statement has that property? The difficulties are apparent.

Suffice it to say, for all its intuitive plausibility, the correspondence theory of truth is surprisingly recalcitrant to intuitive or plausible analysis. That is one of the reasons why the coherence theory of truth has a long history as a contrasting and distinct theory of truth. Coherence theories of truth affirm that a statement is true whenever it coheres with some set of other statements. That is, there is a relation of coherence between some linguistic or mental item and a set of other linguistic or mental items such that if the former bears that relation to the latter then the former is true. The relation of coherence gets spelled out variously in terms of logical relations (entailment, implication, presupposition) among sentences, pragmatic fit among sentences and overall predictive power.

In his work, Nietzsche is most concerned to deny the viability of correspondence theories of truth, although what he says also undermines certain versions of coherence theories. He nowhere denies that we *want to have* correspondence truth or that people often *believe* that there are propositions that are correspondence true. It is consistent with denying that there is such a thing that we have a drive to find it (think of the fountain of youth). Nietzsche goes even further. He thinks we have a *will* to find truth. In *The Genealogy of Morals* it is the will to truth that motivates the generation of genealogies, underlies the rejection of science as the only method via which truth is to be discovered, and warrants the critical appraisal of the value of truth. However, the will to discover statements that correspond to the world, if cultivated without self-deception, leads to the admission that there are no such statements.

Why does Nietzsche think that there are no correspondence truths? One way of getting a handle on his answer to this question is to ask another question: are there *any* statements that bear the right kind of relationship to the phenomena described? Correspondence truth is, recall, composed of three elements: statements; a relation of correspondence; and the world of objects and their properties, and phenomena composed of them. So if we deny that there is any correspondence relation between statements and the world of objects and their properties and states of affairs composed of them, or if we deny that there is a world composed of objects and their properties and states of affairs composed of them there will be no statements that are correspondence true. In the first case, we deny that there is a determinate relation between statements and world, and in the second case, there is no world of objects and their properties and phenomena composed of them to which linguistic or mental entities might bear the relation of correspondence. Either way, there would then be no correspondence truths.

Nietzsche's considered opinion is that both these criticisms of correspondence truth have merit. He thinks, for example, that we have to admit that the entities to which statements are said to correspond are entities *we* have created in order to have something to which our statements might correspond. Hence, he allows that "truth is the kind of error without which a certain species could not live" (*WP* 493) and that "we can comprehend only a world that we ourselves have made" (*WP* 495). One way of thinking about his criticism of correspondence truth is then as follows: he holds the correspondence theory of truth up to itself and asks whether the conditions it lays down as necessary and sufficient for truth are ever met. His answer is negative. Correspondence truth is an error because there are no statements that bear the relation of correspondence to anything in the world, and, where statements do correspond to phenomena, that set is distinct from the set of things required by typical statements of the correspondence theory. He also thinks it is not possible for us to attain the independent standpoint from which we might gauge whether the relation of correspondence has been achieved. Our needs and drives routinely get in the way and we simply cannot find the "view from nowhere" (to borrow a phrase from Thomas Nagel) to judge independently those drives or their role in undermining correspondence truth. In short, whatever knowledge we have is conditioned and perspectival, including our knowledge of true statements.

The plausibility of these claims rests on the plausibility of the claim that humans could not flourish without believing that their statements correspond to the world. Nietzsche is certain that this is the case:

> That a great deal of *belief* must be present; that judgments may be ventured; that doubt concerning all essential values is *lacking* – that is the precondition of every living thing and its life. Therefore, what is needed is that something must be held to be true – *not* that something *is* true. (*WP* 507)

This is a plausible claim. As we have seen, life as a thoroughgoing nihilist is extraordinarily difficult. It is quite plausible to suggest that avoiding nihilism is more salient than defending truth.

Nietzsche's other strategy of criticizing correspondence truth is to deny the existence of objects, properties and states of affairs composed of them. As we have seen, there is no such thing as substance independent of the properties that compose it, and properties are in turn analysed as perspectives or causal effects. But if a thing is the sum of its effects, then there is no antecedent thing that is the subject of causal effects. (We unpack this view in greater detail in Chapter 8.) With the reduction of all substance to bundles of causal effects, the rejection of one version of the correspondence truth falls out neatly. Since there are no substances and no properties independent of perspective, and no states of affairs composed of such things, there are no *things* to which statements and beliefs might correspond and no *states of affairs* composed of those things having certain properties to which statements might correspond. The world is infinitely dense, with no lowest point at which its perspectivity is replaced with anything non-perspectival: no fundamental building blocks that exist independently of perspective. There is nothing independent of perspectives to which statements might correspond.

## Perspectivist truth

If we go along with Nietzsche to this point, we are likely to have some pointed questions. One of them is this: suppose we grant that there is no correspondence truth – does that mean that Nietzsche advocates a kind of coherence theory of truth? Some people have thought so, but the answer is that he does not. Nietzsche nowhere explicitly argues against coherence theories of truth, but that is because he nowhere considers coherence theories of truth at all. Those who have interpreted Nietzsche as a coherentist infer this commitment from all the critical things he says about correspondence truth. Some have gone so far as to claim he is a pragmatist about truth. Here, too, the mistake is thinking that because he disowns correspondence truth he must advocate a pragmatic theory of truth. That is, of course, fallacious, since it is a false dilemma. Well then, if he criticizes correspondence theories of truth *and* pragmatic theories of truth and nowhere advocates any other kind of coherence theory of truth, does it not then follow from the dichotomy between correspondence and coherence theories of truth that Nietzsche is just a nihilist about truth? The answer, surprisingly, is no. He advocates a different view of truth: perspectivist truth. Let us turn to this alternative and investigate it.

We shall say that truth perspectivism is contrary to absolutism. Truth absolutism is, recall, the general view that some statements are true *simpliciter*, true across *all* perspectives. According to truth perspectivism, on the other hand, every statement is true in some perspective and false in some other perspective. It follows almost immediately that if two people occupy different incompatible perspectives, then a statement true for one person in one perspective is false for another person in that incompatible perspective.

It is a little surprising that Nietzsche never bothers to inform his readers what a perspective is. Here is one way to appreciate the problem: are there only supra-individual perspectives (for example, scientific or social perspectives), or are there also inter-individual perspectives (for example, the perspective of individuals with shared visual input at a time), individual perspectives (for example, how ice cream tastes to me), and perhaps even intra-individual perspectives (for example, the point of view of a drive)? Answering this complex question requires answers to two other more basic questions. First, what does Nietzsche think a perspective is? Secondly, how does he think perspectives are to be distinguished from one another? One answer to our questions that will *not* do is to say that a perspective is a belief or a set of beliefs. Suppose that a perspective were a belief. There would then be no difference between a statement being *believed* true in a perspective and a statement *being* true in a perspective. Everything we believe would, simply because we believe it, be true. Nietzsche bluntly rejects assimilating perspectives to beliefs. In *The Anti-Christ*, for example, he writes "truth and the belief that something is true: two completely diverse worlds of interest" (*AC* 23), and, in a note from the *Nachlass*, he insists that there can be false beliefs in perspectives: "a belief, however necessary it is for the preservation of a species, has nothing to do with truth" (*WP* 487). So Nietzsche cannot think that perspectival truths are the same thing as statements being believed.

So if a perspective is not a belief or a collection of them, what is it? Here we have to engage in some speculative interpretation, for Nietzsche is not forthcoming. Nietzsche does claim that a locus of will to power *generates* a perspective. A person, for instance, is such a locus, and Nietzsche thinks that if someone changes herself in the right way she will change her perspective. Given that truths vary across perspectives, a set of true statements will be generated whenever one adopts or creates a perspective. Still, even if perspectives somehow depend on loci of power, it does not provide an answer to the issue of the *kinds* of entities that can have a perspective, or the kind of thing that a perspective *is*. And here we have to admit that Nietzsche is just not very helpful at all. True, he says that "all evaluation is made from a definite perspective: that of the preservation of the individual, a community, a race, a state, a church, a faith, a culture" (*WP* 259). This suggests that all kinds of things can have a perspective. All of these are loci of power for Nietzsche, and so all are entities that adopt or create perspectives. One way of generalizing this view is to say that there is a hierarchy of loci of power, each level of which contains a domain of entities, each one of which has or generates a perspective. But beyond these hints, there is nothing else to go on.

Whatever perspectives turn out to be, one thing that is abundantly clear is that Nietzsche intends truth perspectivism to be a radical departure from traditional theories of truth. We can, if we like, think of it as a two-part theory of truth: statements bear relations of correspondence to various perspectival entities and sets of them, and determining whether statements bear those relations to those entities occurs within perspectives. To see how this works, consider again our banal statement:

Pikes Peak is 14,110 feet tall.

According to Nietzsche, we can determine that this statement is true, but it will take more effort than matching names with things and predicates with properties. First, we have to remember that the entity referred to by the singular term "Pikes Peak" is something we have fabricated; even if there is a world as it is in itself, the thing we call "Pikes Peak" might be there, but it would not be separately identified as Pikes Peak. So, too, the property expressed by "is 14,110 feet tall" is a property that that thing has only because we have perceptual and measurement metrics that are such that Pikes Peak satisfies the predicate utilizing them. Secondly, we have to identify the perspective in or from which the statement is being made. For me, on this date, from this place, the statement is true; for an individual living five hundred years from now, the statement will in all likelihood be false, given erosion rates on granite and the fact that the Colorado Front Range is no longer rising.

Consider next some more controversial statement, say the statement:

Christianity is the only true way to God.

Ignoring what Nietzsche thinks is the patent absurdity of the claim – recall that, for Nietzsche, the Christian God is so absurd a God that he would have to be killed even if he existed – there is still the question whether, if it is true, it is perspectivally true. For Nietzsche, it is at least a real possibility that, for some kinds of Christians, it is true; for other Christians and non-Christians, it is not. Surprisingly, Nietzsche's perspectivism about truth *sanctions* this kind of result. We are not just saying that some kinds of Christians *believe* the statement is absolutely true or that some kinds of Christians have faith that the statement is true. *Those* claims are claims that *any* philosopher would be willing to grant. The question is, instead: supposing that it is true, must it be true absolutely or can it be true perspectivally? To that question, some kinds of Christians will answer that it must be true absolutely if true at all; a God-friendly perspectivist, on the other hand, has the option of saying that the statement is true in some perspectives and not in others.

## Perspectivism and paradox

Even if we can make initial sense of truth perspectivism, it has more than its fair share of problems. It is, for example, the target of an obvious and potentially devastating criticism. A simple version of the argument is this: if perspectivism is itself a perspective, then there are perspectives in which perspectivism is false; if on the other hand perspectivism is not a perspective, then not *every* statement is true in some perspectives and false in others. In short, either perspectivism applies to itself, in which case it is not universally true, or it does not apply to itself, in which case it is not universally true. Either way, it is false.

This version of the puzzle is intuitively plausible. Unfortunately, it is not worked out in sufficient detail. A careful statement of the puzzle makes a distinction between perspectivism as a statement and the conditions in which that statement is true. Here is what I have in mind. Perspectivism is a thesis about the nature of truth as truth applies to statements in a language. The conditions in which the thesis of perspectivism is true specify when we are entitled to say of perspectivism that it captures the behaviour of truth in a language and when it does not. (An analogy might make the distinction clearer. We can distinguish between reference books and books that refer to reference books. In the former, we shall find references to things that are not other books; in the latter, we shall find references only to other reference books. Likewise, most statements in a language speak of things that are not linguistic items, but perspectivism is a thesis about the nature of truth when it applies to statements in a language.)

Given the distinction we can ask: under what conditions is perspectivism as a thesis about truth in a language true? Clearly there are only two possible answers: either when it captures the behaviour of truth in *every* instance when a statement is true; or when it captures the behaviour of truth in *some*, but not all, instances. That is, the thesis of perspectivism is either true absolutely or true perspectivally. In the former, perspectivism about truth is true (or false) in all perspectives; in the latter, it is true in some perspectives and false in others.

The real problem for perspectivism can now be stated clearly. Suppose that perspectivism is true in *all* perspectives. If so, then there is at least one statement – the thesis of perspectivism – that is true in all perspectives. Unfortunately, if there is *any* statement that is true in all perspectives, then absolutism about truth is true, for absolutism just is the claim that there is at least one statement that is true in all perspectives. So, if perspectivism is true in all perspectives, then absolutism is true. Hence, perspectivism is false. That is self-defeating. Well then, suppose that perspectivism is false in every perspective. If so, then absolutism is true again, for if perspectivism is false in *every* perspective, then absolutism is true in *every* perspective. Again, perspectivism is self-defeating.

That leaves only one option: perhaps perspectivism is true in some perspectives and false in other perspectives. Nietzsche certainly thinks this is the way out. In *Beyond Good and Evil* he says: "Supposing that this also is only interpretation – and you will be eager enough to make this objection? – well, so much the better" (*BGE* 22). This answer is just as problematic as any other. Here is why. Suppose that perspectivism is true in some perspectives and false in others. Consider the latter case, a perspective in which perspectivism is false. In such a perspective, the denial of perspectivism – that is, absolutism – is true. Now, absolutism is true only if there is at least one statement that is true in all perspectives. But there is no such statement: not the thesis of absolutism itself, since, by hypothesis, there are perspectives in which it is false and perspectivism is true; not perspectivism, since, again by hypothesis, there are perspectives in which it is false; nor any other statement in the perspective in which absolutism is true, since there are distinct perspectives in which all *those* statements are false. Hence, there is no statement that is true in all perspectives; that is, for every statement there are perspectives in which that statement is true and perspectives in which it is false. But then *perspectivism* is true in *all* perspectives, and this, we have already shown, entails that perspectivism is false.

This self-defeating criticism of perspectivism is a real sore spot. Many of Nietzsche's commentators seem to believe that making perspectivism perspectivally true is the best we can hope for. But that solution is, as just argued, hopeless, for the problem comes back again. Some commentators have attempted more sophisticated rescues. Two of them in particular deserve our attention, if only to see the lengths to which philosophers will sometimes go in saving a cherished claim. One proposal is to think that the paradox of perspectivism can be solved by introducing a distinction between a statement being *actually* false and its being *possibly* false. Here is how Alexander Nehamas, this view's main defender, puts it in his *Nietzsche: Life as Literature*:

> Suppose we characterize Nietzsche's perspectivism as the thesis (P) that every view is an interpretation. Now it appears that if (P) is true, and if every view is in fact an interpretation, this would apply to (P) itself ... But if this is so, then not every view need be an interpretation, and (P) seems to have refuted itself ... If (P) is an interpretation, it may indeed be false. But from the possibility that (P) ... may be false, all that follows is the conclusion that I have

already stated – that is, that not every view need be an interpretation. But (P) does not assert that every view necessarily is an interpretation; it cannot therefore be refuted by showing ... that it is *possible* that some views are not interpretations. To show that (P) is false, we must show that some views are actually not interpretations.

But this involves showing not that (P) may be false ... but that it is *actually* false. Yet our argument can show that (P) is actually false only if we assume that, being an interpretation, (P) may be false and that therefore it is in fact false. This last conclusion would truly refute (P), for if the thesis that every view is an interpretation is in fact false, then indeed some views are actually not interpretations. But the conclusion that (P) is in fact false does not follow from the fact that (P) is itself an interpretation. It is reached only by means of an invalid inference, by means of equating, as above, the fact that (P) is an interpretation and therefore possibly false with the fact that it is actually false.*

This certainly looks as though it gets Nietzsche's perspectivism out of trouble. After all, if perspectivism is not shown to be *actually* false by its being *possibly* false, then the charge that perspectivism is self-refuting is successfully avoided.

Sadly, the proposed solution misfires, for the problem that perspectivism faces has nothing to do with the *possible* falsity of statements. Perspectivism is the statement that all statements are *actually* true in some perspectives and *actually* false in other perspectives. Here is the problem again: if perspectivism is a statement in a language, then, if it is true, it is true either perspectivally or absolutely. If true perspectivally, then there is at least one perspective in which absolutism is true. But absolutism is the claim that there is at least one statement that is true across perspectives. Hence, perspectivism is false. If true absolutely, then perspectivism is true across all perspectives. Hence, there is at least one statement that is true across all perspectives. Hence, absolutism is true. Again, perspectivism is false. If, on the other hand, perspectivism is false in all perspectives, then absolutism is true. Once again, perspectivism is false. No matter what you try, perspectivism ends up being *actually* false. Nehamas's solution is, in fact, rather strange, for it solves a problem that perspectivism is not actually faced with. The problem with the proposal is easily diagnosed: no statement that is *actually* true is shown to be *actually* false because it is

---

* A. Nehamas, *Nietzsche: Life as Literature* (Cambridge, MA: Harvard University Press, 1986), 65–6.

*possibly* false and no statement that is *actually* false is shown to be *actually* true because it is *possibly* true. Thinking that the possible falsity of perspectivism supports its actual truth or falsity is misguided.

Another solution to the paradox of perspectivism has been suggested by Maudemarie Clark in her *Nietzsche on Truth and Philosophy*.* She takes perspectivism to be the claim that our statements about the world do not correspond to things-in-themselves. We have already seen that Nietzsche rejects the thing-in-itself, so it is certainly true that no view of truth that requires correspondence between our statements and things-in-themselves can be Nietzsche's view. From that, however, it does not follow that Nietzsche's truth perspectivism view of truth cannot be run without things-in-themselves.

Clark tries to rescue Nietzsche's perspectivism from the self-referential problems we have outlined above by pointing out that, over time, Nietzsche's thinking about truth developed. He began, in *Daybreak* and *Human, All Too Human*, by rejecting the category of the thing-in-itself. Having jettisoned the thing-in-itself, Clark's Nietzsche is liberated from what she thinks is the real problem with perspectivism; namely, the implication that, if statements are true only in a perspective, then all our statements falsify reality. She calls this the "falsification thesis", and argues that Nietzsche should not, and does not need to, commit himself to it.

However, contrary to Clark, truth perspectivism does imply that all our statements falsify reality. Take some statement, *p*. If truth perspectivism is true, then there is a perspective in which *p* is true and another perspective in which *p* is false. Hence, for any statement *p* in a language, *p* is true in some perspective and false in some other perspective. That is one way of formulating Clark's falsification thesis. Of course, every statement *p* is also such that, if true at all, then it is true in at least one perspective. So, there is also a sense in which the sting of the falsification thesis is immediately undone. But we shall not pursue that here. Suffice it to say, the falsification thesis is implied by truth perspectivism, at least as we are interpreting it here.

Clark thinks, on the other hand, that Nietzsche does not and should not commit himself to the falsification thesis. Her argument is that the falsification thesis is true only if there are things-in-themselves. This is, unfortunately, a mistake. Certainly, *if* there are things-in-themselves of which we can know nothing, *then* all our statements about them would falsify their character or, if that is too strong, all our statements about them would correctly describe their character only by pure unadulterated and

---

* M. Clark, *Nietzsche on Truth and Philosophy* (New York: Cambridge University Press, 1990).

completely unknowable luck. So Clark is certainly right that *if* there are things-in-themselves *then* the falsification thesis is true. Unfortunately, for her argument to be successful she has to defend the claim, not that things-in-themselves are *sufficient* for the falsification thesis to be true, but that they are *necessary* for the falsification thesis to be true. That is, she has to defend the view that *if* there are no things-in-themselves, *then* the falsification thesis is false. And that is not defensible, for even if there are no things-in-themselves, the falsification thesis can still be true. We have just seen how this is the case: if truth perspectivism is true, then there are perspectives in which some statement *p* is true and other perspectives in which *p* is false. Hence, for all statements *p*, there is at least one perspective in which *p* is false. Hence, the falsification thesis is true even if there are no things-in-themselves.

Clark has another argument against the falsification thesis. This argument stems from her attribution to Nietzsche of what she calls the "minimal correspondence theory of truth". The minimal correspondence theory (a theory of great popularity in twentieth-century analytic philosophy) claims that, for any statement *p* of a language L, "*p*" is true if and only if *p*. (Well, we might say, that looks true!) But what does it mean? Take any statement in a language, say, again, the English statement:

Pikes Peak is 14,110 feet tall.

Then, "Pikes Peak is 14,110 feet tall" is true if and only if Pikes Peak is 14,110 feet tall. Now, given that that kind of biconditional is true for *every* statement in a language, it follows that every statement in a language is such that it is true if and only if whatever it says is the case is the case. That is, without question, a version of the correspondence theory of truth, for it is nothing more than a version of Aristotle's dictum that to say of what is that it is is true.

Yet as common-sensical as this minimal correspondence theory of truth is, why think that this is *Nietzsche's* theory? Clark thinks that Nietzsche has to accept the minimal correspondence theory of truth because to reject it is to reject logic altogether. This is, unfortunately, not the case. Here is why. Logic is composed of a *semantics* and a *syntax*. The semantics of a logical system stipulates how the symbols in the language get interpreted; the syntax of a logical system stipulates how symbols are properly put together (its grammar) and the rules for deriving one string of symbols from another (its proof theory). In order for Clark's claim to be true, it must be that if we reject the minimal correspondence theory of truth, then we must reject either the semantics of every logical system or the syntax of every logical system, or both. But Nietzsche does not reject proof theory; he prizes good argumentation. Of course, he correctly recognizes that proof theory is a formal calculus until the symbols get interpreted (we spell this claim out in Chapter 6). And here is where Nietzsche departs from the minimal correspondence theory of truth: he thinks the semantics of any language contains indices to perspectives. It is true that he rejects perspective-independent interpretation, but the only way that would entail rejection of logic is if perspective-independent interpretation is the only way that symbols could possibly get interpreted. And that is false, because Nietzsche has an alternative: his perspectivism! We return to some of these issues in Chapter 6.

## Defusing the paradox

Admittedly, we are now in a peculiar place. Truth perspectivism has a paradoxical result and all the canvassed solutions either do not work at all (thinking that perspectivism is perspectivally true), are not directed against the real problem of truth perspectivism (thinking that perspectivism is a claim about possibility rather than actuality) or are not consistent with Nietzsche's views (thinking that perspectivism is consistent with the minimal correspondence theory of truth). Are we then to conclude that truth perspectivism, because it is paradoxical, cannot be salvaged after all? No. We have to admit that we cannot have our cake and eat it too with truth perspectivism. If we hope to save truth perspectivism from self-defeat, we have no choice but to weaken it, for, as it stands, truth perspectivism yields the problematic result that it can never be true. The way to make the claim palatable is to claim not that *all* statements are true in one perspective and false in another, but that *some* statements are true in one perspective and false in another. This leaves open the possibility – a possibility that has to be defended – that there are some statements that are true in all perspectives. This would be a form of absolutism about the truth of at least some statements.

Suppose we weaken perspectivism to the claim that some statements are true in some perspectives and false in others. Let us distinguish this claim from the claim that generates the problems by calling the weaker claim "weak perspectivism" and the stronger claim "strong perspectivism". Strong perspectivism gets Nietzsche into trouble because it is self-refuting. Weak perspectivism lacks that implication. Suppose weak perspectivism is true for every statement *other than itself*. It then turns out that for the thesis of weak perspectivism, absolutism is true. Why? Because truth absolutism claims that there is at least one statement that is true in all perspectives. Perhaps the only such statement is the thesis of weak perspectivism. Here, then, is a way to rescue Nietzsche's truth perspectivism without abandoning the spirit behind it.

Perhaps there are *other* statements in addition to the thesis of weak perspectivism that are true across all perspectives. That too is consistent with weak perspectivism. And, surprisingly, a case can be made that Nietzsche himself is, at least on occasion, willing to allow that there may be statements that are true for every member of some group. Take the pronouncements of physicists. Nietzsche seriously insists that "physics too is only an interpretation" (*BGE* 14), and yet, especially in the *Genealogy*, he appears to favour physics over any metaphysical system. How can this be? Weak perspectivism helps answer the question. With it, Nietzsche can admit that, for some, Christians for example, their metaphysical systems are true, for they have a perspective and becoming a Christian arguably entails adherence to some of its fundamental principles and metaphysical commitments, such as the existence of God. But Nietzsche can counter that being a Christian, and hence occupying the perspective it demands, is not the only perspective. We can abandon Christianity and opt for the agnostic or atheistic scientific worldview represented by physics. If we do so, we shall find ourselves in the perspective of physics, and its statements are true so long as we remain in that perspective. Yet Nietzsche can apply perspectivism to physics too. Perhaps there is some *other* perspective in which the statements of physics are not true, not because the only alternative to physics is religion, but because there is some as yet to be discovered perspective in which it turns out that the statements of physics are false.

Nietzsche can even permit some true statements to be true across all human perspectives without abandoning his loathing for absolutism. Take the axioms of logic, for example. On occasion, Nietzsche says things that, were he to think that *every* statement is false in some perspective, is flatly inconsistent with that claim. For example, he says at one point that "rational thought is interpretation according to a scheme that we cannot throw off" (*WP* 522). Reflect for a moment on the subtlety of that claim. Nietzsche claims both that rational thought, that is, thought that follows the axioms of logic, is interpretation, and so is a perspective, *and* that we cannot get rid of it. If we think at all, we think within the perspective that logic imposes.

Let us note in passing that there is a particular kind of interpretation of Nietzsche that has been promulgated in the past twenty years that finds statements like this from Nietzsche to be anathema. There are those who think that, with the perspectivity of logic exposed, we can simply think outside logic altogether in a kind of freewheeling continuum of ideas. No doubt Nietzsche's playful style and his chiding of metaphysicians and logicians helps buttress this kind of inference. But Nietzsche himself is more subtle than this, and this view is both bad interpretation of Nietzsche and false. It is false because, as Nietzsche himself notes in this passage, there really is no thinking without logic of *some* kind. We may chafe at "linear" thinking or object to "bipolar" logic, but if we replace them with something else – some have proposed "dialectical" logics, some have proposed "non-linear" logics (premised on certain kinds of mathematical models and equations) or "non-bivalent" logics – *what we shall invariably end up with will still be a logic*. It is as if, having realized that the reasons we wear clothes are social and therefore contingent, we advocate running around without any clothes at all, never realizing that it gets terribly cold in the winter without *something* on.

Admittedly, the view under discussion is tempting and some Nietzsche scholars and many others with various philosophical and political agendas have taken the bait Nietzsche dangles in front of them without recognizing his own circumspection. But resist temptation he does, and his perspectivism justifies his doing so. Consider the above claim again: how can logic (*some* logic – maybe not Aristotle's syllogistic logic) be both a perspective and something we cannot think without? Perspectivism explains it beautifully. Logic is a perspective, one that is shared by all the members of some set, namely, the set of humans. Since logic is a perspective, it is possible that there are perspectives in which every extant logical system is rejected, but such a perspective is, although possible, not conceivable for us.

Suppose we allow that there are many statements that are true across some perspectives, many that are true across most perspectives, many that are false across some perspectives, many that are false across most perspectives, some that are true across every perspective we can conceive of, and some that are false across every perspective we can conceive of. None of this entails that there are any statements that are true *outside* a perspective. The idea of an "absolute truth" has sometimes been thought to be a statement that is true *simpliciter*, true on the face of it, true as a matter of metaphysical or logical fact. Nietzsche has no truck with any view of truth that makes statements true or false without any perspective at all. This is, perhaps, his deepest criticism of the correspondence theory of truth, in particular the minimal correspondence theory of truth we have just discussed. Correspondence theories of truth hold that we can simply hold our statements up to the world and determine whether they are true or false, and this Nietzsche denies emphatically. As he puts it: "as if a world would still remain over after one deducted the perspective!" (*WP* 567). For those who think they can establish absolute truths of this kind, Nietzsche has nothing but scorn. We can never escape the perspective imposed by being members of the human species, so we can never hope to elevate any of the statements that we make to the level of being true outside every perspective.

There is a correlative point that is equally important for Nietzsche. For most of us it proves astonishingly difficult to overcome the perspective imposed on us by being members of various groups: left-handers; men; women; WASPS; Ethiopians; physicists. Nietzsche's perspectivism acknowledges that there may be perspectives that we cannot escape, but it also challenges us at the same time to make the experiment of thinking outside the perspectives we inherit from our families and our cultures and of thinking outside the perspectives we slide into as we mature or those we adopt when we put on our professional blinkers. Like most other philosophers, Nietzsche enjoins us to study hard and to be disciplined in our thinking. Unlike most other philosophers, he makes these recommendations not because he wants us to become narrow-minded experts who intimidate others with our expertise, but because he wants us to recognize the ineliminable *plurality* of perspectives on most topics. He may admit that there are some statements that are true across every perspective, but that they do not pose much of a problem because they are likely to be either banal, "there's at least one rock on every continent"; or abstract, "if $p$ then $q$, $p$, therefore $q$"; or fundamental, "water molecules borrow protons from the vacuum"; or obvious, "$1 + 1 = 2$ in base-10 arithmetic".

For all the other statements that may turn out to be true, Nietzsche's perspectivism requires that we proceed to assess their truth with the humbling recognition that there are other perspectives on them. We shall have to acknowledge those other perspectives and accommodate them in our assessment. And if, after careful and rigorous examination, we conclude that a given statement is true in these and false in those perspectives, intellectual honesty will compel us to confront and admit that uncertainty. The result will be disciplined thinkers who are less prone to overstatement and hyperbole, less likely to get their backs up in debate and less likely to insult when the discussion fails to go the way they want. Nietzsche's kind of thinkers will be independent, circumspect, sceptical, rigorous and, above all and amazingly, liberal, for they do not have the luxury of summarily dismissing points of view with which they disagree.

Nietzsche is without question arrogant on many occasions, and his willingness to make summary judgements about others is both a source of great amusement (when we agree with him) and great anger (when we do not). But there is something startlingly humane about his arrogance. While he calls himself a "destiny" and even analyses his own cleverness in *Ecce Homo*, he also exhibits again and again his abiding concern for those who will not or cannot see that their lives are *theirs* and so end up living according to how *others* say they should live. What is worse, for Nietzsche anyway, is that these same people, having relinquished self-control, then turn around and stamp about with their heads full of what they think are eternal and absolute truths. They act with the confidence that, when they are right, then they are *really right*. After all, everybody else thinks this way too, so they *must* be right.

If there are two kinds of persons Nietzsche cannot stomach, it is the ramrod dogmatist and his willing slave. The serious, certain and ruthless propagandist is Nietzsche's greatest enemy and flocks of happy slaves his greatest source of sorrow. His willingness to judge another is usually a direct function of the presumptuousness of the other to judge everyone else (not always – Nietzsche can be pretty nasty even to some rather underprivileged groups). As he puts it in *Ecce Homo*, "I only attack causes that are victorious" (*EH* "Why I Am So Wise"), and his obvious self-love is a refutation of those who would presume to judge him. His own self-glorification shows us what can result when we refuse to be cowed by those whose arrogance suggests that they know what is true for all of us and so what is best for all of us.

Underlying Nietzsche's rage at dogmatic absolutism and his revulsion with mediocrity is his perspectivism. It certainly is not the only plank in his platform, but it is a necessary one. Without admitting that many of our most cherished beliefs are perspectivally rather than absolutely true, we shall never be able to combat the dogmatists on their strongest ground, namely, their assumption to be trading in absolute truths. Perspectivism challenges not just the content of the dogmatist's claims, but their logical form as well. And, best of all, by challenging the logical form of the dogmatist's claims, the perspectivist defuses the dogmatist's strongest retort as well. The perspectivist does not deny that some of the statements that the dogmatist makes are in fact true, at least in *some* perspectives. She just denies that they are true in *every* perspective. And, if she happens to be in a perspective in which the dogmatist's claim is false, then, given perspectivism, the dogmatist has *no* recourse other than to dig his feet in the sand and raise a lot of dust, insisting on the absolute truth of what he is saying. To that, the perspectivist smiles and walks away: "Poor thing, he really believes what he's saying – such a pity!"

# CHAPTER 6

# Logic and epistemology

Logic studies reasoning and epistemology studies knowledge. The two are obviously linked: being justified in believing something, a topic of epistemology, presupposes for most beliefs that we are reasoning well about the subject of the belief, a topic of logic. Yet logic is a more abstract undertaking than epistemology, for its subject is reasoning in every field of knowledge, whether mathematics, physics or theology. Logic is concerned with, among others, the following questions: what makes a valid deductive argument valid? What makes it sound? What is the difference between the syntax of a language and its semantics? Are there options for syntax and semantics? If so, what are they? Epistemology is concerned with, among others, the following questions: how much do we know? What is it that we know when we know? What are we doing when we know something? How do we know what we know? Nietzsche has interesting things to say about all these questions.

Nietzsche is anything but a fanatical supporter of logic or the traditional epistemological project. The *Nachlass* contains numerous passages asserting the ineliminable falsifications produced by logic. For example, he notes in one passage that "the will to logical truth can be carried through only after a fundamental *falsification* of all events is assumed ... logic does *not* spring from will to truth" (*WP* 512), and, again, "Logic (like geometry and arithmetic) applies only to fictitious entities that we have created. Logic is the attempt to comprehend the actual world by means of a scheme of being posited by ourselves; more correctly, to make it formulatable and calculable for us" (*WP* 516). Likewise, when it comes to the traditional epistemological project of understanding what knowledge is, Nietzsche's hostility is open. For instance, he says in the *Nachlass* that "the biggest fable of all is the fable of knowledge" (*WP* 555) and, in *The Gay Science*, that "delusion and error are conditions of human knowledge and sensation" (*GS* 107).

Such assertions are peppered throughout Nietzsche's published works. However, there is precious little *argument* for these claims. The lack of argument against both logic and epistemology in the published works helps explain why Nietzsche's erstwhile friend, Erwin Rohde, called some of the philosophy contained in Nietzsche's mature published works childish and pathetic. Even if we accept this judgement (and we should not), the same cannot be said about the wealth of notes in the *Nachlass*, where Nietzsche repeatedly gets down to business with direct arguments for and against specific logical and epistemological theses. In this chapter we shall rely on these *Nachlass* notes more directly and more extensively than in other chapters. We begin with a discussion of logic. Nietzsche's various remarks about logic are subtle and far-sighted. Next, we disprove the idea that Nietzsche is a sceptic. Finally, we use that discussion to introduce his perpectivist reflections on knowledge.

## Logic

Nietzsche's criticisms of logic are so strongly worded that some think he advocates rejecting it completely. This is an attractive view for those who find in logic a rigidity that precludes creativity; the field of imagination supposedly opened up as a result of rejecting logic might be liberating. As we have already seen, this view is bad interpretation of Nietzsche, and otherwise absurd. It is mistaken when applied to Nietzsche because he nowhere advocates abandoning logic. He criticizes certain claims of logic, but that is typical for him: he is critical of *many* things. However, he no more abandons logic than he abandons the will, power, morality, truth, knowledge or any of the other things he has, on occasion, been thought to eliminate. And it is absurd because, as Nietzsche himself recognizes, rationality is in some ways essential to thinking. Although we usually think without the more sophisticated branches of logic (how many people routinely think using the insights of second-order intensional logic?) and although we certainly think illogically, we cannot think all the time without any logic of any kind. That is not liberation; it is insanity.

In *Human, All Too Human*, Nietzsche announces that "logic ... rests on assumptions that do not correspond to anything in the real world, e.g., on the assumption of the equality of things, the identity of the same thing at different points in time" (*HAH* 11). In *Twilight of the Idols*, we find a related view:

> science of formulæ, sign-systems: such as logic and that applied logic, mathematics. In these reality does not appear at all, not even

as a problem; just as little as does the question what value a system of conventional signs such as constitutes logic can possibly possess.

(*TI* III 3)

Of course, he also insists that "schooling has no more important task than to teach rigorous thinking, careful judgment, logical conclusions" (*HAH* 256), a sentiment echoed in *Twilight of the Idols*, where he insults German universities on the grounds that "even among students of philosophy themselves, the theory, the practice, the *vocation* of logic is beginning to die out" (*TI* VIII 7). Indeed, he actually claims that "without accepting the fictions of logic ... man could not live" (*BGE* 4). If so, logic, although a fiction, is not only *not opposed* to life, it is actually a *necessary* condition for our kind of thinking life. So, as much as it may appear that Nietzsche denigrates logic, he is not generally sceptical about the importance of logic to our way of living.

Still, there are plenty of specific claims in logic about which Nietzsche is sceptical. One such feature of logic is its dependence upon identity. In *Beyond Good and Evil*, he says that the self-identical is part of a "purely invented world" (*BGE* 4). In *The Gay Science*, he suggests that the origin of logic itself is rooted in a desire to posit different things as being identical (*GS* 111), and he declares that the equation of unequal things is an "erroneous article of faith" (*GS* 110). However, to the extent that these claims are criticisms of anything, they are not criticisms of logic at all, but of ontology. In and of itself, logic is thoroughly neutral about how its squiggles get interpreted, so it is not a question of logic whether those squiggles refer to things that are self-identical at a time or over time or to things that are self-identical neither at a time nor over time. And to the extent that they are ontological mistakes, synchronic and diachronic identity have already been discussed, in Chapter 4. However, there are two other claims that Nietzsche is making in these passages that arguably are criticisms of logic. These are that logic mistakenly presupposes the existence of things and that logic mistakenly presupposes that things are not fictions invented by humans.

According to Nietzsche, logic presupposes the existence of things. What does that mean? On first glance it looks so banal as not to be objectionable. We are tempted to say, "Of course it does. So what?" But Nietzsche is up to something philosophically interesting here. To get an idea about what that something is, recall some of the tools of contemporary logic. Modern logic is, as already noted in Chapter 5, divided into syntax and semantics. The syntax of a language provides the rules for putting symbols together, for manipulating the operators, connectives, quantifiers, predicates, variables and constants of the formal system, for moving the symbols around, and for the derivation of theorems from axioms. These syntactical aspects of logic are completely formal; they tell us absolutely nothing about the world and make absolutely no assumptions about the applicability of the symbols of a formal language to anything at all. A purely syntactical language is an uninterpreted calculus, a bunch of squiggles on paper that obey certain rules. So with respect to the syntax of a logic, reality does not appear even as a problem for logic, as Nietzsche notes in *Twilight of the Idols* (*TI* III 3). But this is not a *criticism* of logic, since it is not the business of syntax to worry about reality or care whether a calculus can be applied to anything. Of course, it is a criticism of any logician who thinks otherwise, and Nietzsche is probably right that the vast majority of logicians of his time made the assumption that a syntactically well-behaved calculus's squiggles applied directly to things in the world. This should hardly be a surprise, for few logicians before the mid-nineteenth century even recognized the distinction between syntax and semantics. Leibniz was one of the few; Nietzsche, of all people, is another.

In addition to the syntax of a language, there is also the semantic aspect of that language. Semantics has to do with the interpretation of the formulae of logic. A semantics for a language specifies a domain of entities for the logic to apply to and offers an interpretation function for the squiggles. Together, the two lead us from squiggles to entities in the domain. Put another way, semantics turns the squiggles of an uninterpreted calculus into symbols, for it provides those squiggles with meaning, and a squiggle of a particular shape with an interpretation is a symbol. The interpretation function assigns an entity in the domain to each singular term, tells us which entities the variables can stand for and provides the extension of the predicates. An example might help. Suppose the domain of entities over which our squiggles range is every person in a particular classroom. Suppose there are 26 people in the classroom, each of whom has a name beginning with a different letter. Then the interpretation function will specify that, for example, $a$ stands for Amanda, $b$ for Bertie, and so on through the members of the class and the letters of the alphabet. Suppose further that we want to say that Bertie is left-handed. Then we interpret a predicate letter, "$Lx$", say, as "$x$ is left-handed". Then, substituting in the name $b$ for the variable $x$, we can say "$Lb$": "Bertie is left-handed". But there may be five left-handed students in the class, so we can also fix the interpretation of another symbol, "$\exists x$", as "there is at least one $x$ such that", and say "there is at least one left-handed student in the class": "$(\exists x)Lx$".

With respect now to semantics, thingness *is* a requirement of logic, for that is just to say that for the symbols and formulae of an uninterpreted calculus to mean anything or have any applicability, there have to be things for them to refer to, properties they have and relations they stand in to one another. The *nature* of these things is a further question and that question is not one that logic can answer. That question is one that ontology has to answer. So it is consistent for Nietzsche to hold both that logic presupposes the existence of things and to hold that logic says nothing about reality. The former is true when interpreted as a claim about semantics, and the latter is true when interpreted as a claim about syntax.

Nietzsche also criticizes two traditional axioms of logic, the law of bivalence and the law of non-contradiction. The law of bivalence is the logical thesis that every statement has a truth-value, and that this truth-value is either true or false. Claiming that the law of bivalence is a logical law entails that denying it is impossible. So, where "∨" means "or", "∼" means "not", "∀" means "for all", "∃" means "there is at least one", and $p$ is a variable for statements, the law of bivalence is:

$$(\forall p)(p \vee \sim p)$$

That is to say, for all statements $p$, either $p$ is true or not-$p$ is true. The denial of the law of bivalence is, then:

$$(\exists p) \sim (p \vee \sim p)$$

That is to say, there is a statement $p$ such that it is not the case that either it or its denial is true. And that is equivalent, by DeMorgan's law, to:

$$(\exists p)( \sim p \mathbin{\&} \sim\sim p)$$

And that is equivalent, by the law of double negation, to:

$$(\exists p)( \sim p \mathbin{\&} p)$$

or:

$$(\exists p)(p \mathbin{\&} \sim p)$$

That is to say, there is a statement $p$ such that both it and its denial is true. And that, to many philosophers, looks impossible: how could a statement be both true and false? But Nietzsche is not most philosophers: he affirms the logical possibility of denying the law of bivalence. He asks:

> Indeed, what forces us at all to suppose that there is an essential opposition of "true" and "false"? It is not sufficient to assume degrees of apparentness and, as it were, lighter and darker

shadows and shades of appearance – different "values," to use the
language of painters?                                        (*BGE* 34)

Nietzsche maintains here that thinking that statements are either true or
false is an item of faith for logicians and he speculates on various
intermediate values of truth as an alternative. From there, one might infer
that he rejects logic itself. But this further step is mistaken, and Nietzsche
nowhere makes it (although some of his interpreters do). That is, even if
the law of bivalence is false, logic does not have to be rejected. In this,
Nietzsche was at least fifty years ahead of his time and has been completely
vindicated by subsequent developments in logic, for, beginning in the
1930s, non-bivalent logics have been developed, logics in which the law of
bivalence is rejected and replaced with another axiom that permits, just as
Nietzsche suggests in *Beyond Good and Evil*, truth-values intermediate
between true and false.

Nietzsche makes a similar argument against the law of non-contradiction.
The law of non-contradiction can be stated thus:

$(\forall p) \sim (p \ \& \sim p)$

That is to say, for all statements, it is not the case that there is a statement
that is both true and false. The denial of the law of non-contradiction is:

$(\exists p)(p \ \& \sim p)$

That is to say, again, there is a statement such that it is both true and false.

Nietzsche points out that the application of the law of non-contradiction
to the world is problematic:

> If, according to Aristotle, the law of contradiction is the most
> certain of all principles, if it is the ultimate and most basic, upon
> which every demonstrative proof rests, if the principle of every
> axiom lies in it; then one should consider all the more rigorously
> what *presuppositions* already lie at the bottom of it. Either it
> asserts something about actuality, about being, as if one already
> knew this from another source; that is, as if opposite attributes
> *could* not be ascribed to it. Or the proposition means: opposite
> attributes *should* not be ascribed to it. In that case, logic would be
> an imperative, not to know the true, but to posit and arrange a
> world that shall be called true by us.
>
> In short, the question remains open: are the axioms of logic
> adequate to reality or are they a means and measure for us to

*create* reality, the concept "reality," for ourselves? – To affirm the former one would, as already said, have to have a previous knowledge of being – which is certainly not the case. The proposition therefore contains no *criterion of truth*, but an *imperative* concerning that which *should* count as true. (WP 516)

This is a philosophical argument against the law of non-contradiction, not a logical argument against it. The argument is directed against the presumption that the law of non-contradiction applies to things in the world free of perspective. Contrary to Aristotle and others who think the law of non-contradiction is bedrock, Nietzsche shows that it is one more stratum in a sedimentary structure of cognitive requirements that have no demonstrable counterpart in the world. Nietzsche's critique of logic is, thus, fundamentally an argument about the semantic interpretation of a logical calculus. He suggests that, contrary to what we typically assume about the relation between logic and the world, there are multiple ways to interpret the symbols of logic. Things referred to by singular terms are constructed out of properties bundled together to satisfy the interests of some perspective. Things are in this way every bit as perspectival as truth. Of course, it is eminently consistent for him to affirm this view and to affirm that logic is necessary for us to think or live. For all his philosophically incisive criticisms of logicians' ontological assumptions, Nietzsche is, as we have already seen, surprisingly generous about the power of logic and its place in human affairs.

### Realism, anti-realism, and idealism

Nietzsche frequently claims that things are fictions invented by humans. Given the distinction between syntax and semantics just drawn, this claim is best interpreted as a claim not about the syntax or proof theory of a logical language but about its semantics. In particular, the statement "things are fictions" can be interpreted as saying that it is not the case that extra-perspectival things are the interpretations of the singular terms in logic. This position is a kind of *anti-realism*, and in suggesting it, Nietzsche anticipates by a hundred years a similar debate in philosophy of language and metaphysics about realism and anti-realism. Now, the term "anti-realism" is pretty clearly contrary to "realism". What then is realism, and how is anti-realism contrary to it? Here are some typical constituent claims:

• the world consists of a fixed number of mind-independent objects (things-in-themselves);

- there is only one complete and true description of that world of mind-independent objects;
- truth is non-epistemic.

Anti-realism is the denial of these claims. Nietzsche denies every one of them, so he is an anti-realist. We have already seen that he does not think the world is composed of stuff that is untinged by the input of perspectives. As we shall see later in this chapter, he celebrates the diversity of descriptions of the world. And his truth perspectivism indexes truth to perspectives, at least some of which include epistemic ingredients.

Nietzsche's anti-realism underwrites a rather enigmatic claim made here and there throughout the last ten years of his productive life, but clearly enunciated in *Twilight of the Idols*: "'Reason' in language: oh what a deceitful old woman! I fear we are not getting rid of God because we still believe in grammar" (*TI* III 5). Can Nietzsche really be claiming that God resides in grammar? What on earth could that mean? Given an understanding of realism and anti-realism we can provide an answer. Realism has often been aligned with God's perspective: the real world, as opposed to the world as it appears in experience, is the world as God would see it, a world composed of mind-independent, determinate, and self-identical things. But with God's death that world implodes. Nietzsche is convinced that realism is one of the last shadows of our belief in God. The logic embedded in our language makes the same ontological commitments to the world of nice, neat, orderly things that God once knew. Since the structure of our language encodes this mistaken metaphysics, neither linguistic analysis nor the construction of a logically perfect language (a dream of early analytic philosophers such as Ludwig Wittgenstein, Bertrand Russell, and Rudolf Carnap) will provide us with an acceptable interpretation of the world. In short, our faith in grammar (the syntax of natural language) generates a faith in logic, and neither is much better than faith in God.

Nietzsche is exceptionally suspicious of any argument that moves from premises concerning the semantic interpretation of our words to any conclusions about what those words talk about. This suspicion extends to *any* language and *any* logic. Nietzsche would certainly have supported the early analytic philosophers who used their linguistic analyses to puncture windy metaphysical systems, but he would turn the table on those same philosophers by suggesting that no syntax and no semantics, no matter how purified, will ever eliminate metaphysical commitments and errors. (The lone exception is Wittgenstein, who turned the table on himself.) For any logically perfect language encodes a commitment to some particular set of things, and Nietzsche is convinced that no single linguistic description is ever unique or privileged over all others.

Nietzsche is equally convinced that there are no ready-made objects out there just waiting around for us to discover and describe. This does not mean that idealism is true, where by "idealism" we understand the thesis that the world is mind-dependent. Nietzsche thinks that idealism is demonstrably absurd. His argument against idealism is stated succinctly in *Beyond Good and Evil*:

> To study physiology with a clear conscience, one must insist that the sense organs are *not* phenomena in the sense of idealistic philosophy; as such they could not be causes! Sensualism, therefore, at least as a regulative hypothesis, if not as a heuristic principle.
>
> What? And others even say that the external world is the work of our organs? But then our body, as a part of this external world, would be the work of our organs! But then our organs themselves would be – the work of our organs! It seems to me that this is a complete *reductio ad absurdum*, assuming that the concept of a *causa sui* is something fundamentally absurd. Consequently, the external world is *not* the work of our organs – ?          (*BGE* 15)

A *reductio ad absurdum* is any argument that assumes a premise *p*, and from *p* derives a contradiction, say *q* & *not-q*. Given the contradiction, we can derive the falsity of *p*. Nietzsche's *reductio* against idealism is succinct. Idealism cannot get off the ground because it claims that the world is the causal result of something that is an inhabitant of that world. But that would make our sensory apparatus (our "organs") a cause of itself, a *causa sui,* which Nietzsche thinks is self-contradictory. So, by starting with the premise that the world is mind-dependent, we derive the self-contradictory conclusion that our sensory apparatus is its own cause.

Nietzsche's claim is, in fact, neither realist nor idealist. His claim is rather that *every* entity has a perspective and every entity with a perspective categorizes its experience in a way that suits its ends and purposes. So, for humans, as for all other species, there is no distinction between objects that "really" exist in and of themselves and those that are invented from some perspective. For Nietzsche, there is a sense in which it is correct to say that every *thing* that we humans think about is an invention or fiction, for everything is a consequence of our imposition of categories on to, and our formation of concepts out of, sensory chaos. As he puts it, "the 'apparent' world is the only one: the 'real' world has only been *lyingly added*" (*TI* III 2). There are, in principle, an infinite number of ways that the raw chaos of sensory experience could have been carved up into objects. We have made the world logical because doing so serves our interests, but there are many other ways to carve the world up according to different logics. Yet it is not idealism, either, for he nowhere reduces the world to the particular perspective necessary for the truth of idealism, the perspective imposed by human sensory and cognitive capacities. For Nietzsche, everything in the world has its own perspective(s), so there are as many worlds as there are perspectives.

Hence, Nietzsche's anti-realism is, strictly speaking, not a logical thesis at all, for although logic presupposes the existence of things, it does not presuppose the existence of *realist* things. The quantifiers of first-order predicate logic can, for instance, range just as easily over constructed objects as over "real" ones. However, one way of reading his criticism of logic is probably true. It is probably true that we can be led easily into thinking that logic lets particular kinds of things in through the back door and keeps others out. This may be what Nietzsche is getting at in this note from the *Nachlass*: "[if we] make of logic a criterion of true being, we are on the way to positing as realities all those hypostases: substance, attribute, object, subject, action, etc.; that is, to conceiving a metaphysical world ... a 'real world'" (WP 516).

## Scepticism

Nietzsche certainly appears to be a sceptic of some kind. He is prone to writing things like "We simply lack any organ for knowledge, for 'truth': we 'know' (or believe or imagine) just as much as may be *useful* in the interests of the human herd, the species" (GS 354). This passage, and others like it, clearly suggests scepticism, if not of the traditional kind (as found in Descartes, for instance), then at least a relative of it. Despite these doubts about knowledge, Nietzsche's scepticism is simply the initial aspect of his by-now familiar argumentative style of critiquing a philo-sophical topic in language so vituperative that we are easily misled into thinking that he rejects all aspects of that topic. But he does not reject all aspects of knowledge, and there are more passages praising knowledge than there are passages criticizing it. For example, Nietzsche writes that "no honey is sweeter than that of knowledge" (HAH 292) and he asserts that "whoever seriously wants to become free ... his will desires nothing more urgently than knowledge and the means to it – that is, the enduring condition in which he is best able to engage in knowledge" (HAH 288). He also connects knowledge with both pleasure and the will to power:

> Why is knowledge, the element of researchers and philosophers, linked to pleasure? First and foremost, because by it we gain

> awareness of our power ... Second, because, as we gain knowledge, we surpass older ideas and their representatives, become victors, or at least believe ourselves to be. Third, because any new knowledge, however small, makes us feel superior to *everyone* and unique in understanding this matter correctly.          (*HAH* 252)

Indeed, not only is knowledge linked with pleasure, but the latter is undesirable without the former: "our drive for knowledge has become too strong for us to be able to want happiness without knowledge ... Knowledge has in us been transformed into a passion which shrinks at no sacrifice and at bottom fears nothing but its own extinction" (*D* 429).

Even in *The Gay Science*, Nietzsche characterizes himself as a lover of knowledge (*GS* 14), a seeker of knowledge (*GS* 380) and someone greedy for knowledge (*GS* 242). *The Gay Science*'s announcement that God is dead is taken to be an epistemological harbinger, for now, "all the daring of the lover of knowledge is permitted again; the sea, *our* sea, lies open again; perhaps there has never been such an 'open sea'" (*GS* 343). This open sea of possibilities is cause for rejoicing:

> and knowledge itself ... for me it is a world of dangers and victories in which heroic feelings, too, find places to dance and play. "*Life as a means to knowledge*" – with this principle in one's heart one can live not only boldly but even gaily, and laugh gaily too.                                  (*GS* 324)

This sort of praise for knowledge continues right up to the end of his productive life. In *The Anti-Christ*, he criticizes Christianity on the grounds that it opposes science and knowledge, characterizing knowledge as "emancipation from the priest" (*AC* 48); and in *Ecce Homo* he writes "Knowledge, saying Yes to reality, is just as necessary for the strong as cowardice and the flight from reality – as the 'ideal' is for the weak, who are inspired by weakness" (*EH* "Birth of Tragedy" 2).

So, despite the nasty things he has to say about knowledge, it is not accurate to describe Nietzsche as a nihilist about knowledge or as a sceptic. A more accurate interpretation of Nietzsche's assessment of knowledge is that what has hitherto passed as knowledge is not knowledge and that whatever can *now* count as knowledge will be denied to be knowledge on the discarded standard. For what can now count as knowledge is perspectival, but knowledge has always been thought to be justified true belief that corresponds to the world. Since there are no correspondence truths, there can be no beliefs or statements that correspond to the world and therefore there can be no knowledge that presupposes that definition of "truth". Towards knowledge of *that* sort, Nietzsche *is* a sceptic. What there can be and is – perspectively true and perspectively justified beliefs and statements – we can now call "knowledge". Toward knowledge of this sort, Nietzsche is not a sceptic. Of course, what we can have – perspectival knowledge – will not qualify on the old standard of knowledge, but there is no such thing anyway, so its loss is no great tragedy.

## Knowledge *de re*

*De re* knowledge is knowledge of things (*res*). As we have already seen, Nietzsche believes that the linguistic and conceptual requirements for synchronic and diachronic identity are probably required for any thinking at all. So there will always be an initial falsification imposed by the preconditions of our thought. However, given that initial falsification, it is certainly *possible* for us to have knowledge of the resulting entities, and that is all that is necessary for *de re* knowledge. Of course, our cognitive abilities are finite, so if there is an infinity of such entities, our *de re* knowledge, where it occurs, will never be complete, for we shall never know everything about all of them. And there is an infinity of such entities, because we are, amazingly enough, capable of creating algorithms for generating sequences of objects, knowledge of which outstrips all our epistemological abilities.

It is important to re-emphasize that Nietzsche is not saying that the world is exhausted by the entities we have created for thinking, even if some of the entities we have created for thinking outreach our capacities for knowing them. Nor is he saying that beyond the entities we have created for thinking there lies another set of entities that are completely unconditioned by any perspective at all. Nietzsche's view is that even those entities that fall outside every human perspective are also conditioned and perspectival, albeit not conditioned by us. So although the world is certainly composed of some entities not conditioned by human perspec- tives, the entities that are not so conditioned are, he thinks, conditioned otherwise by other perspectives. As we shall see in Chapter 8, one of the peculiar aspects of Nietzsche's positive ontological thoughts is that *every* level of existence is perspectival in this way. We shall see that perspectives are part and parcel of the furniture of the world. These ontological speculations – and that is all they are – are among the most extraordinary of Nietzsche's thoughts.

Given this perspectivity, it follows immediately that there are no things- in-themselves. Indeed, this is perhaps Nietzsche's most incisive criticism of

Kant. It is devastating against Kant because, if sound, it demonstrates that what Kant hoped for from the domain of things-in-themselves – namely, that things-in-themselves are beyond relations to *any* knowers – cannot in principle be established. And it is a criticism of any other version of the real world–apparent world distinction because it shows that even when human perspectives are subtracted, what remains is as wrapped up in perspectival interdependence as that which was subtracted. Nietzsche's extension of perspectives into the world is one of the reasons why he can criticize Kant and other defenders of the real world/apparent world distinction without having his own views relapse into a mutant form of the very distinction he rejects. The perspectivity of the non-human balance undercuts every argument on behalf of the real world, for the real world has always been set up as stable, durable and clear, in contrast to the swamp of change and impermanence of the apparent world. That contrast is ruled out by the perspectivity of every level of existence.

We might think that Nietzsche's criticism of the real world is anthropomorphic. After all, he seems to be taking characteristics of our experience of the apparent world – its impermanence, instability and indistinctness – and extending those characteristics to regions beyond our experience. However, this is not what Nietzsche is doing. Nietzsche is not claiming that the rest of existence is as it is because of the way human experience is; the view is rather that human experience is as it is because of the way the rest of existence is. Unfortunately for Nietzsche, taking this position reintroduces the same problem at one level higher, for the careful reader will be certain to notice Nietzsche's presumption to overcome the limitations of the human perspective to speak on behalf of what the world is like outside that perspective. The challenge can be put bluntly: how can Nietzsche affirm both that there is no thing-in-itself beyond the human perspective and that everything that exists – even what exists outside our possible knowledge – is perspectival? No person can get enough epistemo-logical distance from the human perspective to say what the world might be like outside the human perspective.

## Knowledge *de dicto*

We have just investigated Nietzsche's views of our knowledge of things. Consider now what he says about knowledge of statements (*dicta*): so-called "*de dicto*" knowledge. Here is an example of *de dicto* knowledge: Smith knows that George is left-handed. The traditional analysis of *de dicto* knowledge is that Smith knows that George is left-handed if and only if Smith believes that George is left-handed, his belief that George is left-handed is true, and his believing that George is left-handed is justified.

Theories of *de dicto* knowledge vary according to how justification gets articulated. *Foundationalist* theories of justification claim that Smith is justified in believing that George is left-handed whenever that belief is either implied by or is a foundational belief, where a foundational belief is a belief that is either indubitable, incorrigible, infallible, immediately justified, self-justified or non-inferentially justified (which you choose determines what kind of foundationalist you are). *Coherentist* theories of justification claim that Smith is justified in believing that George is left-handed whenever that belief coheres with others of Smith's beliefs. Various candidates for that coherence are live options, including implication, mutual implication, pragmatic fit and others (again, which you choose determines what kind of coherentist you are). *Contextualist* theories of justification claim that Smith is justified in believing that George is left-handed whenever that belief is justified within a context of belief. Various candidates for that contextual justification are live options, including various causal relations.

Nietzsche is clearly not a foundationalist about justification. Take one, predominant, strain of foundationalism, according to which foundational beliefs are those that result from self-presenting states, where a self-presenting state is a cognitive psychological state whose content cannot be doubted. An example is that, right now, as I write this sentence, it seems to me that I am looking at a computer screen. Now, suppose I believe that I am looking at a computer screen. That belief would be justified, and hence be knowledge, on this kind of foundationalism, if it were inferred from the self-presenting state of seeming to be looking at a computer screen. Nietzsche cannot be this kind of foundationalist, if for no other reason than that he thinks there are no beliefs that qualify as self-presenting states. As we shall see in Chapter 7, he thinks that the inner world of beliefs is full of error and illusion. No category of belief is immune to this error, so there is no such thing as an indubitable self-presenting state. Hence, for Nietzsche, there are no foundations of this sort for justification. Hence, foundationalism of this sort fails. He could make similar arguments against every other foundationalist proposal.

It is much better to think of Nietzsche as a contextualist. With the contextualist, Nietzsche concurs that the justification of a belief can vary across context. After all, if two individuals, *a* and *b*, both believe that George is six feet tall and *a* believes it of George of the Jungle and *b* believes it of George Costanza of the *Seinfeld Show*, who is shorter than that, then *a*'s belief will be well justified and *b*'s belief will not be well justified. But Nietzsche goes well beyond typical contextualist theories, for he is willing to countenance two much more radical possibilities: first, a single belief can be justified in one perspective and unjustified in another, regardless of perceptual input; and, secondly, the *truth* of a belief can vary as a function of perspective.

One implication of Nietzsche's epistemic perspectivism is that our justification for a belief varies as a function of the number of perspectives that can come into play about that belief. As he notes in *The Genealogy of Morals*:

> But precisely because we seek knowledge, let us not be ungrateful to such resolute reversals of accustomed perspectives and valuations ... to *want* to see differently, is no small discipline and preparation of the intellect for its future "objectivity" – the latter understood not as "contemplation without interest" (which is a nonsensical absurdity), but as the ability *to control* one's Pro and con and to dispose of them, so that one knows how to employ a *variety* of perspectives and affective interpretations in the service of knowledge .... There is *only* a perspective seeing, *only* a perspective "knowing"; and the *more* affects we allow to speak about one thing, the *more* eyes, different eyes, we can use to observe one thing, the more complete will our "concept" of this thing, our "objectivity," be. (*GM* III 12)

For instance, if simple perceptual beliefs have *n* relevant perspectives for determining their justification, more complex beliefs will no doubt have many more perspectives that are relevant for determining their justification. Of course, Nietzsche is not advocating that justification consists simply in adding up a bunch of available perspectives and announcing that we have considered 15 contexts in which the belief is true, and *therefore* the belief is justified, for some perspectives will be true but irrelevant, some will be relevant but false and some will be relevant but uninteresting.

The radical consequences of Nietzsche's perspectivism have led many to conclude that he is a relativist. In one sense this is undeniable, since both truth and justification are indexed, or relative, to perspectives. Recall, truth perspectivism is the view that the truth of knowledge claims is indexed, or relative, to a perspective, and epistemic perspectivism is the doctrine that the justification of knowledge claims is also indexed, or relative, to a perspective. A statement is known whenever it is believed, is true in a perspective and is justified in a perspective. The relativistic implications of this view are apparent: if truth and justification are relative to a perspective, then anyone can know any statement whatsoever, so long as it is true in *their* perspective at *that* time and justified in *their* perspective at *that* time.

We can admit that Nietzsche's perspectivist accounts of truth and justification imply the relativism of both. From the relativity of truth and justification it does not, however, follow that every statement is as true or is as justified as the next. Even if truth is indexed to perspectives, there are, as we have seen, statements that are true across many perspectives. Likewise, even if justification is indexed to perspectives, there are statements that are justified in many perspectives. Hence, one measure of a statement's justification is whether it can be submitted to, and pass, cross-perspectival adjudication. So, Nietzsche need not admit that an implication of his relativism about truth and justification is that every statement is as true, or is as justified, as any other. Of course, he must admit that his relativism about truth and justification does imply that every statement other than those true or justified in every perspective will be false or unjustified in some perspective. However, the mere existence of such a perspective will never alone be sufficient to undermine confidence that the vast majority of our statements will retain whatever truth-value or justification they had prior to the relativization to Nietzschean perspectives. And those statements whose truth and justification are revealed to be dubious upon relativization to Nietzschean perspectives are statements whose truth and justification probably should be analysed with care anyway.

Objections to Nietzsche's epistemic perspectivism are likely to come from the opposite quarter as well. If he is right, then, we might argue, there can be no absolute knowledge of any kind. But there is absolute knowledge of at least some things. So, Nietzsche's epistemic perspectivism is wrong. Nietzsche has an excellent rejoinder to this kind of criticism. If this objection uses the term "absolute knowledge" to refer to beliefs that are true outside any perspective, believed to be true outside any perspective and justified outside any perspective, then he will readily admit that there is no absolute knowledge. For Nietzsche denies that there are any extra-perspectival truths, denies that there are any extra-perspectival beliefs and denies that there are any extra-perspectival justifications for our beliefs. However, there may be statements that are true *across all* human perspectives, and some of those statements may be believed by *every* human, and justified in *every* human perspective. Those statements would, even on Nietzsche's epistemic and truth perspectivisms, be instances of absolute knowledge. Whether there are any such beliefs is a matter of debate. As we have seen, Nietzsche flirts with the idea that some statements of logic are candidates, but he persistently denies that there are many other candidates, and the statements offered up by philosophers are almost certainly not among them.

## The perspectivity of science

In the past few years, some interpreters have insisted that Nietzsche advocates science and the results of science as the only exemplars of knowledge. However, he is not such an advocate. He certainly thinks science is preferable to other perspectives, religion and morality in particular, but he has a number of complaints about science that, together, entail that he cannot think it is uniquely privileged over every other kind of knowledge. The first kind of complaint is directed against practising scientists. The second kind of complaint is levelled against what he thinks are inherent problems with science itself.

One criticism of scientists takes them to task for their alleged character flaws. One such flaw is myopia. Scientists root around in their specialities, digging "quietly under their molehills" (*D* 41), never wondering about the value of their work and never connecting it to the larger contexts, personal and social, in which that work occurs. This trait distinguishes scientists from philosophers, for whom nothing is impersonal (*BGE* 6). Nietzsche's second, and more serious, complaint against scientists is that they are ascetics. Recall from Chapter 1 that the ascetic ideal is a kind of self-mortifying decadence. Fine, we might say, but why think that *scientists* are ascetics? Nietzsche's argument in *The Genealogy of Morals* (III, 24) is that science places unquestioned faith in the value of truth, and that that unquestioned faith makes truth a stand-in divinity for God after he has died. Truth thus becomes the object to which all sacrifices must be made. Hence we have scientific labourers who practise humility before the truth and who, by suppressing their desires in order to devote their lives to their research, their labs, and their books, practise chastity and poverty as well. Thus the practice of science is practical asceticism.

Still, we might respond, that *scientists* are flawed does not mean that *science* itself is flawed. However, Nietzsche also complains about science itself. His first criticism is that it is mistakenly governed by a set of mechanistic principles that are not only false but perniciously so. He writes in *The Gay Science*:

> Do we really want to permit existence to be degraded for us like this – reduced to a mere exercise for a calculator and an indoor diversion for mathematicians? Above all, one should not wish to divest existence of its *rich ambiguity*: that is a dictate of good taste, gentlemen, the taste of reverence for everything that lies beyond your horizon ... an interpretation that permits counting, calculating, weighing, seeing, and touching, and nothing more –

> that is a crudity and naiveté, assuming that it is not a mental illness,
> an idiocy.                                               (GS 373)

Nietzsche drives the point home with an example from music. There is, he notes, more to music than the measurement of frequency and amplitude of sound waves. Now, to the extent that science reduces to mechanism, to that extent this criticism is sound. But does science make the reduction as Nietzsche alleges? Certainly in the nineteenth century, mechanism was more widespread than it is now and there were certainly unguarded propagandists who advocated reducing everything to that which could be studied mechanistically. So, in that way, the criticism is fair.

Of course, to the extent that the criticism is restricted to mechanistic science, it misses against contemporary science, because contemporary science has abandoned mechanism. But this glib response misses Nietzsche's real objection, which is to reductionism in science: the view that we can identify fundamental categories and explain everything in terms of them. Even today there are plenty of reductionists in science. Review the past hundred years of psychology, for example. Until the so-called "cognitive revolution" in the 1960s, the most widespread theoretical framework in psychology was a reductionist form of behaviourism, according to which the explanatory domain of psychology was exhausted by observable behaviour. Behaviourism was replaced by computationalism, which insisted that all cognition had to be reduced to computational activity. Computationalism is now generally thought to be false for some kinds of cognition, for a very good reason: computers are qualitative zombies and we are not. There is *something* that *we* have – phenomenological character to our experiences – that computers lack. So, from mechanism to behaviourism to computationalism, psychology has had its fair share of proposed reductions. Apparently, we have still not learned our lesson. The current reductionist flag-waving surrounds evolutionary psychology, according to which a psychological phenomenon is best explained as the result of that phenomenon's survival value. Nietzsche is already standing at the end of *this* reduction; recall from Chapter 3 his objections to Darwin. So, in this way too, Nietzsche's larger point is also made: science, not just scientists, is routinely blinkered and self-interested.

However, we should be careful about drawing too many conclusions from this line of criticism and careful, too, about interpreting Nietzsche's own conclusions. Consider that from the fact that mechanism does not capture *everything* in music it does not follow that it captures *nothing* in music. Music certainly is waves of particular wavelengths and particular amplitudes. But it is more than that, too, since those sound waves are structured in particular ways. And, in general, from the fact that some scientific theory $X$ does not capture *everything* about the things it studies, it does not follow that $X$ captures *nothing* about those things. Nietzsche, of course, is careful not to draw any dismissive conclusions about science. In the section of *The Gay Science* immediately following his criticism of mechanism, he suggests that there may be infinite perspectives to adopt. In this way, his criticism of science can be seen to be an instance of his general attitude about most things, namely, that we are well advised to refrain from dogmatic over-assertion on behalf of our beliefs. That attitude is, of course, a direct implication of perspectivism. Perspectivism does not need to deride specific perspectives such as science; it just insists that they are not the *only* perspective to take on a subject. Other perspectives may enrich our lives in different ways from those found in science. The mistake is thinking that the perspective of science is unique.

Nietzsche's second criticism of science is that it rests upon a faith in extra-perspectival truths that hold independently from any human perspectives. He writes in *The Gay Science* that:

> We see that science also rests on a faith; there is simply no science "without presuppositions." The question whether *truth* is needed must not only have been affirmed in advance, but affirmed to such a degree that the principle, the faith, the conviction finds expression: "*Nothing* is needed *more* than truth, and in relation to it everything else has only second-rate value." (GS 344)

He is not terribly clear here as to whether the faith of science is in the extra-perspectival nature of truth or in the *value* of truth as an object of pursuit. To the degree that it is the former, to that degree is Nietzsche critical of science.

That there can be a perspectivist science for Nietzsche implies that there is something in science that Nietzsche admires. In fact, there are a number of things that he admires about science. One such feature is the scientific method, which Nietzsche regards as producing a much-desired mental rigour. He even applies this methodology to his own philosophy in *The Gay Science*: "But we, we others who thirst after reason, are determined to scrutinize our experiences as severely as a scientific experiment – hour after hour, day after day. We ourselves wish to be our experiments and guinea pigs" (GS 319). A related positive feature is that adherence to the scientific method staves off superstition. This feature is cause for some of Nietzsche's greatest praise and it is the source of some of his greatest sorrow, for scientific method was in place in Greek and Roman culture and then was "sucked dry" by the "*covert ressentiment*" of Christianity (AC 59). What the Greeks and Romans recognized, and what "we have won back for ourselves today with an unspeakable amount of self-constraint" is the Greek discovery of scientific method (*AC* 59). Those methods, "one must repeat ten times, *are* the essential, as well as being the most difficult, as well as being that which has habit and laziness against it longest" (*AC* 59). Simply for the mental hygiene science permits, Nietzsche recommends that everyone learn at least one science (*HAH* 635). Finally, science does not commit a variety of common errors found in other perspectives. For example, since science deals with the apparent world alone, it does not commit itself to the false division of the real *versus* the apparent world, and in its attention to only natural phenomena, science is non-moral, so, in that way, beyond good and evil. It is no wonder that dogmatic moralists and religious types, popular Nietzschean targets, are compelled to attack science. Nietzsche makes the point as follows: "it is all over with priests and gods if man becomes scientific! – *Moral*: science is the forbidden in itself – it alone is forbidden. Science is the *first* sin, the germ of all sins, *original* sin" (*AC* 48).

In short, although Nietzsche does not want to abandon science, he does want to warn against its creeping absolutism, especially in the hands of its ascetic practitioners. For Nietzsche, science is discovery about ourselves, our perspectives, and our needs and desires. In *The Gay Science* he writes:

> Let us introduce the refinement and rigor of mathematics into all sciences as far as this is at all possible, not in the faith that this will lead us to know things but in order to *determine* our human relation to things. Mathematics is merely the means for general and ultimate knowledge of man. (GS 246)

Like all knowledge, science is a "regulative fiction" (*GS* 344). We shape our world, according to Nietzsche, and then come to know it. What we know is a world made calculable by us for us. Having "made" this world, however, we *can* know it. And, thanks to its methodological rigour, science is a valuable contributor to our body of knowledge. There is, Nietzsche thinks, no domain to which his kind of science can contribute more than psychology, so let us turn to it.

# CHAPTER 7

# Psychology

Perhaps no other philosopher has as many interesting things to say about the self as Nietzsche. His reflections on the metaphysical status of the self, on consciousness and on some of the darker elements of human psychology have had a dramatic impact both in philosophy and, through the work of Sigmund Freud and others, also in psychology. For all his insight into the role of the unconscious in determining our character, and subtlety in debunking the pretentious claims philosophers make on behalf of consciousness, what Nietzsche is most remembered for is his commitment to the will to power as a psychological explanatory principle. Once it takes hold of his philosophical imagination, he does not waver from the perspective the will to power imposes, and this gives all his mature psychological reflections their characteristic bite.

In this chapter we shall investigate Nietzsche's meta-psychology, that is, his views about the composition and individuation of the self. This meta-psychological investigation will focus primarily on his claims about consciousness and his analysis of the composition of the self. Nietzsche repeatedly argues that consciousness is a relatively unimportant aspect of our psychological lives, and we shall analyse these arguments, showing how his views are best interpreted as claims about the unimportance of what we have already referred to, in Chapter 4, as reflective consciousness. We shall also discuss Nietzsche's notion of drive, distinguishing between conscious and unconscious drives, and discussing the relation between cognitive and non-cognitive psychological states. We shall then examine Nietzsche's proposal that the self is perspectival and non-substantive. Our focus will be on his claims that the self is a bundle of drives coming together in the service of certain ends. In conclusion, we shall note how this bundle view of the self supports the perspectivity of synchronic and diachronic identity. Then, in Chapter 8, we shall see how the will to power folds into this meta-psychology.

135

## Consciousness

Nietzsche rejects a substantive self and criticizes the role that consciousness has played in establishing the existence of a substantive self. Yet, although he repeatedly says that conscious *things* are illusory and that our *identity* is not determined by consciousness, he rarely denies that many psychological events are conscious. He readily admits that feelings, intentions, valuations, thoughts, perceptions, hopings, willings, and pain and pleasure can all be conscious. Most of the time, what he means by saying that psychological events are conscious is that they are the objects of some other, reflective, psychological event.

Nietzsche's starting point in explaining conscious experience is *access consciousness*. He is prepared to allow that it is the logical and causal precursor of reflective consciousness and that both access consciousness and reflective consciousness are perspectival. The objects we are access conscious and reflectively conscious of are multiply mediated and simplified by the time they reach the level of even access consciousness. Nietzsche agrees here with Kant and Leibniz on the causal structure of access conscious perceptual experience. Both Kant and Leibniz draw a distinction between the passivity of the reception of sensory input and the activity of the mind in categorizing or conceptualizing input as presented by our sensory apparatus. Sensory input and cognitive categorizing yield the perceptual experience that we are all familiar with in access consciousness. Nietzsche also agrees with Kant and Leibniz on another point: there is a distinction between the ineliminable particularity of sensory input and the generality of conscious experience. Were we to have no concept of *table*, for example, our sensory experience of *that* would be only of *that* and of nothing relevantly similar and would never rise to the level of perceptual experience of a table. Finally, all three agree that the activity of the sensory organs is unconscious. Where they differ is on how much of cognitive activity is unconscious. With Leibniz and against Kant, Nietzsche thinks that most of our cognitive activity is unconscious.

These distinctions yield the following picture: our sensory apparatus passively and unconsciously receives a manifold of particular sensory inputs, and our mind actively and un-reflectively interprets those sensory inputs as instances of kinds and categories. Nietzsche suggests this view in the following passage from *Beyond Good and Evil*:

> The spirit's power to appropriate the foreign stands revealed in its inclination to assimilate the new to the old, to simplify the manifold . . . – just as it involuntarily emphasizes certain features and lines in what is foreign, in every piece of the "external world," retouching

and falsifying the whole to suit itself. Its intent in all this is to incorporate new "experiences," to file new things in old files.

(*BGE* 230)

In typically free-flowing style, this passage presents Nietzsche's view of experience: we start with a manifold of passively received and unconscious sensory inputs; we then retouch and falsify them with our involuntary emphasis on certain features and lines, our preconscious conceptualization of the manifold; and the result is delivered to conscious awareness as the accomplished incorporation of new experiences into old and familiar conceptual systems.

In one way, Nietzsche's view of perception is a kind of phenomenalism, where by "phenomenalism" we understand the view that statements about the physical world are equivalent to statements about sensory experience. As in other phenomenalisms, Nietzsche's view starts with the unconscious raw sense-data of experience, working them up to conscious experience of the world. Unlike most phenomenalisms, however, Nietzsche's views are thoroughly perspectivist as well. The retouching and falsifying we subject our sensory experience to is a function of our human perspective. Thus may we understand what Nietzsche is up to in this dense passage from *The Gay Science*:

> This is the essence of phenomenalism and perspectivism as *I* understand them: owing to the nature of *animal consciousness*, the world of which we can become conscious is only a surface- and sign-world, a world that is made common and meaner; ... all becoming conscious involves a great and thorough corruption, falsification, reduction to superficialities, and generalization.
>
> You will guess that it is not the opposition of subject and object that concerns me here: This distinction I leave to the epistemologists. ... It is even less the opposition of "thing-in-itself" and appearance; for we do not "know" nearly enough to be entitled to any such distinction. (*GS* 354)

Sense can be made of this passage because Nietzsche's kind of phenomenalism is perspectivism, not idealism. It would be idealism were he to hold that the only entities in the world were mind-dependent. However, Nietzsche's phenomenalism agrees with empiricism that sensory experience is passive reception of inputs from the world. And it agrees with Kant and Leibniz because the mind plays a role in working up those inputs into the perceptual experience of access consciousness. This is why he is not concerned with the opposition between subject and object; *both* are required on his view. And it is also why he is not talking about the thing-in-itself and appearance; *his* phenomenalism is a perspectivism that rules out talking about things-in-themselves altogether.

Although reflective consciousness introduces *new* perspectives, its activities only bring *additional* interpretations to those already introduced at pre-access-conscious levels. Contemporary science supports Nietzsche's speculative hypotheses. Contemporary theories of perception have revealed that perception is largely a matter of unconscious and preconscious causal mechanisms that transmit data from the environment to various locations in the brain. At these locations, representations of objects are worked up and translated into our conscious experience of a unified field of perception. Nietzsche is aware, if not of the details of this largely unconscious set of perceptual mechanisms, at least that they must be there.

Nietzsche is also aware that, if these perceptual mechanisms are doing what he thinks they must do, their presence entails the end of the claimed *objectivity* on behalf of perceptual beliefs. If, as Nietzsche states, consciousness is a kind of "language" (*WP* 479), a mediated and symbolic simplification and interpretation on the psychological event that it models (itself already an interpretation), then no perceptual belief can be objective. Again, this looks like idealism. This is not the case, however, because idealism ignores both the sensory input from the world and the inherent perspectivity of conscious states. We have already assessed the impact of the first point, so consider the second. Nietzsche agrees with idealists that there is a cut between the world and our conscious experience of it, but the idealist uses this cut to conclude that the most, indeed only, reliably known things are the products of consciousness. Nietzsche uses that cut to support the contrary conclusion, namely, that the contents of conscious states are among the least reliably known things. This conclusion follows directly from the inherent perspectivity of consciousness.

Nietzsche believes that not only are the objects of consciousness perspectival, but conscious processes and events are also perspectival. Nietzsche thinks that our beliefs about the temporal sequencing of conscious events and their causal behaviour are all interpreted after the fact and prone to error. For instance, consider the temporal sequence of conscious thought events. Although conscious thoughts come after the preconscious psychological events that are their causes, Nietzsche claims that they are often mistakenly believed to be temporally prior to them. An example is sensory after-images. In *Human, All Too Human*, he notes that the figures and shapes that reason conforms the formless colours into when our eyes are closed are often taken to be the cause of the colours. As he puts it there:

> The imagination keeps pushing images upon the mind, using in their production the visual impressions of the day ... That is, the supposed cause is deduced from the effect and imagined after the effect. All this with an extraordinary speed, so that, as with a conjurer, judgment becomes confused, and a sequence can appear to be a synchronism, or even a reversed sequence.     (HAH 13)

The mistakes of which such mis-sequencing is an instance are endemic to our descriptions of our psychological lives. Even our conscious experiences of our internal world – our thoughts, hopes, memories and dreams – are subject to systematic mistaken description. Accordingly, he claims that "nothing is so much deception as this inner world" (WP 478).

Given Nietzsche's pervasive perspectivism about consciousness, his commitment to its epiphenomenality is more plausible than it might otherwise seem. There should be no doubt that Nietzsche claims that reflective conscious activities are epiphenomenal. An epiphenomenon is an event that is caused but has no causal consequences of its own. For example, he claims that conscious thoughts are "terminal phenomena" and he notes that:

> We believe that thoughts as they succeed one another in our minds stand in some kind of causal relation: the logician especially, who actually speaks of nothing but instances which never occur in reality, has grown accustomed to the prejudice that thoughts *cause* thoughts.     (WP 478)

Nietzsche thinks that between any two conscious thoughts "all kinds of affects play their game" (WP 477). In short, what the logician sees as a sequence of conscious thoughts linked to the next in neat, logical relations simply does not exist. Nietzsche makes similar claims about the feelings of pleasure and pain. For example, although "we believe ... that pleasure and pain are causes of reactions", we should instead "concede that everything would have taken the same course, according to exactly the same sequence of causes and effects, if these states 'pleasure and displeasure' had been absent" (WP 477). Pleasure and pain are "epiphenomena with a quite different object than to evoke reactions; they are themselves effects within the instituted process of reaction" (WP 478).

Nietzsche asserts here that conscious thoughts are terminal phenomena that have no subsequent conscious causal consequences. Although we may be tempted to attribute to him the stronger claim, that *all* psychological events are epiphenomenal, such a move is not Nietzsche's. That's a good thing, too; it would be hard to conceive of ourselves were global epiphenomenalism of the psychological true. Imagine the consequences: no pain ever causes flinching, no caress ever causes pleasure, no memory ever causes remorse or joy, no desire ever causes action, no one ever intentionally crosses the street. If global epiphenomenalism were true, we would be *massively* wrong about ourselves. Worse, our being wrong about ourselves would be *undiscoverable*, for were global epiphenomenalism of the psychological true, *every* psychological event would be a terminal phenomenon. We could never reach the level of reflective consciousness required to assess our beliefs or determine that we have made a mistake about *anything*, including our being wrong about the causal efficacy of conscious thoughts.

The difficulties with global epiphenomenalism of the psychological for Nietzsche's own views would be just as awful. All his complaints about the baleful consequences of *ressentiment* and the liberating consequences of the new philosopher's sceptical turn would be false; the bad conscience would not be a disease; distinguishing between kinds of morality would be pointless; ranking individuals according to their psychological types would be a waste of time; praising certain souls for their health would be like praising rocks for their mass; and advocating emotional discipline would be as effective as advocating that beavers cut down only those trees they actually need. Luckily, Nietzsche does not claim that all psychological events are epiphenomenal. His claim is that *reflective conscious* psychological events are epiphenomenal. This amounts to the claim that no psychological event can cause a psychological or non-psychological event because of its reflective conscious properties. Nietzsche's counter is that unconscious drives and other affective events are much more important than conscious thoughts in explaining our actions. These claims are difficult enough to defend, but let us at least try.

Here is an interpretation of what Nietzsche is saying. Suppose we have a chain of reflective conscious thoughts, that is, a chain of cognitive states of which we are aware. Nietzsche's view is that between any two such thoughts drives, passions and instincts always intrude. There are two ways of looking at this intrusion. First, the thoughts may be events that are caused by temporally prior drives and do no further causal work of any kind; they do not cause any other thoughts, emotions, affects, passions, instincts or other psychological events. On this view, reflective thoughts are caused by drives or by phenomenal or access conscious thoughts but cause nothing at all in turn. Each such reflective thought is a dead end, both cognitively and affectively, a complete epiphenomenon. Alternatively, reflective thoughts may be caused by temporally prior drives and in turn may cause temporally succeeding drives, but do not cause any temporally succeeding thoughts. On this view, a drive causes a thought and that thought causes a subsequent drive, but no thought causes another thought. So reflective thoughts are not individually epiphenomenal but members of causal sequences containing nodes not widely acknowledged. Nevertheless, this also is a kind of epiphenomenalism, for no reflective thought ever causes another reflective thought without the intrusion of an intervening drive. So thoughts are cognitively epiphenomenal, but not affectively epiphenomenal.

Something like this latter view is the best interpretation of Nietzsche. We have already seen, in Chapter 4, that reflective consciousness is an accidental property of experience. It is not shocking, then, that psychological events are not causally efficacious in virtue of their being reflective conscious. However, that does not rule out their being causally efficacious in virtue of some other property they have, and Nietzsche nominates an event's affective or drive properties as those causally efficacious properties. As we have seen, he repeatedly insists that *all* our psychological events are nothing more than refined drives and affects, and drives and affects do have causal effects. Reflective thoughts may not cause anything because they are reflective, but they certainly do cause something because they are also and at the same time drives or instincts. This is enough to salvage the causal potency of the psychological and still maintain the epiphenomenality of reflective consciousness.

## Self-identity

Nietzsche's reflections on self-identity are fascinating yet unsatisfying. They are fascinating because he understands the troubling implications of adopting a bundle theory of the self. They are unsatisfying because, in the end, he stumbles over the biggest problem with bundles theories of the self: how to account for identity over time, that is, diachronic self-identity.

Nietzsche repeatedly claims that the self is a bundle composed of experiences, actions, drives, impulses and what is thought, wanted, needed and done. The self is a "communality" (*WP* 492) or an "aristocracy" (*WP* 490) or a "social structure" of such phenomena (*BGE* 12). Since drives and affects need not be reflective conscious and it is not in virtue of their being so that they are causally efficacious, we begin to understand how the Nietzschean self is so different from substantial accounts of the self and other bundle theories. Insisting that *drives* are the building blocks of the self underwrites Nietzsche's perspectival view of the self. He does not deny that there is a self that is a collection of drives and other affective psychological events, but this view of the self is straightforwardly inconsistent with an ego or "I" of the kind assumed by Descartes and others. Nietzsche has nothing but scorn for *that* kind of self. There is no core *thing* that has experiences or drives. Just as importantly, Nietzsche's claim that drives and other affective psychological states compose the self pushes consciousness away from the core of the self. This is contrary to considerable swathes of philosophy that claim instead that consciousness is the very centre of who we are. By draining reflective consciousness of causal potency, Nietzsche lays the ground for his contrary claim that thoughts, beliefs, drives and instincts are far more frequently not conscious. Further, even when they are conscious, it is not in virtue of being conscious that thoughts have their causal potency.

Nietzsche's proposal that the self is composed of drives and other affective states provides a nifty solution to a problem that dogs most philosophical views of the self. This problem, known as the "mind–body problem", emerges as the implication of the assumption that the mental and the physical are distinct ontological realms. Descartes is the most notorious advocate of this view, although he is far from alone. Descartes's arguments are compelling and clear. He notes that the properties of thought and the properties of the objects that make up the physical world are not just distinct but disjoint. Thoughts are not extended in space and have no mass; objects are both extended in space and have mass. Hence, the mind is distinct from the body. If this were the case, however, what is the nature of the relation between thoughts and body? How does a non-extended, massless thought ever cause muscles to move? Descartes's answer – that very fine movements in the brain's pineal gland initiated by thoughts are sufficient to result in muscular movement – is not a satisfactory one.

Nietzsche thinks the mind–body problem is a pseudo-problem. At the most fundamental level, the Nietzschean self is a unity of *forces* organized around a living body itself constituted of forces, whose functional organization is as a "mode of nutrition" (*WP* 641). He elaborates:

> The body and physiology the starting point: why?– We gain the correct idea of the nature of our subject-unity, namely as regents at the head of a communality, also of the dependence of these regents upon the ruled and of an order of rank and division of labor as the conditions that make possible the whole and its parts. The most important thing, however, is: that we understand that the ruler and his subjects are of the same kind, all feeling, willing, thinking – and that wherever we see or divine movement in a body, we learn to conclude that there is a subjective, invisible life appertaining to it. (*WP* 492)

Nietzsche clearly states in this passage that the mental is not different from the physical. Nor is he saying, as contemporary reductionists would have it, that the mental is *identical* to the physical or that the mental *emerges* from the physical. Nietzsche is suggesting that the terms "mental" and "physical" do not refer to distinct ontological realms at all, but refer instead to the *same* category of entity; namely, collective forces of willing, feeling and thinking. The physical realm is nowhere contrasted with the mental realm, so no relation between them needs ever be specified. There is no mind–body problem for the simple reason that there is nothing mental and nothing physical between which relations have to be established. As he puts it, "If there is nothing material, there is also nothing immaterial. The concept no longer contains anything" (*WP* 488).

Grant, then, that the self is composed of drives and other affective states. How do we distinguish two such bundles, be they contemporaneous or not, that is, how do we individuate selves at a time and over time? Nietzsche's advocacy of a bundle view of the self makes this a question he really has to answer. As we have seen earlier, he rejects one answer popular in the philosophical tradition, namely, that the self is a substance. According to this view, the self is simple and its identity intuitively known. However, since Nietzsche thinks that the self-atom is a myth, he does not have access to that kind of answer. Nor, perhaps surprisingly, can he appeal to *bodily unity* as the criterion of the self. One might think that his frequent stress upon the body represents a view of this sort, and, indeed, he does claim that "a multiplicity of forces, connected by a common mode of nutrition, we call 'life'" (*WP* 641). This seems like a brief for the view that bundles of forces are unified by nutrition. However, while the emphasis on nutrition and the body reveals Nietzsche's perspectival take on the functional structure of organisms, we should remember that bodily unity, its states and dispositions and the explanations that invoke them, are all also subject to interpretation. The body is a unity of forces and so a unity of entities, each one of which is at the same time a perspective. The body and explanations that start from it are, thus, subject to distinct perspectives given distinct interests. Hence, even the body is an entity subject to genealogical study. Thus, physiological reductions of the self to the body are also ruled out. Thus bodily continuity cannot suffice for personal identity over time.

Infrequently, as in this passage from *Daybreak*, Nietzsche considers the possibility that *other people* individuate us: "The great majority do nothing for their ego their whole life long: what they do is done for the phantom of their ego which has formed itself in the heads of those around them and has been communicated to them" (*D* 105). But it is clear from the context that he does not favour such a view; a life in which we are at the mercy of others culminates in "a strange world of phantasms – which at the same time knows how to put on so sober an appearance!" (*ibid*.). (Worse still, it is irredeemably circular. Take a world of only two individuals, *a* and *b*: if *a* is individuated by $b$, then $b$ is individuated by $a$. Prior to being individuated by $b$, $a$ is not a self and prior to being individuated by $a$, $b$ is not a self. But then $a$ is individuated only if $b$ is and $b$ is individuated only if $a$ is. Hence, $a$ and $b$ are both individuated only if the other is.) The considered judgement must be that Nietzsche also rejects this kind of view. Another option he considers only to reject is the Kantian favourite, reflective consciousness. That option claims that because all of the members of a set of drives can become the objects of a particular set of reflective thoughts, those drives are the components of a single self. Nietzsche rejects this suggestion too. In order to see why, we have to step back just a bit to note the connections between the development of reflective consciousness and Nietzsche's view that the self is composed of drives.

According to Nietzsche, reflective consciousness evolves with our enculturation; it is an effect of the inwardly directed will to power that abjures subduing other bodies in favour of subduing one's self. The drives and instincts of which we are composed were originally engaged in direct attempts to maximize power over others, but as we became members of social units they turned inwards instead of outwards. "A solitary beast of prey," Nietzsche writes in *The Gay Science*, "would have not have needed [consciousness]" (*GS* 354). So a self cannot be the self it is because it is reflectively aware of an ensemble of drives, since there are selves that predate the development of consciousness.

Although reflective consciousness is not the unifier of the self at a time, Nietzsche is interested in how reflective consciousness ever emerged in the first place. He offers two candidate explanations for the development of reflective consciousness. The first is that human beings were for aeons the most endangered animal and needed protection of compatriots. As a result, we needed to express our needs and make ourselves understood to others via spoken communication. This in turn required that we ourselves know what those needs were and how we felt about them, and knowing these matters entailed the development of the reflective capacity that forms attitudes about psychological events. The second explanation is that it was a specific subset of needs that required communication, namely, those that arose in competitive interaction with others: "As soon as one animal sees another it measures itself against it in its mind, and men in barbarous ages did likewise. From this it follows that every man comes to know himself almost solely in regard to his powers of defense and attack" (*D* 212). Here Nietzsche suggests that reflective consciousness arose as a result of our need to calibrate ourselves against those human and non-human others with whom we came in contact.

At this point, a careful reader is likely to ask: why does the internalization of drives and instincts result in reflective consciousness anyway? Let us agree with Nietzsche that there is something uncanny introduced into the world with the emergence of reflective consciousness. As he notes, there is no obvious need for it at all: "we could think, feel, will, and remember, and we could also 'act' in every sense of that word, and yet none of all this would have to 'enter our consciousness'" (*GS* 354). Still, why did reflective consciousness emerge as the end result of internalization? Again, we can grant that the redirection of drives whose objects were originally external generates new internal objects against which to struggle. But drives whose objects are external events are not reflective conscious, so why should those whose objects are internal be so? An answer to this question has either to say that all drives with internal objects are reflective conscious or that all drives with internal objects provide the necessary conditions for the emergence of reflective consciousness. The former will not work since there are non-conscious drives with internal objects, such as those connected with the autonomic functions of the body. Unfortunately, Nietzsche never explains the second alternative. (In his defence, let us admit that, to this day, no one else has a good explanation of the emergence of reflective consciousness either. Even contemporary evolutionary psychologists are circumspect about the matter. The difficulty is that even if we can demonstrate the survival value of reflective consciousness, that survival value does not establish the genetic mechanism by which reflective consciousness is inherited. No one has yet identified that mechanism.)

In *The Genealogy of Morals*, Nietzsche offers an account of how drives, perceptions, sensations and affects get bundled together into persons that is a variant on reflective consciousness but not really reducible to it. This variant is the memory criterion of personal identity, and is widely thought to be the most viable criterion of personal identity. Let us investigate Nietzsche's version of it, for it is characteristically peculiar.

The second essay of the *Genealogy* is, as we have already seen in Chapter 1, devoted to explaining how "an animal with the right to make promises" has been bred. The essay discusses the origins of guilt, a sense of moral responsibility and conscience. Nietzsche argues that it is impossible for a creature to have a moral sense, or feel guilt, unless that creature first has a belief in diachronic identity. If the debtor does not believe that *he* borrowed the money, then *he* cannot feel any compunction to repay. Primitive humans lack this ability. Nietzsche considers primitive humans to be "slaves of momentary affect and desire" (*GM* II 3) who might each morning wake up as new persons. Memory is then required for the sense of a unified self that persists through time. The debtor remembers a person who borrowed something and comes to identify himself with that person. The development of memory is no small matter, however. A powerful force or impetus is needed to overcome the drive to forget. Nietzsche puts the question clearly in *The Genealogy of Morals*: "How can one create a memory for this human animal? How can one impress something upon this partly obtuse, partly flighty mind, attuned only to the passing moment, in such a way that it will stay there?" (*GM* II 3). His answer to the question is, recall, simple and painful: "If something is to stay in the memory it must be burned in: only that which never ceases to *hurt* stays in the memory . . . pain is the most powerful aid to mnemonics." Should the debtor fail to recall the debt owed and neglect payment, the creditor could cut from the body of the debtor whatever seemed appropriate for the size of the debt.

We can agree with Nietzsche that without memory we could not be diachronically identical, for that is only to say that memory is necessary for diachronic identity. But memory alone is not enough to establish diachronic identity for, if it were, then I could say that whenever I have a memory of something, then I am the same person now as I was then. Unfortunately, there are false memories, memories that we have of things that in fact never happened to us. So it cannot be that if I have a memory of doing something that that alone is enough to establish that I am now the person who once did the thing I now remember. After all, it could be that what I now remember happening then did not occur to me at all. Perhaps it did not occur at all; perhaps it occurred to someone else.

Nietzsche does have other thoughts about self-identity and they typically cluster around the idea that there be some principle of individuation for the self that is intrinsic to it. There must, he thinks, be some central drive or central set of drives in the service of which other drives are organized. This explains his imperative to "'give style' to our character" (*GS* 290). It also presupposes that a bundle of drives be identified independently of the perspectives taken on it by others. Of course, intrinsically individuating selves will be – must be – a complex affair, because doing so is not a matter of finding an existing subject atom and triumphantly announcing that we have discovered the self. Rather, identifying a self, our own self included, is an achievement, accomplished over a significant amount of time and with considerable remembering and reconfiguration. Consider, then, how such self-individuation of a bundle of drives takes place, both at a time and over time.

The first thing to admit is that Nietzsche's list of the components of the self, namely drives and instincts, is really peculiar. Along with the obvious, such as sex, hunger and preservation, there are drives to doubt, to negate, collect and dissolve (*GS* 113); to laugh, lament and curse (*GS* 333); for truth (*WP* 585); for curiosity, dialectical investigation and contradiction (*UM* III 6); for distinction (*D* 113); for beauty (*WP* 800); for pride, joy, health, love of the sexes, enmity and war, beautiful gestures and manners, strong will, high spirituality, discipline, gratitude to the earth and life, beneficence and transfiguration (*WP* 1033); for compassion, anger and revenge (*WP* 929); for magnanimity and heroism (*WP* 388); for decadence (*WP* 401); for the herd (*GS* 50); for weakness (*GS* 347); for hatred, envy and covetousness, (*BGE* 23); for enterprising spirit, foolhardiness, vengefulness, craftiness, rapacity and lust for rule (*BGE* 201); for sentimentality, nature-idolatry, the anti-historical, the idealistic, the unreal and the revolutionary (*TI* IX 49); and, of course, for power (*WP* 720). One thing that cannot be said about this list is that its members are all merely *affective*. Drives for dialectical investigation, for the revolutionary, for negation and for doubting are all drives with significant *cognitive* content. They may originate from internalized and redirected drives of a more primitive nature that are not themselves cognitive, but they have developed in such a way that they are now much more complex than them.

So, then, what makes one collection of drives and affects the Queen of England and another collection a rancher in Calhan, Colorado? Nietzsche thinks that the self is neither a substance nor simply the body, that it is not identical to our consciousness, and that it is not identical to what other people say it is. Now we can see that the fact that each collection of drives has different components at a time is also insufficient for individuating a self. A difference in drives may show why the Queen of England is not a rancher in Calhan, but it does not show why a particular group of drives composes a person at all, much less a specific person, such as the Queen. So, even if we have part of an answer, we do not yet have a complete answer.

In fact, Nietzsche does not and cannot have a complete answer. Here is why. According to Nietzsche, the origin of the diachronic unity of the self was "like the beginnings of everything great on earth, soaked in blood thoroughly and for a long time" (*GM* II 6). The spectacle of watching others suffer leads to the development of memory and the unification of previously dissolute drives and desires into a self. That suggests that certain needs and requirements lead to the development of those psychological qualities that serve as the unifying glue of the bundles of drives and affects that constitute persons. Unfortunately, all the problems that confront the reflective consciousness criterion of personal identity re-attach to Nietzsche's alternative as well. What explains the unity of the drives that we remember? Nietzsche has no answer to this question other than that the self is a confederation of drives and affects, a hierarchy of them, and which drives and motivations are uppermost at any one time and over time is mutable. This reveals the deep perspectivity of the Nietzschean self: the self is held together by whatever drives are currently dominant. It is in terms of, and in service of, the dominant component that the other elements of the bundle are organized and maintained. A unified self is an accomplishment not yet within reach rather than an accomplishment we have already reached because we have memory.

We may think that the lack of a unified self spells the death of agency, that sense of ourselves as the initiator of actions for which we are responsible. If what we require for agency is a unified deliberator, then Nietzsche is happy to watch that self die, for that is only the doer behind the deed one more time. But, as we shall see, that there is no doer does not entail for Nietzsche either that there is no deed or that there is no self that does things. The Nietzschean self is a self, just not a unified substance. Let us turn, then, to his view of the constitution of the self.

## Drives, free will and the Nietzschean subject

Nietzsche thinks that human beings are "*included* among the most unexpected and exciting lucky throws in the dice game of Heraclitus's 'great child,' be he called Zeus or chance" (*GM* II 16). We are interesting because our capacity to conjoin drives and impulses is almost infinite. Sadly, that very capacity is also reason for despair. Although our potential is enormous, most of us are either vapid conformists or too disorganized ever to amount to much.

For all of us, some drives dominate others. Some of us are dominated by the desire to succeed materially, some of us are obsessed with sex, some of us are prisoners of our pasts and some of us just love watching television. Selves are always eccentric and skewed in some direction. Such eccentricities are, Nietzsche thinks, unavoidable for being a self at all, and he takes great pleasure in spinning out the implications of being dominated by particular emotions or drives. A note from the *Nachlass*, entitled "To what extent interpretations of the world are symptoms of a ruling drive", for instance, articulates the differences in the interpretations of experience in those dominated by, respectively, the aesthetic drive, the scientific drive, the religious drive and the moral drive. For someone dominated by the aesthetic drive, for example, contemplation of life and playfulness are fundamental; for one dominated by the scientific drive, it is the drive to make comprehensible and practical or exploitable that is basic; for the religious person, it is the drive to constraint and subjection that is key; and for the moral person, it is the drives to social classification and coordination that are fundamental. In each case, "the ruling drives want to be viewed as the highest courts of value in general, indeed as creative and ruling powers" (*WP* 677).

Although Nietzsche thinks that there must be a ruling drive in the service of which the other drives organize, he also recognizes that it is a rare achievement for the relations between the drives to result in something interesting. At one point, for example, he notes that the drives are subject to certain deformations:

1. the dominating passion, which even brings with it the supremest form of health; here the co-ordination of the inner systems and their operation in the service of one end is best achieved – but this is almost the definition of health!
2. the antagonism of the passions; two, three, a multiplicity of "souls in one breast": very unhealthy, inner ruin, disintegration, betraying and increasing and inner conflict and anarchism – unless one passion at last becomes master. Return to health –
3. juxtaposition without antagonism or collaboration: often periodic, and then, as soon as an order has been established, also healthy. The most interesting men, the chameleons, belong here; they are not in contradiction with themselves, they are happy and secure, but they do not develop – their differing states lie juxtaposed, even if they are separated sevenfold. They change, they do not *become*. (WP 778)

Those in whom the drives are not coordinated under a single dominating drive, or a small cluster of dominating drives, are bound to result in a failed self: "where [drives] *all* seek gratification, a man of profound mediocrity must result" (WP 677). It is therefore crucial that the drives be disciplined. A famous passage in *Beyond Good and Evil* claims that, "what is essential 'in heaven and earth' seems to be ... that there should be *obedience* over a long period of time and in a *single* direction" (BGE 188). As should be expected, viewpoints that deny the importance of disciplining the drives come in for some of Nietzsche's nastiest attacks. Recall his criticism of Christianity's assumption that the drives are so uncontrollable that the only effective means of disciplining them is to get rid of them altogether. Nietzsche's retort is biting: "to *exterminate* the passions and desires merely in order to do away with their folly and its unpleasant consequences – this itself seems to us today merely an acute form of folly" (TI V 1).

Nietzsche thinks to the contrary that the drives *can* be disciplined for the greater realization of power. Such self-direction requires enough reflective self-awareness to think of oneself as capable of change. With reflective consciousness comes the abilities to reflect on our self and to turn the drives hitherto directed outwards on to our self in schemes of internal ravishing and cruelty. Of course, reflective consciousness is subject to all the deformation and promise of other internalized drives, but it would be a mistake to think that, given its mixed legacy, Nietzsche would like to return to a world of non-conscious barbarians. Our reflectiveness cannot be undone by wilful reversions of evolution. It is here to stay and its mixed legacy is to be accepted. That legacy is one of sickness *and* new forms of health. No one can doubt that reflective consciousness provides the conditions in which self-doubt, guilt and the other accompaniments of the bad conscience flourish. Yet those same reflective capacities also provide the needed capacities for other, healthier, kinds of projects of power.

There is a problem lurking here in Nietzsche's claims about self-discipline that must be addressed. Suppose that reflective consciousness does in fact result from the internalization of some set of drives. Suppose also that guilt, remorse, memory, responsibility and a sense of sin develop with reflective consciousness. Suppose, finally, that self-discipline requires memory and a sense of responsibility. That appears to require in turn that reflective consciousness is an active player in self-discipline. However, attributing to reflective consciousness the power of disciplining other drives appears on all accounts to grant causal powers to them, and this appears to contradict Nietzsche's commitment to the epiphenomenality of reflective consciousness, discussed at length earlier. This problem can be solved, but to do so requires further comment on what Nietzsche takes discipline to be and what role, if any, he grants to willing and conscious reflection in discipline.

Nietzsche rightly thinks that we *are* capable of disciplining our drives. In *Daybreak*, he identifies six different strategies for disciplining drives:

- avoid opportunities for gratification of the drive;
- impose upon oneself strict regularity in a drive's gratification;
- give oneself over to the unrestrained gratification of a drive;
- associate a drive's gratification with a painful thought;
- impose on oneself some particularly difficult and strenuous labor;
- weaken and depress one's bodily organization. (D 109)

By adopting the first strategy, we eventually end up in a state in which the drive is forgotten and no longer operative. By adopting the second strategy, we eventually end up in a state in which the drive is periodically ineffective and is so for increasing lengths of time. The third strategy will, rather like the Buddhist sect that recommends engaging in sexual activity until we despise it, ultimately result in disgust with the object of the drive. The fourth strategy results in the conflation of gratification of the drive and the painful thought. The fifth strategy compels us to redirect our psychological energy away from the drive so that it becomes increasingly less compelling. Finally, the sixth strategy results in a generally depressed state in which none of the drives, including the particular drive over which we seek control, are active.

For Nietzsche, it is not the rational ego or conscious self that directs all this disciplining. Rather, "what is clearly the case is that in this entire procedure our intellect is only the blind instrument of *another drive* which is a *rival* of the drive whose vehemence is tormenting us: whether it be the drive to restfulness, or the fear of disgrace and other evil consequences, or love" (*D* 109). Indeed, although we think that there is a self that is distinct from the drives and does the complaining about them, "at bottom it is one *drive which is complaining about another*" because "for us to become aware that we are suffering from the *vehemence* of a drive presupposes the existence of another equally vehement or even more vehement drive" (*D* 109).

This passage and others like it provoke serious questions. Nietzsche's insistence to the contrary, the activity of coordinating impulses and disciplining drives appears to *entail* a subject distinct from them who effects, via reflective consciousness, that coordination and discipline by acts of will. Nietzsche repeatedly asserts that this is not the case; there is no doer behind the deed. But has he an alternative explanation of coordination and discipline? If he does, is that alternative consistent with his rejection of the self and his commitment to the epiphenomenality of reflective consciousness? To answer these questions, attention must turn to his discussions of the will.

Nietzsche categorically rejects the will as a simple thing or faculty, but he couples that rejection with qualified endorsements of willed actions. So despite writing that "there is no will" (*WP* 46) and despite calling the will a "phantom" (*TI* VI 3), he also claims that "in willing it is absolutely a question of commanding and obeying, on the basis . . . of a social structure composed of many 'souls'" (*BGE* 19), a claim that, were there no willing of any kind, would make no sense. One way to untangle Nietzsche's approval of willing from his criticism of it is to note that he thinks that willing is "above all something *complicated*, something that is a unity only as a word" (*BGE* 19). As he goes on to argue, the word "will" refers not singly to an identifiable capacity or faculty but plurally to a melange of sensations (of moving towards and away from something and of muscular tension), thoughts (of what is to be accomplished and how it is to be accomplished), and affects (of command and obedience). Willing is thus a complex of distinct kinds of psychological states, no one of which is identifiable as *the* will. We have run these distinct kinds together into one kind, thereby ignoring, as we do in the case of thoughts, the myriad of intervening states.

There are two other problems with free will that Nietzsche has in mind when he objects to it. The first is that the philosophical tradition has typically assumed that the free will is exempt from other efficient causal chains. Free will has been the mechanism by which humans *introduce* causal chains into the world, but it has also been a closed door to past causal chains. It is, after all, free, not conditioned by the past, and it is that freedom in virtue of which we are responsible agents. Nietzsche denies this property of the will outright. The second problem with free will is that it presupposes reflective consciousness. The structure of the free will is similar to that of any drive. There is a subject, an intentional object, and an attitude towards that intentional object. But in willing, the intentional object is always conscious. And that, of course, is inconsistent with Nietzsche's counter claim that we are not reflectively conscious most of the time. So he rejects the will for this reason as well.

The myth of free will is, Nietzsche thinks, motivated by decadence and *ressentiment*. The doctrine is promulgated so as to separate us from the actions we engage in, which in turn makes us susceptible to guilt and answerable to the priest and moral philosopher (*TI* VI 7). The priest thinks that we can be held accountable to the higher law of Christianity only if we have free will and we have free will only if there is a faculty of willing separate from the actions we engage in. Hence, the priest concludes, there is a faculty of willing. Nietzsche claims to the contrary that free will is nothing more than a prerequisite for decadent priestly machinations. He agrees that a free will entails a faculty of the will. Hence, he concludes, there is no such faculty.

Willing is nevertheless a state that is, as are all psychological states, a drive. As argued earlier, every psychological state is causally potent in virtue of being a drive that is accurately characterized as a will. Recall:

> The question is in the end whether we really recognize the will as efficient, whether we believe in the causality of the will: if we do – and at bottom our faith in this is nothing less than our faith in causality itself – then we have to make the experiment of positing the causality of the will hypothetically as the only one. (*BGE* 36)

As such, willing is both a constitutional part of the furniture of the world and nothing at all; every puff of existence is a striving for power, but that striving is not separable as a thing, much less as a faculty distinct from drives. Each drive *is* a willing, but there is no such *thing* as willing, so no *faculty* of willing. This view of willing is, surprisingly, consistent with

Nietzsche's epiphenomenalism of reflective consciousness. Every reflective conscious state is causally potent not in virtue of being reflective but in virtue of being a drive, and every reflective conscious state has only non-conscious consequences. Hence, in those cases where willing is reflective, it is a causal power in virtue of being a drive and whatever consequences it has will be non-conscious consequences.

Moreover, it is consistent for Nietzsche to advocate this view of willing and to attribute to it some unique causal potency. And he does just this: he claims that reflective purposes are *directing* rather than *driving* causes. A passage from *The Gay Science* makes the distinction: "people are accustomed to consider the goal (purposes, vocations, etc.) as the *driving force*, in keeping with a very ancient error; but it is merely the *directing* force – one has mistaken the helmsman for the steam" (*GS* 360). Reflective conscious states are, thus, causally efficacious, but as causes that constrain and shape drives that would attempt to realize their aims of augmenting power even were that constraining and shaping not to occur. This is as should be expected, for although every reflective conscious state has only non-conscious consequences, there are some reflective conscious states that have no consequences at all.

Thus is the general problem posed earlier about the causal power of reflective conscious psychological states also solved. Reflective conscious willing states are not the only kinds of reflective conscious states; others include reflective thoughts, beliefs, desires, hopes and all the rest of the contents of our psyche. If what is suggested here about willing is correct, it is also possible for Nietzsche to affirm that such states are epiphenomenal. Reflective conscious states that reflect on the conscious and unconscious drives and affects provide the direction for cultivating them along certain routes. Hence, they can have *some* causal consequences, for they cause certain other drives to implement the direction they provide. But only the drives themselves implement those directions and it is not in virtue of any of those drives' reflective conscious properties that such implementation occurs.

We may well ask of Nietzsche's version of epiphenomenalism whether the metaphor of helmsman and steam – hence the distinction between directing and implementing causes – avoids the problems it is designed to solve. One of the problems facing Nietzsche's views is that reflective conscious directing causes must, if they are epiphenomenal, cause some change in another psychological state that initiates a chain of implementing causes that realizes the directing cause's instructions. Grant that, subsequent to the causal nexus between directing and initial implementing cause, every causal nexus is between drives that are not reflective conscious. Consider the causal nexus between directing and initial implementing cause itself:

what kind of causal nexus is *it*? By hypothesis, it is not a causal nexus between two implementing causes. For, if it were, then there would be no distinction between directing and implementing causes. But can it be anything *other* than a causal nexus between two implementing causes? For were it not, then Nietzsche seems to commit himself to a unique form of causation that occurs only between some members of the subset of psychological causes that are reflective conscious and those that are not. Advocating such a view – even if it is grounded in the obvious Nietzschean need to explain how reflective thought can change our character – sits poorly with his attempt at analysing all causal power in terms of drives and will to power.

This is not the only difficulty facing Nietzsche's views on mental causation. That there is no unitary willing faculty is also a bit of a problem, for he continues to talk about strong and weak and free and unfree wills. Consider the free–unfree will contrast. When he disparages this contrast in *Beyond Good and Evil*, his reason is that there is no such thing as the will, and consequently neither a free nor an unfree one. The former is a "boorish simplicity," the latter a piece of "mythology" (*BGE* 21). Still, something can be saved from the idea of a free will, namely the "affect of superiority in relation to him who must obey" (*BGE* 19). Despite *Beyond Good and Evil*'s claim that it is always "only a matter of strong and weak wills" (*BGE* 21) it is more accurate to say that a weak will no more exists as an identifiable faculty than does a strong will. The term "weak will" refers to "the multitude and disgregation of impulses and the lack of any systematic order among them" (*WP* 46). Likewise, the term "strong will" refers not to a faculty or capacity that is strong but to a set of impulses being coordinated "under a single predominant impulse" (*WP* 46). It is, then, nothing other than the coordination of affects, thoughts and drives that constitutes what is misleadingly called "strong-willed" and the lack of such coordination that constitutes what is called "weak-willed".

The view of willing outlined here is a restatement of the view at work in Nietzsche's discussion of disciplining the passions outlined in *Daybreak* (*D* 109). Hence, the need to answer the question posed in that discussion about the logical entailment of a subject is now acute. The answer is that disciplining the drives does *not*, according to Nietzsche, entail a subject distinct from the drives because the task the subject is supposed to perform is shouldered by each and every drive or set of drives that go into composing the self. *Every* individual drive and every set of drives is an instance of forces that attempt to domineer all the others, so there is no need for a subject distinct from them that engages in the domineering.

This view needs to be explained in greater detail because its initial attractiveness may only be superficial. Nietzsche appears to think that every person is nothing but a collection of drives, that every drive attempts to dominate all others, that there are different levels of drives and that drives cooperate with one another to achieve certain ends or goals. Take the first claim, that we are nothing but drives. Is that true? Probably not, unless we countenance the idea that bones and fingernails are drives. Nietzsche is willing to countenance that, as we have already seen in Chapter 4 and will see again in Chapter 8. But this ontological claim is, strictly speaking, unnecessary for Nietzsche's psychological project, for all he here requires is that whatever explanatory uses the self substance has can be equally shouldered by a drive self. And those explanatory uses have always centred around the need for a subject of desire, a subject of passions, a subject of thought that can exist even as the desires, passions and thoughts change. Nietzsche invokes the drive self as a replacement for that subject, so all he requires is that the drive self be capable of being a subject of desire, of passions and of thought. It is at least plausible that a drive self can satisfy this goal, for all desires are structured with a subject, an intentional object and the relation of desire between subject and intentional object. For example, if $s$ loves chocolate, the drive is $s$'s loving chocolate, where $s$ is the subject of the drive, love is the kind of drive and chocolate is the intentional object of the drive. All Nietzsche must deny is that the subject of desire exists independently of all of its desires. He must affirm rather that, when the drives are removed, there is no subject. That looks reasonable in at least one way: there is no self after all drives are gone.

Take the second claim, namely, that every drive attempts to dominate all others. Suppose we have a drive-constituted individual, three of whose drives are $a$, $b$ and $c$. Suppose that $a$ is the drive to eat chocolate cake, $b$ the drive to sleep eight hours a night and $c$ the drive to procreate. Then the drive to eat chocolate cake will, according to Nietzsche, try to dominate the drive to sleep for eight hours a night and the drive to procreate, and each of the other drives will do the same. They may work together to achieve mutual goals. For example, $b$ may work with $a$ to achieve $c$. Believing that procreation is best achieved by eating chocolate cake and getting eight hours of sleep, the self composed of those drives may eat chocolate cake until 10 o'clock at night, go to sleep and in the morning have the strength and energy to resume the drive to procreate. Of course, every self is more complex than this. Moreover, even if we consider only the drives that have external states of affairs as their intentional object to eating cake, sleeping and procreating, there will be, in addition to these *first-level* drives, also *second-level* drives; drives that operate on first-level drives or groups of them. So in addition to $a$, $b$ and $c$, we might also have a second-level drive $d$ of being embarrassed by $a$ and of wanting to eliminate it. Then $d$ will try to dominate $a$, $b$ and $c$. Perhaps $d$ and $b$ will cooperate together to thwart $a$ in the service of $c$. Nietzsche's position is that in all this cognitive and affective activity, no subject distinct from the subject of drives is ever entailed. Discipline is accomplished, when it is accomplished, by drives or sets of them and the relations they bear to one another. Hence, a case can at least be made that disciplining the drives does not entail the existence of a subject distinct from them who does the disciplining. Hence, it is not the case that disciplining the drives entails a subject who engages in the activity, and Nietzsche's claims on behalf of a view of the self as constituted entirely of drives is vindicated.

Assume that we can make sense of the drive self. Together with his other commitments about consciousness and the will, Nietzsche's views on the kind of thing we are and our psychological dimensions reveal a self that is thoroughly de-deified and de-reified. The Nietzschean self is a bundle of drives, some of which dominate, some of which are subservient, some of which are strong, some of which are weak, some of which are reflectively conscious, and most of which are reflectively unconscious. All the "higher" purposes that philosophers and theologians have thought we strive for, all the divine and non-natural properties that they have tried to attribute to us, all the certainty they have assured us we are entitled to when it comes to knowledge of ourselves, all of it is, if Nietzsche is right, chimerical. We are natural beings through and through, albeit natural beings capable of the most unnatural flights of aspiration and the most amazingly anti-natural evaluations of our fellows and ourselves.

The depth of our self-deception is frightening and, once revealed, it is likely to lead to nihilism. After centuries of believing that we have souls and that our consciousness and faculty of will are divine gifts, Nietzsche's deflationary analysis of the self may leave us feeling lost: if we have no soul, if our reflective consciousness is epiphenomenal and if we have no will, how, one might ask, are we any better than a dog? Nietzsche worries about this too, seeing both the enormous promise to demystify the human species and the great threat that we shall be tempted to advocate a return to the apes. Dangle as we do between our bizarre, blood-soaked past and a future shorn of stable meaning, the threat of nihilism is real. Nietzsche thinks he has a solution to it, and that solution begins with recognizing that even without God and all the structure he provided to our hopes and desires there is another structure by which we can organize ourselves. That structure is, of course, the will to power.

# CHAPTER 8

# The will to power

The will to power is Nietzsche's most infamous contribution to philosophy. It is also among his most poorly articulated and defended concepts. To begin with, he never decided what will to power was: was it a psychological category of explanation, a reduction base for causal relations or an overarching ontological category? He says things that support all three alternatives. Nor did he ever determine how the will to power could be consistent with his rejection of the will or causality, for that matter. Moreover, he neither needed it nor used it for many of his philosophical undertakings and, where he did use it, he was, until his collapse, still working out its details. In fact, his uncertainties about the will to power were so great that, just before his collapse, he abandoned the project that had the will to power at its core. It was only his sister's sifting through the scraps of paper he left behind that provided the material that would become, under her peculiar editorship, the book published as *The Will to Power*. The will to power was, until the end, an experiment, and Nietzsche was more tentative and mixed up about it than he was about most other things. However, since will to power has incited so much blather from his sister, his commentators, his detractors, his exploiters and his epigones, we cannot simply ignore his reflections on the subject either.

In this chapter, we trace Nietzsche's various thoughts about the will to power in the later writings to get an idea of the scope of his experiments with it. We begin by considering those passages that appear to take will to power as a fundamental ontological category. On this reading, the will to power characterizes every mote of existence. We show how this reading is supported by the texts and trace some of the implications of the view. Next, we assess a reading of will to power that takes it as a replacement for the tradition's concept of cause. On this reading, the will to power is a property of events and collections of them. We show how this reading is supported by the texts and trace some of the implications of the view.

Next, we discuss the passages in which Nietzsche takes the will to power to range over psychological phenomena. Finally, we analyse the relation between the will to power and another controversial claim; namely, the claim that the world eternally recurs. We use the distinction between will to power as an ontological category and will to power as a causal and psychological category to defuse some of the more outrageous claims made on behalf of the eternal recurrence.

## Will to power as an ontology

Despite the paucity of appearances in the works Nietzsche prepared for publication, we should not be tempted to infer that Nietzsche places *no* weight on the will to power. There really can be no argument that in the last six years of his life Nietzsche struggled long and hard to develop the will to power as a fundamental category of ontology, causality, psychology and methodology. Some of the results of that development make it into his books on a number of occasions and in a number of different contexts. Beginning with *Daybreak* and extending right through to *Twilight of the Idols* and *The Anti-Christ,* we find repeated uses of the term "will to power" and "power", and, even where it is not mentioned explicitly, we also find arguments that clearly presuppose it.

The most famous discussion of the will to power is, however, a note from the *Nachlass*. In this note, dated 1885, written as he was preparing part 4 of *Thus Spoke Zarathustra*, Nietzsche lays out the will to power as an ontological category, that is, as a category of existence. The passage is worth quoting in full, since it is one of Nietzsche's most amazing:

> And do you know what "the world" is to me? Shall I show it to you in my mirror? This world: a monster of energy, without beginning, without end; a firm, iron magnitude of force that does not grow bigger or smaller, that does not expend itself but only transforms itself; as a whole of unalterable size, a household without expenses or losses, but likewise without increase or income; enclosed by "nothingness" as by a boundary; not something blurry or wasted, not something endlessly extended, but set in a definite space as a definite force, and not a space that might be "empty" here or there, but rather as force throughout, as a play of forces and waves of forces, at the same time decreasing there; a sea of forces flowing and rushing together, eternally changing, eternally flooding back, with tremendous years of recurrence, with an ebb and a flood of its

158

forms; out of the stillest, most rigid, coldest forms toward the hottest, most turbulent, most self-contradictory, and then again returning home again to the simple out of this abundance, out of the play of contradictions back to the joy of concord, still affirming itself in this uniformity of its courses and its years, blessing itself as that which must return eternally, as a becoming that knows no satiety, no disgust, no wariness: this, my *Dionysian* world of the eternally self-creating, the eternally self-destroying, this mystery world of the twofold voluptuous delight, my "beyond good and evil," without goal, unless the joy of the circle is itself a goal: without will, unless a ring feels good will toward itself – do you want a *name* for this world? A *solution* for all its riddles? A *light* for you, too, you best-concealed, strongest, most intrepid, most midnightly men? – *This world is the will to power – and nothing besides!* And you yourselves are also this will to power – and nothing besides!

(*WP* 1067)

We get it all in this passage: Nietzsche's fantastic use of language, his dynamic style and the clearest statement possible of a proposed reduction of all ontological kinds to one kind, the will to power. I have to admit to a certain fondness for the view, even if it is wacky, for in some ways it is nothing more than a philosophically free expression of the contemporary scientific worldview. Of course, there are two radical features of the proposal: first, Nietzsche claims that even the subatomic and atomic levels of existence are nothing but instances of *will*; secondly, he thinks that even the conscious and intentional levels of existence are nothing but instances of *power*. The first addendum suggests one of the most outrageous forms of panpsychism ever proposed; the second suggests one of the most unforgiving reductions ever proposed.

Nietzsche ruminates over the proposal made here in numerous other notes from the *Nachlass*. He repeatedly works though the hypothesis that the world is ephemeral, energetic, transient and constantly in motion, that it is composed of events, and that events are nothing more than "a determination of degrees and relations of force" (*WP* 552). Take two examples:

The degree of resistance and the degree of superior power – this is the question in every event ... A quantum of power is designated by the effect it produces and that which it resists. The adiaphorous state is missing, though it is thinkable. It is essentially a will to violate and to defend oneself against violation. Not self preservation: every atom affects the whole of being – it is thought away if one thinks away this radiation of power will. That is why I call it a quantum of "will to power": it expresses the characteristic that cannot be thought out of the mechanistic order without thinking away this order itself.                                                                     (*WP* 634)

... no things remain but only dynamic quanta, in a relation of tension to all other dynamic quanta: their essence lies in their relation to all other quanta, in their "effect" upon the same. The will to power not a being, not a becoming, but a *pathos* – the most elemental fact from which a becoming and effecting first emerge.
                                                                     (*WP* 635)

We can glean some crucial components of Nietzsche's ontological version of the will to power hypothesis from these two passages. First, there are nothing but logically atomic events of power, referred to by the terms "quanta of power" and "dynamic quanta"; secondly, these power events are identified and distinguished from each other by the effects they produce and those they resist; thirdly, their essence consists in their being a relation of effecting and resisting other such events; fourthly, they are essentially experience, or, as he puts it, a *pathos* (the Greek term "*pathos*" may be translated as "experience"); and, fifthly, they are related to one another in relations best characterized as relations of tension.

Suppose that we tolerate the proposal long enough to ask some questions about it. Here are two: what does Nietzsche mean by the terms "force" and "power"? And why does he think that there is some connection between power and willing? Take the first. Nietzsche holds that force is an amount, or quantum, of outwardly directed energy, where energy is a primitive. A passage in *The Genealogy of Morals*, for example, claims that "a quantum of force is equivalent to a quantum of drive, will, effect – more, it is nothing other than precisely this very driving, willing, effecting" (*GM* I 13). A note makes the connection between willing and energy explicit:

The victorious concept "force," by means of which our physicists have created God and the world, still needs to be completed: an inner will must be ascribed to it, which I designate as "Will to power," i.e., as an insatiable desire to manifest power; or as the employment and exercise of power, as a creative drive, etc.
                                                                     (*WP* 619)

So quanta of force are reduced to outwardly directed energy effects on other quanta of force and, since a quantum of force is directed outwards, it is apparently accurately described as a quantum of willing. On the basis of these two premises, he concludes that force is nothing but will to power.

These reflections are the beginning of an argument, but they are not the whole argument. We should immediately be suspicious of what appears on all counts to be a view of power that makes it a mysterious metaphysical category beyond experience. If so, then the will to power would seem to be subject to the same objections against mysterious metaphysical categories as Nietzsche deploys against substance, the ego, and identity. Luckily, this concern can be defused. The only view Nietzsche needs to commit himself to is the colourless view that once the effects of force are experienced we have experienced all there is to force. This is a metaphysically neutral view, for it is consistent with there being many ways that the effects of force are experienced.* Nietzsche puts this point this way in the *Nachlass*: "the 'world' is only a word for the totality of these actions. Reality consists precisely in this particular action and reaction of every individual part toward the whole" (*WP* 567). The more troubling problem, however, is this: why does Nietzsche think that because energy is directed outwards it is an instance of *willing*? We can grant that outwardly directed energy is a kind of force, but what justifies the proposed identification of efficient causality with willing? We shall return to this question in the next section.

Having speculated about the nature of relations between atomic quanta of power, Nietzsche builds the world up out of them. He thinks, for example, that quanta of power cooperate to form structured bundles or alliances of power, each such alliance concerned with extending its power. Thus, he notes that every specific body "continually encounters similar efforts on the part of other bodies and ends by coming to an arrangement ('union') with those of them that are sufficiently related to it: thus they conspire together for power" (*WP* 637). Of course, more complex bundles of power are only contingently cooperative and have only as much unity as would any organization or cooperative, which is to say not very much, given that their membership regularly changes when quanta terminate the cooperation of the arrangement. So, except in a "loose and popular" sense, units do not reach a stable identity over time.

---

* Nietzsche's demystification of force is congruent with the views of the American pragmatist Charles Saunders Peirce, who likewise claimed that:

> the idea what the word "force" excites in our minds has no other function than to affect our actions, and these actions can have no reference to force otherwise than through its effect. If we know what the effects of force are, we are acquainted with every fact which is implied in saying that a force exists, and there is nothing more to know. (C. S. Peirce, "How to Make Our Ideas Clear", in *Charles S. Peirce: Selected Writings* (Values in a Universe of Chance), P. Weiner (ed.) (New York: Dover Press, 1958), 129.)

Most of the bundles of power are simple and inorganic, but some form more complex and organic living entities. Of those, some form even more complex entities, such as living molecules and all the other organizations that make up organs (kidneys), systems (muscles), the brain and its neurons, even bodies. For instance, Nietzsche claims that all life, even a form as simple as protoplasm (*WP* 551), is "a will to the accumulation of force; life strives after a *maximal feeling of power*"(*WP* 689). The following note explains the emergence and functioning of bodily organs:

> Greater complexity, sharp differentiation, the contiguity of developed organs and functions with the disappearance of the intermediate members – if that is perfection, there is a will to power in the organic process by virtue of which dominant, shaping, commanding forces continually extend the bounds of their power and continually simplify within these bounds.
>
> (*WP* 644)

As at inorganic levels, diachronic identity of these organic units obtains only loosely. For instance, he notes that "living unities continually arise and die ... the 'subject' is not eternal" (*WP* 492). This should be expected, for the bundles that are an organic entity, not just the quanta that constitute them, can themselves change.

This construction continues right up to the human being, an entity that is, Nietzsche is willing to admit, the most complex bundle of forces. After all, humans can expand their power against other inorganic, organic, and human entities and also, via various schemes of *self* overcoming, against themselves as well. Nietzsche suggests that the self that is engaged in such activities is compositionally a society of relations between forces united by a mode of nutrition. This view is stated in some passages from the published writings (for example, *BGE* 12), and is made explicit in the *Nachlass*. He suggests in one note that:

> the assumption of one single subject is perhaps unnecessary; perhaps it is just as permissible to assume a multiplicity of subjects, whose interaction and struggle is the basis of our thought and our consciousness in general? A kind of aristocracy of "cells" in which dominion resides? To be sure, an aristocracy of equals, used to ruling jointly and understanding how to command?     (*WP* 490)

Nietzsche's view here that the self is composed of bundles of power directly entails rejecting subject atoms. More, the bundle view of the self also implies rejecting the distinction between doer and deed. So long as the entities that compose the self are quanta of outwardly directed energy, his claim that "there is no ... substratum; there is no 'being' behind doing, effecting, becoming; 'the doer' is merely a fiction added to the deed – the deed is everything" (GM I 13) follows directly from the complex composition of the self.

We have already seen, in Chapter 4, that Nietzsche rejects self-substances and egos as the agents of action and as responsible moral agents. However, rejecting the self-substance is not the same as denying the self altogether, and Nietzsche suggests that even the word "soul" might be salvaged for reuse:

> Between ourselves, it is not at all necessary to get rid of "the soul" ... the way is open for new versions and refinements of the soul-hypothesis; and such conceptions as "mortal soul," and "soul as subjective multiplicity," and "soul as social structure of the drives and affects," want henceforth to have citizen's rights in science.
>
> (BGE 12)

In Chapter 7 we saw some of the implications of this view. Recall our defence of Nietzsche's claim that there need be no entailment from the organization of drives to a soul or subject of thought. We can now see that Nietzsche's decomposition of the self into an aristocracy of drives is driven not just by his hostility towards decadent metaphysicians who want there to be something mysterious that only they can have control over, and not just by his conception of the self as a bundle of drives, but also by his own monism of power.

Nietzsche's ontological version of the will to power has certain precursors in the history of philosophy. Its closest cousin is what is known as bundle theory. Typical statements of bundle theory identify objects with sets of properties such as redness, hardness, mass and so forth. Since properties are usually treated as abstract entities, the everyday world of concrete phenomena ends up being constructed out of abstract entities, and trying thus to construct the concrete out of the abstract has its fair share of odd consequences. One of the things that distinguishes Nietzsche's version of the bundle theory from standard versions is that it does not rely on properties. So, to the extent that the problems associated with bundle theory are a consequence of properties being abstract entities, Nietzsche's version avoids those consequences. This is not to say that his version is free of problems. Quite the contrary: his version poses almost intractable problems. Let us see why.

The first problem for bundle theories is that, if things were sets of properties, then, since properties exist necessarily and sets exist necessarily if all their members do, things would be *necessary* things. But contingent things are not necessary things, and there are many contingent things. Nietzsche can escape this criticism easily. Admittedly, he is unclear about the entities that compose his bundles. There are, for example, isolated passages in which he seems to be offering a traditional bundle view in which things are built out of properties. If so, then Nietzsche is subject to the first objection. However, Nietzsche's preferred conception of things is not as sets of properties but as bundles of power quanta. Power quanta are, as we have seen, primitive units of force that form their own non-abstract ontological category. Power quanta are not abstract entities because, unlike abstracta, they are neither multiply instantiable by particulars nor repeatable; that is, power quanta are instantiated only once. If so, then, since power quanta are concrete entities rather than abstract entities, they do not necessarily exist. Hence, the entities they compose are not necessary entities either. Hence, the first criticism misses its mark.

The second consequence is much more challenging. Assume that bundle things are composed of quanta of power. If so, then any bundle at all, no matter how arbitrary, appears to fulfil the conditions for being a thing. But there are many sets of properties that are not things. For example, the aggregate composed of my computer mouse and a blade of grass in Siberia would, if the bundle theory were true, be every bit as much of a thing as a tree. This form of the bundle theory asserts that any conjunction of two or more entities of a given ontological category constitute a whole of which they are its parts. As hard as it may be to believe, Nietzsche actually considers this view in the *Nachlass*:

> ... the world, apart from our condition of living in it, the world that we have not reduced to our being, our logic and psychological prejudices, does not exist as a world "in itself"; it is essentially a world of relationships; under certain conditions it has a differing aspect from every point; its being is essentially different from every point, every point resists it – and the sum of these is in every case quite incongruent.                    (*WP* 568)

Nietzsche claims here that once we subtract the interpretations imposed on a segment of reality by external interpreters (human or otherwise) what remains is naught but a world of relationships. Every quantum is related to all other quanta, and this implies that every combination of quanta, no matter how bizarre, is a bundle thing.

Happily, this is not Nietzsche's preferred alternative. A second view that he considers affirms that bundles of quanta of power are the bundles they are because they are so interpreted in the perspective of an external interpreter. Again, in the *Nachlass*, Nietzsche tries this view out. For instance, he asserts: "That things possess a constitution in themselves quite apart from interpretation and subjectivity, is a quite idle hypothesis" (*WP* 560). Of course, individuating power bundles from outside does not obviously solve the problems that plague bundle theories. After all, why are those interpreters capable of being bundlers? What power do these interpreters have? How is it used? And, most troubling of all, why is it not the case that interpreters are themselves individuated as objects only by *other* interpreters? What makes them unique in being capable of bundling others but not being bundled by others? This looks very much like the "oldest and most long-lived psychology" (*TI* VI 3), which takes the subject as the only actor in the world. Nietzsche, of course, rejects such claims, so we must conclude that this is not Nietzsche's considered view either.

Luckily, he has yet another option. At various points in the *Nachlass* Nietzsche suggests a view along the following lines. Each unit of will to power "strives to become master of over all space and to extend its force", and each encounters "similar efforts on the part of other bodies". This war of all against all ends in a truce, in which the units of power come "to an arrangement ('union') with those of them that are sufficiently related". Having thus formed a new and more complex bundle, these quanta "then conspire together for power" (*WP* 636). On this view, it is the interaction and collaboration of quanta of power that form complex bundles of power. Not all combinations of quanta reach an appropriate arrangement with each other, so the arbitrariness problems of the first alternative for bundle individuation are avoided, and at no point is an external bundler necessary, so the problems with the second alternative for bundle individuation are also avoided.

That an external bundler is not *necessary* for bundle individuation does not entail that external bundlers are not *possible*. Our human perspectives present an obvious case in which entire worlds are created by external bundlers. It is, as we have already seen in Chapters 4 and 6, consistent for Nietzsche to affirm both that there is a world independent of our perspectives and that we construct worlds by our perspectives. The world is perspectival all the way down and all the way up, so it is certainly possible for one set of perspectives to be laid on top of another, the latter of which is laid on top of yet another set. All that Nietzsche requires is the claim that some bundles of power compose themselves independently of human perspectives, and he is able to affirm this because he thinks that *every* quantum of power maps to a perspective:

> Even in the domain of the inorganic an atom of force is concerned only with its neighborhood: distant forces balance one another.

> Here is the kernel of the perspective view and why a living creature is "egoistic" through and through.     (WP 637)

And: "Every center of force adopts a perspective toward the entire remainder, i.e., its own particular valuation, mode of action, and mode of resistance" (WP 567). Admittedly, this is a radical position, for it amounts to nothing less than a monism of power-perspectives. If we are to take Nietzsche seriously here, *every* thing, down to the level of subatomic particles and up to us, is either a quantum of power-perspective or a bundle of such quanta organized for maximal power.

It is a compliment to Nietzsche that he traces the various implications of these remarkable views in his notes. His reflections on the third problem with bundle theories provide another example of his willingness to follow his views out to some of their stranger logical conclusions. The problem is this: if things were sets of properties, then they could not change any of their properties and remain the same things. But if things could not change their properties, they could not change. Hence, if things were sets of properties, there would be no change. But there is change. So things must not be bundles of properties. Nietzsche recognizes this consequence and accepts it. It is true that a bundle-thing cannot shed or add even a single quantum of power without ceasing to exist as *that* thing, and, as we have already seen in Chapter 4, Nietzsche agrees with this conclusion. Things do not change, or, to put the point another way, there is no thing to which change occurs. As Nietzsche himself notes, "'Changes' are only appearances" (WP 545). Let us see why this must be true.

On the view that every collection of power quanta composes some object, change becomes purely a matter of perspective because every combination of power quanta is always realized already at any given time. So there is never any *new* combination that could be the result of change. Only the perspectives on bundles offered by interpreters change. On the view that power bundles are the things they are because some other thing interprets it, change is, again, a function of interpreters. As perspectives change, revisions to what were once things may well result in those things no longer being things or may well result in things becoming different things. However, there is nothing intrinsic to a thing in virtue of which it remains the same thing from one time to another while undergoing change. Finally, the view that bundles of power quanta are unified into a thing by an intrinsic principle has a similar conclusion. Again, take a simple bundle composed not of properties such as $P$, $Q$ and $R$, but of power quanta $\alpha$, $\beta$ and $\gamma$. That bundle – $<\alpha, \beta, \gamma>$ – cannot change any of its members and remain the same bundle. For were we to subtract a quantum – say $\gamma$ – the resulting bundle will be a distinct bundle, since $<\alpha, \beta, \gamma> \neq <\alpha, \beta>$. Likewise, if we were to add a quantum $\delta$,

$<\alpha, \beta, \gamma> \neq <\alpha, \beta, \gamma, \delta>$. So, again, there is no change to any thing over time.

The fourth criticism of traditional bundle theories is that properties are essential to the bundles of which they are parts. But, the criticism goes, not all properties are essential to the things that have them, so bundle theory is wrong. Applied to Nietzsche's power ontology, this criticism amounts to the following: each quantum of power is an essential member of any bundle of which it is a part, but that cannot be true, so his bundle theory must be wrong. Nietzsche meets this criticism head on, agreeing that every part or element of a bundle is essential to it. That is, after all, one way to ground his startling adherence to *amor fati*: "My formula for greatness in a human being is *amor fati*: that one wants nothing to be different, not forward, not backward, not in all eternity" (*Ecce Homo* "Why I am So Clever" 10). This desire is the source of greatness for the very simple reason that to want any change in one's character is to want not to be who one is at all. Only those who are decadent contemplate changing themselves. And it is clear why only the decadent do this: they are anti-life.

Well, we may say, wait a minute. What does that psychological attitude have to do with the claim against bundle theories that, if they are true, every power quantum is essential to the whole of which it is a part? The two seem, if not worlds apart, then at least continents apart. However, the two issues are tightly linked in the following manner: if every element of a bundle is essential to it, then no bundle can remain the bundle it is across change in composition. When we apply that to the case of a person who wants to be different than who he has become or who wishes that he had not done something he has done, the relationship to *amor fati* becomes clear. To want to be *different from who we are* is, given the claim that every quantum of power is essential to the whole we are, to want *not to be who we are*, and that is equivalent to wanting *not to be at all*. Simply put, the desire to be other than who we are is a desire to not be at all, since *any* change to who we are entails the end of the person who forms the desire to want to be different. So Nietzsche's bundle theory strongly supports *amor fati*. Whether that bundle theory is necessary for *amor fati* is a question we shall return to in the last section of this chapter, where we discuss the eternal recurrence.

There are other, more general, problems with the ontological reading of will to power. Since language refers only to that which is created within a perspective, that which is referred to is never extra-perspectival. But now apply this thought to the language of Nietzsche's power ontology. The terms of a will to power ontology, such as "force" and "quantum of power" (to name two), also do not refer to anything outside a perspective. Yet, since ontology hazards a general theory of the constituents of reality, and since no term of such an ontology could ever refer to an extra-perspectival constituent of reality, it looks as though there can be no will to power ontology. This certainly appears to be a problem, but, surprisingly, it is not. Suppose we grant that, with Nietzsche's will to power ontology, the world is perspectival all the way down. If so, then from the most fundamental levels of ontology up, there are no things except those composed entirely of quanta of power, each of which and each bundle of which has perspectives. Hence, a will to power ontology implies the very claim invoked to reject it: that there is no reference to anything outside a perspective. Every term of a will to power ontology will refer to an entity that is fundamentally also a perspective, so, of course, there can be no reference from any word in any language, including those words in Nietzsche's will to power ontology, to anything but a perspectival entity.

The objector has a response to this argument. The response is that linguistic terms refer only to entities within a *human* perspective. That everything is perspectival in some *other* sense is irrelevant. Our rejoinder is that the restriction to human perspectives also follows from a will to power ontology. What else *could* it be? It is human beings who formulate ontologies and we do so in language. This fact does not show that we cannot devise ontologies, since we do. Nor does it show that it is impossible for our ontology to be wrong, since the only case where it would be impossible for our ontology to be wrong is the case in which, *pace* Nietzsche, the world collapses into the human perspective. Finally, nor does it show that it is impossible for our ontology to be right, since the only case where it would be impossible for our ontology to be right is the case in which, *pace* Nietzsche, there were a world of things-in-themselves that served as an unknown, unknowable and unusable criterion of ontological error.

A final problem for a will to power ontology is that, as we have seen, Nietzsche claims that identity is foisted upon the world by conceptual thought, so we cannot attribute any ontology to him since *any* ontology requires identity. However, we have already argued that diachronic bundle identity is clearly perspectival, so Nietzsche's will to power ontology is consistent with the rejection of diachronic identity. What then of synchronic identity? Does a will to power ontology require its rejection? The answer is simple: no. A will to power ontology must reject the claim that (i) there are, at a time, any two power constituted bundles that are strictly identical at that time, but not the claim that (ii) there are, at a time, power constituted bundles that are self-identical at that time. The first is what is known as the "identity of cases", and Nietzsche does reject it. However, rejecting the identity of cases only entails that two things are never one thing, and that is hardly a surprise. The second claim is another matter. We have already encountered the passage in the *Nachlass* in which

Nietzsche rejects the law of identity:

> Supposing there were no self-identical "A", such as is presupposed by every proposition of logic (and of mathematics), and the "A" were already mere appearance, then logic would have a merely apparent world as its condition ... the "A" of logic is, like the atom, a reconstruction of the thing. (WP 516)

It is undeniable that what Nietzsche is rejecting here is the law of identity, which is an axiom of most logics. We suggested earlier that, once interpreted in light of his rejection of substances, the claim amounts to rejecting self-identical substances outside the domain of phenomena. Nietzsche has no reason to proscribe the diachronic identity of objects either bundled together as perspectives or bundled together via perspectives. Such identity is, of course, perspectival, but that is not a problem either.

## Will to power as causality

Nietzsche's ontological reflections on the will to power are found primarily in the *Nachlass*. When it comes to the published works, what we typically (not always) find are claims about the causal efficacy of the will to power and its explanatory efficacy in psychological and biological domains. One way into this alternative perspective on will to power, causality and explanation is to consider *Beyond Good and Evil*, section 36, a passage in which Nietzsche moves from the moral and psychological levels through the biological level and all the way down to the mechanical level of explanation.

Suppose, Nietzsche suggests, that we assume only our passions, desires and affects as categories of causes. Given those categories, do we have everything required for biological and mechanistic (or material) causality? His answer is "Yes". Everything from our noblest passions to the exchange of mitochondria across cell walls is a symptom or ramified development of "a kind of instinctive life in which all organic functions are still synthetically intertwined along with self regulation, assimilation, nourishment, excretion, and metabolism" (*BGE* 36). He uses this generalization about causality at the biological level as support for a consolidation of *every* form of causality presumed by the metaphysician:

> The question is in the end whether we really recognize the will as efficient, whether we believe in the causality of the will: if we do – and at bottom our faith in this is nothing less than our faith in

causality itself – then we have to make the experiment of positing the causality of the will hypothetically as the only one. "Will," of course, can affect only "will" – and not "matter" (not "nerves," for example). In short one has to risk the hypothesis whether will does not affect will wherever "effects" are recognized – and whether all mechanical occurrences are not, insofar as a force is active in them, will force, effects of the will. (*BGE* 36)

He concludes with a statement of the doctrine of the will to power as a causal force that is as clear as one might hope to find:

> Suppose, finally, we succeeded in explaining our entire instinctive life as the development and ramification of one basic form of the will – namely, of the will to power, as my proposition has it; suppose all organic functions could be traced back to this will to power and one could also find in it the solution of the problem of procreation and nourishment – it is one problem – then one would have gained the right to determine all efficient force univocally as – will to power. The world viewed from inside, the world defined and determined according to its "intelligible character" – it would be "will to power" and nothing else. (*BGE* 36)

Here, Nietzsche bluntly affirms that efficient causality is reducible to will to power. He also appears to affirm more than this, of course, by claiming that the world is defined and determined by will to power. But the ontological claim that the world is composed of entities that are bundles of power quanta and the claim that all efficient causality is nothing but will to power are, in fact, distinct. The ontological version entails the causal version, but the causal version can be affirmed without the ontological version. Let us then investigate this latter option.

Nietzsche's bundle theory is, recall, composed of claims about bundle *constitution* and bundle *individuation*. With regards to the first component, it is best to interpret Nietzsche as holding that everyday objects are bundles composed of quanta of power rather than properties. Now, if everything is nothing more than a bundle of power quanta, then, since power quanta are understood by Nietzsche to be quanta of causal effect, it falls out immediately that bundles of power are nothing more than bundles of causal effects. So the ontological version of will to power immediately entails the causal version of will to power.

We have seen that Nietzsche considers three different possibilities for individuating bundle objects: that any and every collection of power quanta constitutes an object; that only those bundles bundled together by some external perspective are properly objects; and that power quanta compose themselves into objects to acquire greater power. Nietzsche believes that the first two alternatives will have pretty strange consequences and any causal version of the will to power presupposing these alternatives will inherit those strange consequences. On the first alternative, there are distinct objects composed of every distinct collection of quanta of power, and any and every bundle, no matter how gerrymandered, is a thing. But then no *new* objects ever come into existence, since every object that *can* exist *does* exist. Hence, no quantum of power or bundle of power can cause any new quantum of power or bundles of power to come into existence or cause any change in already existing bundles. This consequence is pretty bizarre. After all, we might reasonably think there are new objects and new events that are outcomes of causal processes. But on this alternative, there are neither new objects nor new events of any kind, since the world is maximally impacted already. Works of art, bottles, babies and plants all already exist at times when most of us would be inclined to say they do not since the quanta of power that compose them already exist prior to them assuming their particular structure. Whatever change there is consists entirely in new *arrangements* of quanta of power and distinct perspectives taken on quanta of power and bundles of them. This consequence is a decisive objection and a decisive reason to reject this alternative.

The second approach to bundle individuation has equally strange consequences. If causality is a perspective taken by some quantum or society on another quantum or society, then, as Nietzsche suggests, things are the sum of their effects (WP 551). Yet, on the alternative under consideration, things are not the sum of effects *they* have on *other* things; rather, everything is the sum of effects *other* things have on *them*. Suppose, for instance, that my glasses fall on the floor, and a lens breaks. On this alternative, bundles of quanta distinct from those composing the lens of my glasses take perspectives on and so compose the bundle of my lens, and take the perspective that when that bundle hit the floor (also a perspective composed bundle) the former bundle shatters as a result. This is not a particularly promising view either.

That leaves the alternative on which bundles of power compose themselves somehow. This alternative is the only one that supports a plausible extension to the causal version of will to power. Indeed, this alternative immediately entails the causal version without any loss or peculiarity at all (except, of course, for the overall peculiarity of the will to power hypothesis). After all, as just argued, that in which things consist is also that in virtue of which quanta bundle themselves together: augmentation of power. So things that are sums of their effects are things composed of power quanta conspiring together for greater power. Hence, Nietzsche's account of causality is a direct implication of this version of the will to power ontology. This alternative also has clear benefits over the other two alternatives. Quanta organize together with certain, not every, other quanta into bundles, so not every possible bundle that can be formed actually is formed. Hence, new things and new events can come into existence and can be the result of causal processes. Likewise, bundles have a character that is not reducible to the set of perspectives taken on them by other bundles, so no bundle is beholden for its causal effects *only* on what other bundles say about them. This is not to say that the character bundle objects have is non-perspectival or non-relational, for, again, each of the constituent power quanta of the bundle is itself a perspective on the other constituent power quanta, and hence there are myriad perspectival relations between the constituents of the bundle. So this alternative is consistent with passages such as this *Nachlass* note, which claims that once "all the relationships, all the 'properties,' all the 'activities' of a thing" are removed, "the thing does not remain over" (WP 558).

Although the ontological version of the will to power entails the causal version, the converse is not true. We can reject the claim that things are identical to bundles of power quanta and nevertheless affirm that the causal relations things enter into with other things are identical to relations of power. Or, if even that is too strong, we could say that perhaps it is only the causal relations between the *organic* things of the world, or between the *animated* things, or even between the *conscious* things, that are reducible to relations of power. The numerous options available to Nietzsche defuse some of the criticism directed his way that the will to power is a quasi-mystical and nutty panpsychist alternative to the scientific worldview. However, that there are options available does not, without additional argument, determine the appropriate extension of the causal will to power hypothesis. Determining just how far into the non-human world the causal will to power hypothesis extends requires determining just what Nietzsche thinks the fundamental explanatory categories of desires, passions and affects are. Knowing that will, in turn, help determine whether the evidence Nietzsche cites for thinking that efficient causality is identical to a kind of willing is compelling.

In Chapter 7 we investigated an issue that will help us answer these questions. We said there that drives are structured psychological entities that have a subject, an intentional object and an affective attitude relating subject to intentional object. For instance, if s loves chocolate, then s is the subject, chocolate the intentional object and loving the affective attitude that s has to chocolate. The way this helps us is as follows: suppose the triadic intentional structure attributed to drives also applies to desire, passion and affect. Then we would have good reason for thinking that all psychological events can be modelled as realizations of will to power. More, if that structure can be generalized to instances of efficient causality other than the psychological, then we would have reason for thinking that all realizations of efficient causality can be modelled as realizations of will to power. This is a fundamental issue, so let us proceed carefully.

To begin, then, the structure attributed to drives can also be attributed to passions, desires and affects, for passions are passions of some subject for some intentional object or objects, desires are desires of some subject for some intentional object or objects (however obscure), and affects in general are non-cognitive attitudes taken by some subject towards some intentional object. (There are complications here with which we need not be concerned. For example, suppose the object of desire is an abstract entity, such as death (not *my* death, just death). Or suppose the object of passion is an object that cannot exist, such as the perfect woman or man. This is the stuff of philosophy of psychology.) So at least the overall triadic intentional structure applies equally to all the psychological event types that Nietzsche investigates. The more serious issue for Nietzsche is this: why think that this kind of *psychological* structure applies to anything *other* than events found in the psychological domain? To think that it does appears to be just another instance of that "oldest and longest-lived psychology" according to which we have "*created* the world on the basis of it as a world of causes, as a world of will" (*TI* VI 3).

Nietzsche's best answer to this challenge is to say that his is not a case of spreading human agency into the world but of structuring human agency as an instance of a structure found everywhere there are causes. The structure of intentional psychological events:

$$<\text{subject} \to \text{affect} \to \text{intentional object}>$$

is, on this interpretation, an instance of a more general structure that is plausibly instantiable by non-conscious, non-animated and perhaps even non-living entities. Nietzsche is proposing that psychological events are structured in a manner isomorphic to that exemplified by all efficient causal relations. Suppose there is a power-constituted but non-intentional event $\alpha$ at a time $t_1$, say, a rock sitting in the sun. Suppose, next, that the sun warms the rock and the rock emits heat energy. That emitted heat energy is an outwardly directed packet of energy, $e$. Suppose that $e$ is emitted by $\alpha$ at $t_2$. Suppose, finally, that there is another event, say $\beta$ at $t_3$, of a moth's legs overheating on the rock. Then we have the following causal structure:

$$<\alpha \text{ at } t_1 \to e \text{ at } t_2 \to \beta \text{ at } t_3>$$

This triadic causal structure is isomorphic to the intentional structure of psychological states. Of course, the causal structure is a temporal structure and the psychological structure is a logical structure, so, for strict isomorphism, we would have to eliminate the temporal indices from the causal structure to yield the logical structure of causal relations:

$$<\text{event } \alpha \rightarrow \text{energy packet } e \rightarrow \text{event } \beta>$$

There, it is done. Nietzsche's proposal is, then, that intentional psychological events are nothing more than special instances of a structure instantiated by all efficient causal events: that of being composed of an object or event, a quantum of outwardly directed force and another object or event. Hence, despite all appearances to the contrary, Nietzsche's proposal is not the anthropomorphic proposal of reading the structure of human intentionality *into* efficient causal events but the naturalistic proposal of precipitating human intentionality *out* of efficient causal events.

Still, why think that the triadic structure of efficient causality has enough resemblance to the triadic structure of intentional psychological events to label the former as instances of willing? For that matter, why think that the triadic structure of intentional psychological events is sufficient to call *them* instances of willing? Take the questions in reverse order. The answer to the second question is that everything that can be safely salvaged with the word "willing" is captured by the triadic structure of intentional psychological events. Nietzsche is arguably right about this. It is certainly true that a large part of what the philosophical tradition has always wanted from willing is an explanation of how we can be efficient causal forces. Our faculty of will has been the tradition's candidate for the causal mechanism by which we effect changes in the world, and the triadic structure of intentional psychological events can capture that (with some tweaking – make the intentional object a future object of desire and derive from it, in Aristotelian fashion, a practical syllogism). Willing thus reduces to a directed transfer of energy towards an intentional object. To that extent, then, Nietzsche is arguably on safe ground in reclaiming the word "will" for a psychological view without faculties of willing. Of course, the philosophical tradition has also wanted much *more* from the will than a mechanism for effecting change, for it has wanted to saddle that faculty with the property of being free. As we have already seen above and will see again in Chapter 9, Nietzsche rejects that part of the tradition's use of "will".

Attributing the property of being an instance of willing to the triadic structure of intentional psychological events is, thus, vouchsafed. Yet, again, why think that all efficient causality is on a par with the causality of the will? Recall Nietzsche's hypothesis in *Beyond Good and Evil*:

> The question is in the end whether we really recognize the will as efficient, whether we believe in the causality of the will: if we do – and at bottom our faith in this is nothing less than our faith in causality itself – then we have to make the experiment of positing the causality of the will hypothetically as the only one. (*BGE* 36)

The issue here is not whether there is something *similar* to willing that is found in efficient causality. Of course there is *something* shared between the two. But similarity is not identity. Nor is the question whether willing is just *one* kind of efficient causality; it is, rather, whether efficient causality is the *same* kind as willing. Consider contemporary debates about the applicability of computer models of the mind. Here, too, there can be no doubt there is *something* shared between cognition and computation, but that is not enough for concluding that the mind *just is* a computer. There may be properties of minds that computers lack; the qualitative character of experience is thought by many to be such a property. Similarly, there may be properties of certain kinds of realizations of the triadic structure of efficient causality in human beings that are not shared by all others, and it may be just those properties that warrant calling those realizations "willings".

We can now answer this challenge. Nietzsche's argument is that all that can be reclaimed from the category of willing is the affective directed transfer of energy from subject to intentional object. That triadic intentional structure is mirrored across the non-conscious world in efficient causal processes, which are also instances of directed transfers of energy from object to object. So to the extent that we are prepared to call any realization of this intentional structure an instance of willing, we may call any realization of any efficient causal structure an instance of willing. Nietzsche is prepared to extend the compliment throughout the biological realm and even into non-living realms. We may balk at such extensions. In the end, the plausibility of Nietzsche's extension depends on our willingness to go along with him that the triadic structure of efficient causal events is sufficient or reveals something that allows us to attribute to them certain properties from otherwise dissimilar realizations of that structure.

To begin with, we should eliminate the triadic structure itself as a candidate for identifying these properties, for this structure, although shared, is neutral across the psychological and the non-psychological. There are *plenty* of things that have a triadic structure that are not plausible instances of willing, but that there are is neither here nor there. Here is one: my left little toe is to the left of my left big toe. I, for one, am unwilling to attribute much efficient causal force to the spatial relation between my left little and my left big toe; much less am I prepared to call that spatial relation structure an instance of willing. So it is not the triadic structure of intentional psychological events and efficient causal events that grounds whatever differences there might be between the two. We are looking, not for any similarity, but for a salient similarity. A salient similarity between the intentional structure of psychological events and the structure of efficient causality is that, in each case, there is something *forceful* about the relation between the relata. Spatial relations are not forceful, whereas causal relations of outwardly directed energy and psychological attitudes to intentional objects are arguably both kinds of forces. So, extending willing to non-intentional causal relations reduces to whether causal relations share the relevant property of directed energy transfer possessed by intentional willing relations.

Here is a defence of Nietzsche. Recall the *Nachlass* note where he broaches the idea of calling efficient causal relations instances of willings:

> The degree of resistance and the degree of superior power – this is the question in every event ... A quantum of power is designated by the effect it produces and that which it resists. The adiaphorous state is missing, though it is thinkable. It is essentially a will to violate and to defend oneself against violation. Not self preservation: every atom affects the whole of being – it is thought away if one thinks away this radiation of power will. That is why I call it a quantum of "will to power".           (WP 634)

Nietzsche appears to think that a quantum of outwardly directed – "radiating" – energy is identifiable by the amount of effect it produces and resists. Calling a quantum of power a quantum of "will to power" means, then, that every quantum is both productive of and resistant to causal effects. If so, extending the term "willing" to non-intentional events is arguably justified, for this characterization strips it of any requirement that it be reflectively conscious or access conscious, that it be a property of a thinking subject, or even that it be the result of any thought at all. Willing amounts to outwardly directed transfers of energy and resistance to other such transfers.

So, being productive and resistant to directed transfers of energy is a kind of willing. But now put the reverse problem on the table: is being productive and resistant to directed transfers of energy all there is to willing, at least as Nietzsche uses that term? Arguably, it is. Recall from Chapter 7 that Nietzsche recommends that the intentional activity the faculty of willing is supposed to be responsible for can be accomplished by each and every drive of which we are composed. Each drive is a striving for mastery over and a resistance to other drives' similar strivings. So, a case can be made that will to power and efficient causality are, as Nietzsche claims, identical causal structures. Of course, Nietzsche need not deny that there are properties had by psychological realizations of the causal structure that are not shared by non-psychological realizations of the structure. For it is consistent to affirm that the entities that are the relata of the relation have unique properties, and that both intentional relations and efficient causal relations are identical in causal potency. Provided those unique properties play no role in grounding the causal relations between the relata, there is nothing in virtue of which they need differ causally.

## Will to power as psychology

The most restricted version of the will to power, but also the version that Nietzsche makes most use of, ranges over only psychological domains. Beginning with *Human, All Too Human* and extending through *Twilight of the Idols*, Nietzsche's use of the will to power as a psychological category of explanation is consistent and his *Nachlass* notes from 1879–88 are full of reflections about the explanatory utility of the will to power at the psychological level. In his books from the 1870s, power contrasts with reason and moral goodness, but this contrast presupposes that power is *worldly* power represented by wealth, political control over others and social prestige. With *Human, All Too Human*, this conception of power begins to retreat into the background and Nietzsche starts to recognize the explanatory strength of a drive describable as a less restrictive kind of power. In *The Gay Science*, he is willing to announce this alternative conception of power outright, and in *Thus Spoke Zarathustra*, *Beyond Good and Evil*, *The Genealogy of Morals*, *Twilight of the Idols* and *The Anti-Christ*, he uses it to explain a wide range of psychological and moral phenomena.

We have already introduced a number of the constituent claims that go into Nietzsche's will to power psychology. We have, for example, analysed his claims that: there is no substantial self, the self instead being composed of a hierarchy of drives, every one of which is reducible neither to being mental nor to being physical; reflective consciousness plays a rather unimportant role in our psyche; drives have a particular kind of structure; willing is not a faculty of a thinking subject but a property of every drive; and disciplining the drives is the hallmark of a healthy psyche. Here, let us add more of the details to the view.

It is tempting to interpret Nietzsche's will to power psychology as the claim that we strive for power all the time. But if we are blanking out in front of the television, the idea that we are then engaged in power-enhancing activity is comical. Worse, how can Nietzsche differentiate between valuable and stupid realizations of power? If our lives really are all power all the time, then your striving for perfecting your piano skills is no more interesting than my striving to count every pine needle on the Ponderosa down by the barn. This is, of course, silly, so it is a good thing that it is not Nietzsche's view.

Recall that the fundamental psychological unit to which Nietzsche attributes will to power is a drive, where a drive is an intentionally structured psychological event with a subject, an intentional object and a relation between subject and intentional object. This monism of psychological event types has certain benefits. Whereas a contemporary philosopher or cognitive scientist might distinguish between cognitive psychological events, affective psychological events, representational psychological events, non-representational psychological events, conscious and unconscious psychological events and phenomenological and non-phenomenological psychological events, Nietzsche lumps them all together in the category of drive. So, for instance, every psychological event has some affective or phenomenological character because it is a drive. That is appealing as a reminder of our psyche's fundamentally energetic nature. There are drawbacks too. It is not particularly clear in Nietzsche's work how representational events or cognitive events can be analysed as nothing more than refined non-representational and non-cognitive events. We shall have to leave that issue unresolved.

The version of will to power that takes us to be aiming at power all the time takes the intentional object of every drive to be the conscious intention of augmenting power. This is not very promising. To begin with, it is false. Not all intentional objects are conscious and power is not the only possible intentional object of a drive. If we are thinking of Vienna, the intentional object of our drive is Vienna rather than power. If we have an instinct for danger, the intentional object of that instinct is not conscious and it is danger, not power. This is an inaccurate reading of human motivational psychology as well, for not every kind of motivation is motivation for power, any more than pleasure is, as psychological hedonists would have it. (In fact, Nietzsche's power alternative is arguably less persuasive than hedonism. Ask a hundred people what they are motivated by and the most prevalent answer will probably be pleasure. Of course, they could be self-deceived. They may really be motivated by power and not pleasure, even if they do not admit it to themselves. If so, the burden is on Nietzsche to show that this is the case.) Happily, this debate is a red herring, since Nietzsche's views do not require that power is always a conscious intentional object or the only intentional object. Recall from Chapter 7 the sampling of Nietzschean psychological drives. They range from the drive for sex to the drive for rapacity, from the drive for humour to the drive for good manners, from the drive for beauty to the drive for revolution. Thinking that power is the intentional object of each of these drives is dotty. Rather, Nietzschean drives have their own intentional objects, some of them conscious, some of them not. So we can at least safeguard the diversity of our psychological economy.

By safeguarding the diversity of our drives, however, Nietzsche's claim that power provides a global psychological principle appears to lose its purchase. For suppose power is but one of many different intentional objects, as Nietzsche himself sometimes says, as in *The Genealogy of Morals* (III 18), where he claims that the will to power is "the strongest, most life-affirming drive". If so, then there are plenty of *other* intentional objects as well, and so plenty of other drive types. Yet, then power seems to recede from being a global psychological principle. This sits ill with virtually everything else Nietzsche ever says about power in psychological contexts. What is required is an interpretation that allows a multiplicity of intentional objects, so a multiplicity of drive types, and yet preserves the global psychological importance of power. We can defend Nietzsche, but doing so requires digging deeper into the way power functions in psychological contexts. In the ontological version, power is an outwardly directed quantum of energy and in the causal version power is a directed quantum of energy transferred from one entity to another. So if the psychological version of power is relevantly similar to these other two versions, and if that similarity is sufficient for weaving will to power into psychological explanations without entailing that it is the only possible intentional object of drives, then we shall have succeeded.

Power in the psychological context can be interpreted along the same lines as the ontological and causal versions. Bracket the more extreme implications of the ontological version of power and consider the causal version of power. The causal version identifies will to power with efficient causal relations in which an object transfers or fails to transfer a quantum of energy to another object and accepts or resists such efforts from other objects. Suppose, now, that we have a drive, say the drive for sex. It, too, can be interpreted as transferring energy from the subject towards the intentional object of having sex. After all, there is a considerable amount of time and effort devoted to realizing the goal. That model can be generalized to a wide array of psychological drives, so for any one of those drives, the will to power is a general principle underlying the clout that explanations invoking it have. There is, of course, no need for such drives all to be reflectively conscious; in fact, it is even possible to say that some of them are not even access conscious, much less reflectively conscious.

Although we have carved out a place for will to power in psychological explanation, it is an almost empty room, for, to this point, power in psychological explanations amounts only to describing the transference of affective energy from a subject to an intentional object. If *that* is all there is to Nietzsche's position, we have laboured mightily to bring forth a mouse. Luckily, there is more to be said. A clue to what else there may be comes from Nietzsche's insistence that, at least at every level of explanation higher than the inorganic, power is internally related to both *form-giving* and *self-overcoming*. Take the former. Nietzsche is convinced that the essence of life is will to power and that, in the organic and animal domains, this is "the spontaneous, aggressive, expansive form-giving forces that give new interpretations and directions" (*GM* II 12). Concerning the latter, Nietzsche urges us to remember that "All great things bring about their own destruction through an act of self-overcoming; thus the law of life will have it, the law of the necessity of 'self-overcoming' in the nature of life" (*GM* III 27). Well, we might say, we are in a fine place now, for we appear to be adding to the vacuous claims about power already made some new and thoroughly obscure ones! What are *form-giving* and *self-overcoming*, and how do they help us understand what Nietzsche has in mind for power in psychological explanations?

Form-giving is a modification of the energy we discharge in realizing the goal of a drive or, alternatively, a manner of the activity constitutive of realizing our intentions. Form-giving is taking the activity imposed by any desire, drive or passion and cultivating that activity in a focused, organized, disciplined and inventive manner so that engaging in that activity gives new shape and structure to the intentional object, to itself as activity and to the subject who has the desire. If, for example, we want to learn to climb, we must first learn the rudiments of climbing safety – rope handling, protection placement, balance, foot and hand placements, varieties of physical leverage – and we must then practise them to become competent. But in cultivating the activity of climbing, our technique becomes nuanced and subtle, matching moves to rock with increasing refinement until our movement on the rock is supple and without overt intention; until the goal of learning to climb is absorbed into and disappears in the activity of climbing; and until the activity of climbing becomes its own end and we are transformed into a climber. This process is part of what Nietzsche has in mind by claiming that a drive is an opportunity for form-giving, for expressing power. Power enters into the explanation of what happens psychologically as a particular kind or mode of the activity of a drive.

Of course, there are many modes of climbing, as there are for any drive. We can climb badly or hesitantly or stupidly; each of them is also a mode of the activity constitutive of climbing. Power is clearly something more than *any* old modification of activity. We have tried to suggest the unique qualities of power in the above description of climbing by focusing on the internally transformative character of the modes in which Nietzsche is interested. We can add to that description by focusing on self-overcoming as another aspect of psychological power. Consider climbing again. Climbers who reach a level of competence regularly report that things change for them. In becoming competent or expert as a climber, the goal of climbing becomes overlaid with other consequences that would never have been experienced without the activity of climbing but which were neither foreseen nor intended. Once experienced, these unforeseen and unintended consequences become their own goals and sometimes replace the goals we had when we started climbing. The initial goal of being a climber overcomes itself and becomes the means to some other goal, if it becomes a means to anything at all. Self-overcoming is like that in general: in realizing a drive or intention, the activity itself, if cultivated in a form-giving manner, can result in our overcoming our goal in pursuing it. This happens not because the goal is discarded or because the goal becomes merely a stepping-stone for some loftier goal, although both can certainly occur. It is more that the original goal is incorporated and synthesized by engaging in the activity required to achieve it in a form-giving manner, thus altering the goal, the activity and the subject so completely that neither we, nor our activity, nor the goal we once had are the same.

This characterization of the manner in which power finds purchase in explanations about climbing can be generalized to other psychological explanations, and so to other drives and passions. Power is a second-order property of having and trying to realize a drive in a particular way, of engaging in the activity constitutive of the drive in a form-giving and self-overcoming manner. If we like, we can recall the language of Chapter 7: power is a directing force but not a driving force, for it is, like a directing force, "the cause of acting in a particular way, in a particular direction, with a particular goal" rather than "a quantum of damned-up energy that is waiting to be used up somehow, for something" (*GS* 360). We have to be careful, however, for a directing force, since it is directed to a goal, is conscious in a way that willing psychological power need not be. We shall return to this in Chapter 9.

In claiming that power functions in psychological explanations in this way, Nietzsche is not claiming that power is nothing but the ultimate goal or highest end of all our other drives, that is, that satisfying various drives is a means to achieving the ultimate goal of power. It can be, but its fundamental explanatory power does not require it to be such. On these grounds, we can distinguish Nietzsche's power psychology from other, superficially similar, views. Take psychological hedonism, the empirical claim that we are motivated by and directed towards pleasure. The relation between instrumental ends and highest ends is found in hedonism, for pleasure is the ultimate explanatory end, the goal that explains why we do the enormous variety of things we do. We eat, drink and are merry because we want to maximize our pleasure; we sleep, work and are responsible because we want to eat, drink and be merry because we want to maximize our pleasure; and we make the bed because we want to sleep better because we want to eat, drink and be merry because we want to maximize our pleasure. Power is typically not an ultimate goal or highest end in this way. Power infuses the way we realize the drives we already have as a modality of that drive. In the maximal cultivation of itself, a drive eventually overcomes itself, sublimates itself and morphs into something else, thus also changing the subject of the drive. We shall return to this theme as well in Chapter 9.

That the will to power is not primarily a first-order intentional object of a drive does not entail that it cannot be such an object, and that the will to power is not an ultimate goal or highest end does not entail that it cannot on occasion be such a goal. Power can certainly be the intentional object of a first-order drive and it can equally well serve as the goal of a second-order drive. If, for instance, the set of drives that dominate my character are hell-bent on disciplining my other drives so that my power over my dog is maximized, there is a clear sense that power over my dog is the intentional object of a second-order drive that has a variety of first-order drives as the instrumental means to that end. However, from the fact that power can *sometimes* serve as an intentional object in a first- or second-order drive, it does not follow that power is *always* such an object or that it is the *only* such object. So, Nietzsche's will to power drive psychology is vindicated on this score as well. We shall also return to this theme in Chapter 9.

Nor should we think that just because power is not the intentional object of every drive, we can never be self-deceived about the intentional objects of our drives. We might be tempted to think that, since only a few first-order drives have power as their intentional object, Nietzsche's insistence that power is globally important must be false. However, this view assumes mistakenly that if power is not a conscious intentional object of a first-order drive, it can play no other role in psychological explanation. We have just seen that this is false. Worse, it deflects attention away from the possibility that we can be self-deceived about the way power permeates our psyches. We can be self-deceived about this, and the ministrations of religion and decadent metaphysicians offer entire regimes of self-deception. It is not just that religion provides an interpretation of physiological exhaustion that glorifies it, or that the peculiar behaviour of the ill-constituted is mistaken for strength, or even that the decadent can provoke themselves to derangement and madness. The chief means religion employs in breeding self-deception is its uncanny ability to tap into rituals and rites that provoke psychological intoxication. Nietzsche recognizes, respects and admires the ecstatic trances that religious activities can induce in their practitioners. But he suggests that the ecstatic states encouraged by religion are easily mistaken for the equally ecstatic states of the realization of power. So, for example, in a *Nachlass* note, he points out that "the experience of intoxication proved misleading. This [intoxication] increases the feeling of power ... therefore, naively judged, power itself" (*WP* 48). The distinction is crucial. The feeling of power is not power itself, and the experience of ecstatic intoxication runs the two together, for the feeling of power found in intoxication can be caused either by our experience of ourselves as powerful or by artificial means (those used by religion, for instance). Taken by itself, the experience of intoxication can easily mislead us into thinking that whatever causes the feeling is unitary, when, in fact, the causes of a single psychological event can be diverse and even contrary to one another. Once again, we shall return to this issue in Chapter 9.

## The eternal recurrence and *amor fati*

Before turning to ethical issues, we have to fulfil an earlier promise to discuss *amor fati* and eternal recurrence. The eternal recurrence and *amor fati* are often run together with will to power, as if the three form a single set of mutually entailing doctrines. We need not and should not concur with this assessment.

We have already encountered *amor fati* in our discussion of the ontological version of will to power, and we shall return to it here and again in Chapter 9. But we have not yet discussed eternal recurrence in any detail. First appearing in *The Gay Science* and popping up infrequently in his other books, the eternal recurrence finds its way into a small number of discussions on a smaller number of topics, which are mostly ethical. In its most outrageous form, the claim is that everything that happens during our lifetime will happen and has already happened an infinite number of times exactly as it does in this lifetime. The only passage that even approaches being a proof for the eternal recurrence appears in a *Nachlass* note:

> If the world may be thought of as a certain definite quantity of force and as a certain definite number of centers of force – and

every other representation remains indefinite and therefore useless – it follows that, in the great dice game of existence, it must pass through a calculable number of combinations. In infinite time, every possible combination would at some time or another be realized; more: it would be realized an infinite number of times. And since between every combination and its next recurrence all other possible combinations would have to take place, and each of these combinations conditions the entire sequence of combinations in the same series, a circular movement of absolutely identical series is thus demonstrated: the world as a circular movement that has already repeated itself infinitely often and plays its game *in infinitum*. (WP 1066)

Here we have a proof for a cosmological thesis, that is, a thesis about the nature of the cosmos as a whole. However, even if we accept the ontological version of will to power, this cosmological version of the eternal recurrence is not, contrary to what Nietzsche claims here, entailed. And it is a good thing, too, for the cosmological version of the eternal recurrence is, to put it bluntly, bunk.

Suppose that the world is compositionally nothing but power quanta and collections of such. Suppose that the number of quanta is finite and that time is finite. Then the number of societies of such quanta is also finite. If so, then at any time $t_1$ there is a finite number of power quanta and societies of power quanta. At $t_2$, there will also be a finite number of power quanta and societies of them. And so on for all $t_n > t_1$. Now, consider a particular society of power quanta, call it "Fred", at $t_1$. If the eternal recurrence is to be true, it must be possible for Fred at $t_1$ to occur at $t_2$. It would not follow immediately that the eternal recurrence is true, of course, for there may be other premises that would also have to be true for the eternal recurrence to be true. However, if this premise is false, then the eternal recurrence cannot be true. That is to say, the premise:

it must be possible for Fred at $t_1$ to occur at $t_2$

is necessary for the eternal recurrence to be true. Since it is necessary for the eternal recurrence, demonstrating that it is false is sufficient to undermine the eternal recurrence. And the premise is false: it is not possible for Fred at $t_1$ to occur at $t_2$. For, if so, then it would have to be possible that Fred at $t_1$ = Fred at $t_2$. However, for all time pairs $<t_n, t_{n+1}>$, whenever $t_n < t_{n+1}$, then $t_n \neq t_{n+1}$, so, in general, Fred at $t_n \neq$ Fred at $t_{n+1}$, and, in particular, Fred at $t_1 \neq$ Fred at $t_2$. Now, consider the generalization of that claim: *every* society of power quanta is just like Fred, so every society of power quanta is such that

184

it never remains identical across time. *A fortiori*, for every society of power quanta, that society never recurs. Hence, one premise necessary for the truth of the eternal recurrence is false, and the proof for the eternal recurrence fails.

Note that this argument, if sound, does not require any supplementary premises about the finite or infinite number of power quanta, about the nature of societies of power or about the principles of putting societies of power quanta together. Even if the cardinality of the power quanta is infinite, the conclusion still follows. The premise that drives the conclusion is Nietzsche's own rejection of diachronic identity, which we have considered in Chapter 4 and earlier in this chapter. Eternal recurrence presupposes that there is *something* to recur at some later time than the present, but Nietzsche denies that anything is diachronically identical. Given that nothing continues through time, there is nothing to occur again at some future time. In brief, because there is nothing to recur, there is no recurrence of anything, eternal or otherwise. Hence, the cosmological version of the eternal recurrence is false.

We may object to this argument as follows. Surely, we might say, time is not finite, as is assumed in the above argument. Time is infinite so, surely, if there is a finite number of power quanta, then some society of them at some time will *have* to occur again at some later time. But this is false. For, again, consider some such society, say $<\alpha, \beta, \gamma, \delta>$ at $t_1$. Even if $<\alpha, \beta, \gamma, \delta>$ at $t_1$ and $<\alpha, \beta, \gamma, \delta>$ at $t_{14}$, $<\alpha, \beta, \gamma, \delta>$ at $t_1 \neq <\alpha, \beta, \gamma, \delta>$ at $t_{14}$, since $<\alpha, \beta, \gamma, \delta>$ at $t_1$ has the property of existing at $t_1$ and $<\alpha, \beta, \gamma, \delta>$ at $t_{14}$ has the property of existing at $t_{14}$. So, even where time is infinite, the eternal recurrence fails, and this is true whether there is a finite number of power quanta or an infinity of them.

Suppose, instead, that time is circular, that is, at some point in the future, we start the time cycle all over again. Then, at least if the number of power quanta is finite, the eternal recurrence could be true, for then there can be a $t_n$ such that $<\alpha, \beta, \gamma, \delta>$ at $t_1$ happens *again* at $t_n$, where $t_1 = t_n$. So, if exactly the same point in time can be replayed an infinite number of times, then, given certain assumptions about the cardinality of power quanta and certain other assumptions about bundling them together, eternal recurrence can be sustained. But rejecting the linearity of time is an extraordinarily high price to pay, and there is no reason, either philosophical or scientific, for paying it. Of course, the interpretive question for Nietzsche is whether *he* accepts the circularity of time. And it is to be admitted that on certain occasions he does. In the *Nachlass* note quoted above, he refers to the cosmos as a circular movement, and, presumably, this includes time. Likewise, in *Ecce Homo* he refers to the "doctrine of the 'eternal recurrence,' that is, of the unconditional and infinitely repeated circular course of all things" (*EH* "Birth of Tragedy" 3). Presumably, he intends to include time in all things. If so, then, as occasionally happens elsewhere with Nietzsche's claims, we cannot go along with him.

To be kind to Nietzsche, the cosmological version of the eternal recurrence is usually unveiled as a rhetorical counterpoint to metaphysical real worlds and religious heavens. For example, Nietzsche throws it down on the table in his longest note on nihilism as a trump card against any hope that we might try to salvage from the disillusionment of religion. In this note, he discusses, among other things, the nihilism that results from accepting the meaninglessness of existence once we admit to ourselves that the religious-metaphysical interpretation of the world that gave it meaning is false. In that nihilistic moment, Nietzsche rubs salt into our wounds by suggesting that not only is that old interpretation wrong, but the meaninglessness uncovered by the admission that it is wrong is only a precursor to a deeper nihilism, that which follows upon acknowledging the eternal recurrence of meaninglessness:

> Duration "in vain," without end of aim, is the most paralyzing idea, particularly when one understands that one is being fooled and yet lacks the power not to be fooled.
>
> Let us think this thought in its most terrible form: existence as it is, without meaning or aim, yet recurring inevitably without any finale of nothingness: "*the eternal recurrence.*"
>
> This is the most extreme form of nihilism: the nothing (the "meaningless"), eternally! (*WP* 55)

Here, then, is a way of tolerating the eternal recurrence, as a counterpoint to the meaningful and ordered world of the religious persona and the metaphysician.

This interpretation of the eternal recurrence is neutral on the truth of the cosmological thesis and comports well with his other uses of the term. In *The Gay Science*, for example, the eternal recurrence is used as a counterfactual for determining the value of a life. Consider the passage:

> *The greatest weight.* What, if some day or night a demon were to steal after you into our loneliest loneliness and say to you: "This life as you now live it and have lived it, you will have to live once more and innumerable times more; and there will be nothing new in it, but every pain and every joy and every thought and sigh and everything unutterably small or great in your lie will have to return to you, all in the same succession and sequence – even this spider and this moonlight between the trees, and even this

moment and I myself. The eternal hourglass of existence is turned upside down again and again, and you with it, speck of dust!"

Would you not throw yourself down and gnash your teeth and curse the demon who spoke thus? Or have you once experienced a tremendous moment when you would have answered him: "You are a god and never have I heard anything more divine." If this thought gained possession of you, it would change you as you are or perhaps crush you. The question in each and every thing, "Do you desire this once more and innumerable times more?" would lie upon your actions as the greatest weight. Or how well disposed would you have to become to yourself and to life *to crave nothing more fervently* than this ultimate eternal confirmation and seal?

(GS 341)

Here the truth of the cosmological version of the eternal recurrence is completely beside the point. The point of this passage is to ask whether we would be crushed or would rejoice were the eternal recurrence to turn out to be true. In this sense, the eternal recurrence is a litmus test for the worth of our lives, not a litmus test for the truth of the will to power hypothesis. As others have observed, the eternal recurrence is the Nietzschean equivalent to Kant's categorical imperative to act only so that the maxim of our action can be willed to be a universal law of nature. The Nietzschean equivalent is: act only so that the eternal recurrence of that action can be willed.

We may ask, finally, about the relation between *amor fati* and the eternal recurrence. Suppose the cosmological version of the eternal recurrence is, as we should admit, false because nothing recurs, either once or eternally. Does the falsity of the eternal recurrence as a cosmological thesis entail the falsity of *amor fati*? Surprisingly, the answer is "no". Recall, *amor fati* is a thesis about our individuation and identity over time. Healthy individuals love their fate because they know that were they to change anything in their past, they would not be the person they are now. This follows from the ontological version of will to power, for which every constituent is necessary for the whole of which it is a part. But Nietzsche's will to power ontology is inconsistent with eternal recurrence because will to power ontology rejects diachronic identity. Consider: if Fred at $t_2$ wills *amor fati* about himself, then Fred at $t_2$ is able to affirm that, necessarily, Fred at $t_2$ has Fred at $t_1$ as his ancestor. That is to say that were Fred at $t_2$ to have had some *other* ancestor at $t_1$, then he, Fred at $t_2$, would be distinct from who he is at $t_2$. Note that, in order for Fred to be able to will *amor fati* about himself, it is not necessary that Fred at $t_1$ = Fred at $t_2$. In fact, it is consistent with Fred willing *amor fati* about himself that Fred at $t_1 \neq$ Fred at $t_2$, so long as Fred at $t_1$ is the ancestor of Fred at $t_2$. But that it is possible that Fred at $t_1 \neq$ Fred at $t_2$ is inconsistent with the cosmological version of eternal recurrence, which, if true, entails that, necessarily, Fred at $t_1 =$ Fred at $t_2$. So *amor fati* can be true where the cosmological version of eternal recurrence cannot be true. Hence, it is not the case that the truth of eternal recurrence is necessary for the truth of *amor fati*. Indeed, *amor fati* can be true only if the cosmological version of eternal recurrence is false.

# CHAPTER 9

# Life, virtue, politics

Having been introduced to the range of Nietzsche's philosophical views, we are in a good position to return to his positive thoughts about ethics and social life. These thoughts are spread across every book he wrote. Of course, as we should expect by now, his views change over time and he nowhere lays out a definitive statement of his positive views, so it is not possible to identify his ethical or political *theory*. In fact, he does not have theories about these topics at all, if by "theory" we understand a systematic view with reductive principles and derivations from them. Instead, we find a number of comments and extended passages on ethical, social and political topics that, together, add up to something more than a loose collection but something less than a theory. They all presuppose Nietzsche's commitment to a psychology of drives and affects, his commitment to a distinction between health and sickness or decadence, his insistence on the deleterious effects of the herd on some individuals and his hope for liberation from herd thinking.

We shall begin our investigation by looking at Nietzsche's reflections on the relation between ethical values and life and will to power. Despite all appearances to the contrary, this relation is not an instance of a naturalistic fallacy, the fallacy of deriving an "ought" from an "is". In the second section of the chapter, we expand on the psychological role of drives by focusing on a subset of valuable ones, the virtues, and by showing how those virtues can be ordered so as to augment power in a wide variety of different healthy lives. Finally, we discuss Nietzsche's troubling hierarchical views about social and political organization.

## Life, value, ethics

Nietzsche's commitment to ridding us of supernatural and otherworldly elements in our thinking is nowhere clearer than in his reflections about ethical values. It is impossible to avoid his repeated insistence that there is no higher ethical goal than the enhancement of *life*. Look at *Twilight of the Idols,* for instance: "when we speak of value we do so under the inspiration and from the perspective of life: life itself evaluates through us *when* we establish values" (*TI* V 5). Or, again:

> I formulate a principle. All naturalism in morality, that is all *healthy* morality, is dominated by an instinct of life – some com-mandment of life is fulfilled through a certain canon of "shall" and "shall not", some hindrance and hostile element on life's road is thereby removed. (*TI* V 4)

This claim, that ethical values are valuable only in so far as they promote life, is alone enough to differentiate his views from many other ethical theorists, for whom such grounding would never occur even as an appropri-ate question. It smacks too much of a naturalistic fallacy, of trying to derive the ethical value of some action or behaviour from the fact that it happens. Admittedly, this hardline stance against ethical naturalism has weakened a little in the past twenty years. The emergence of evolutionary psychology and sociobiology has given new life to the hypothesis that evolutionary explanations can extend into the domain of ethical values. Yet these attempts, propounded by ambitious scientists and scientific reporters, have come in for withering criticism from philosophers (and other scientists), often precisely because they purport to derive the ethical value of some action or behaviour from its evolutionary pervasiveness across humans.

It is quite tempting to interpret Nietzsche as nothing more than a precursor to evolutionary ethics and so quite tempting to accuse him of violating the fact–value distinction. That we routinely come across passages that appear to be evolutionary or sociobiological explanations of ethical values is undeniable. For example, he claims in *Beyond Good and Evil* that "for all the value that the true, the truthful, the selfless may deserve, it would still be possible that a higher and more fundamental value for life might have to be ascribed to deception, selfishness, and lust" (*BGE* 2). Again, in a *Nachlass* note, he insists that, "altruistic [actions] are only a species of egoistic actions" (*WP* 786). These look suspiciously similar to sociobiological reductions that explain altruism as nothing more than the concern of an organism to perpetuate a gene lineage: the so-called "selfish gene" hypothesis. Nor in good intellectual conscience can we avoid a passage such as this:

> There are *only* immoral intentions and actions; – the so-called moral ones must be shown to be immoral. The derivation of all

affects from the one will to power: the same essence. The concept of life: – in the apparent antithesis (of "good" and "evil") degrees of power in instinct express themselves, temporary orders of rank under which certain instincts are held in check or taken into service.                                                    (WP 786)

We could, on the basis of these passages and the dozens like them, conclude that Nietzsche is a straightforward evolutionary reductionist about ethical values and, on the basis of that attribution, slap him with a fine for violating the fact–value distinction. However, he is not a Darwinian reductionist and his reasons for rejecting Darwin actually undermine the fact–value distinction presupposed by those who commit the naturalistic fallacy. So, a case can at least be made that he avoids the fallacy.

Recall that Nietzsche objects to Darwinian evolutionary theory on three grounds. First, he denies that the instinct of self-preservation is prior to the instinct of self-expansion; secondly, he claims that the struggle for existence is exceptional rather than normal and that the struggle for power is normal rather than exceptional; and, thirdly, he rejects Darwin's optimism that natural science produces objective truths. Were it not for this third objection, Nietzsche would be an evolutionary reductionist, albeit an idiosyncratic one. For even though he replaces self-preservation with self-expansion, and even though he thinks the struggle for power is more prevalent than the struggle for survival, these are still within the ambit of a generalized evolutionary reduction. Nietzsche's suggestion would then represent a change in the reduction *base* of ethical values to certain kinds of facts, rather than a denial that such reduction is *possible*. However, Nietzsche's objection to Darwin's optimism that evolutionary theory produces objective truth does entail rejecting reductionism. As we have seen, Nietzsche is convinced that empirical science no more produces perspective-independent statements than religion. (Of course, scientific perspectives are *better* than religiously based claims, but even physics is, he is prepared to admit, a perspective.) Whatever science produces is, contrary to its own presumption, perspectivally rather than objectively true. So, although Nietzsche claims that "the value for *life* is ultimately decisive" (WP 493), this cannot be, as the claims of sociobiology and evolutionary psychology pretend to be, an objective truth, for Nietzsche's truth perspectivism undermines the grounds on which any such claim could stand. And even if the statement "life is *ultimately* decisive when it comes to value" is true across *every* human perspective, we can never get outside ourselves to establish that it is an objective truth. The perspectivity of truth trumps those arrogant enough to think they can find an objective basis for ethical evaluation.

We can no more evaluate the value of life than we can think without logic or know anything about the thinking subject. In all three cases, we would have to step outside our own living skins to engage in the kind of reflection required. However, we cannot occupy that perspective:

> One would have to be situated *outside* life, and on the other hand to know it as thoroughly as any, as many, as all who have experienced it, to be permitted to touch on the *value* of life at all: sufficient reason for understanding that this problem is for us an inaccessible problem. (*TI* V 5)

We are living beings, so we cannot find an unbiased perspective for evaluating life. In the end, the judgement that we cannot find or occupy a perspective for evaluating life grounds his deepest criticism of the decadent. The decadent presumes that he can affirm that life is not worth living, but Nietzsche thinks to the contrary that it is not even possible for anyone to coherently assert the statement "life is not worth living". His question is: how *can* the decadent say that? It is like saying "I do not exist" – in the act of asserting the statement, the statement is revealed to be false. Therefore, as Nietzsche notes, the decadent cannot but be a liar: "[T]he moral lie in the mouth of the *decadent* says: 'nothing is worth anything – *life* is not worth anything'" (*TI* IX 35).

Insisting that we must occupy an interested position in any attempt to evaluate life is a funny move in Nietzsche's dialectic, but it is also proof positive that he was sufficiently self-reflective about his own position as to avoid obvious charges of self-referential inconsistency. Our evaluation of life is perspectival, not objective. That does save Nietzsche from jumping over the fact–value divide, but the means by which he avoids the jump leaves him forever on the evaluative side of the divide. This is unavoidable. Nietzsche's commitment to our lives here on earth being the criterion of ethical values entails that we can look nowhere else *but* our lives as the criterion of value. That means that not even natural science can overcome the perspective its being *our* product entails.

Although Nietzsche does not think we can successfully deny the value of life, he does think that plenty of things can be said *about* life. Not surprisingly, what he has to say about life is that it is will to power. So, in the *Nachlass*, he asks, "But *what is life*? — Here we need a more definite formulation of the concept 'life.' My formula for it is: life is will to power" (*WP* 254). Again:

> The wish to preserve oneself is the symptom of a condition of distress, of a limitation of the really fundamental instinct of life

which aims at the *expansion of power* and, wishing for that, frequently risks and even sacrifices self-preservation … in nature it is not conditions of distress that are *dominant* but overflow and squandering, even to the point of absurdity. The struggle for existence is only an *exception*, a temporary restriction of the life-will. The great and small struggle always revolves around superiority, around growth and expansion, around power – in accordance with the will to power, which is the will to life.

(*GS* 349)

We have seen this before, in his discussions both of ontology and human psychology: life is a set of activities for the acquisition of power.

In creatures less sophisticated than we are, that acquisition takes the form of expanding power over others of one's kind and over other kinds. Human life, especially the life that we have inherited over the past few millennia, is more tortured, self-referential and self-aware. No better description is to be found than this one, from *Beyond Good and Evil*:

That commanding something which the people call "the spirit" wants to be master in and around its own house and wants to feel that it is master; it has the will from multiplicity to simplicity, a will that ties up, tames, and is domineering and truly masterful. Its needs and capacities are so far the same as those which physiologists posit for everything that lives, grows, and multiplies. The spirit's power to appropriate the foreign stands revealed in its inclination to assimilate the new to the old, to simplify the manifold, and to overlook or repulse whatever is totally contradictory – just as it involuntarily emphasizes certain features and lines in what is foreign, in every piece of the "external world," retouching and falsifying the whole to suit itself. Its intent in all this is to incorporate new "experiences," to file new things in old files – growth, in a word – or, more precisely, the *feeling* of growth, the feeling of increased power. (*BGE* 230)

Given that life is the criterion of value and given that this is our kind of life, Nietzsche thinks that this description of life can serve as a criterion of value. Where life as described is enhanced, that is, where power is enhanced, we have goodness and where life, that is, power, is thwarted, we have badness. *The Anti-Christ* puts it into an infamous slogan: "What is good? All that heightens the feeling of power, the will to power, power itself in man. What is bad? Everything that is born of weakness" (*AC* 2).

193

Many of us will, and we all should, find Nietzsche's views troubling. Grant that our kind of power is not as brutal as that of other species or even our ancestors. Grant, too, that our kind of weakness is not physical but psychological weakness, that is, the inability to give form, to assimilate the foreign, to repulse the contradictory. Still, why think that enhancing life so described is *good*? Nietzsche's answer is blunt: there is no choice – life as he describes it is all we have. Once the supernatural realms of moral goodness have gone up in smoke, all we have left is our life, a life informed and enriched by our decadent attempts to escape from it or our healthy attempts to embrace it. We can, if we try hard enough and are sufficiently self-reflective, instantiate the power of life itself, for now we can finally recognize that we give form to what is formless, that we give value to what is valueless. Since this is life, we who have survived the disillusionment of nihilism make it our ideal:

> Whatever has *value* in our world now does not have value in itself, according to its nature – nature is always value-less, but it has been *given* value at some time, as a present – and it was *we* who gave and bestowed it. Only we have created the world *that concerns man*! (GS 360)

## Health and virtue

Nietzsche believes that life and will to power are coextensive and that, to enhance our lives, it is valuable to enhance power. How, then, are we to understand this imperative? We shall suggest that Nietzsche's mature ethical views are couched in terms of virtue ethics. Let us see what this view comes to and let us begin that project by acknowledging that here, as elsewhere in his work, Nietzsche has plenty of nasty things to say about virtue. In a *Nachlass* note, for instance, he insists that modern virtue is a "form of sickness" (*WP* 50) and in *The Gay Science* he contends that the praise of moral virtues is the "praise of instincts that deprive an individual of his noblest selfishness and the strength for the highest autonomy" (*GS* 21). Still, *Beyond Good and Evil* contains an entire section devoted to virtue, and he is also willing to list solitude, courage, insight and sympathy as noble virtues (*BGE* 284). Here, as everywhere else, Nietzsche speaks both critically and positively, so we have to be careful with what we attribute to him. The best view to attribute to him is that which criticizes the category virtue as it has been poisoned by herd thinking and praises virtue to the extent that it resists herd thinking.

Virtue ethics finds its first, and still best, expression in Aristotle, the Stoics and other Greeks. European moralities such as are found in Kant and Mill typically do not discuss virtue in great detail and, where they are discussed, these moralities eliminate essential properties of virtue that Nietzsche thinks must be retained. Kant, for example, talks about virtue in a number of places, but what he refers to with the word "virtue" is so rarefied as not really to be a psychological trait at all. What Nietzsche takes from the Greek concept of virtue is that it is a psychological state, a character trait, disposition, skill, habit or capacity whose cultivation and development constitutes human flourishing. In Aristotle, for example, a person who has the virtue of being honest is someone disposed to telling the truth because it has become habitual. Nietzsche says, along the same lines, that virtue is a "way of thinking and behaving that, once it has become habit, instinct, and passion, will dominate" (*GS* 21). In *Beyond Good and Evil* he notes that virtues are "drives" and "inclinations" (*BGE* 201), and in a note he claims that virtues are "physiological conditions . . . refined *passions* and enhanced states" (*WP* 255).

Given Nietzsche's drive psychology, it should be no surprise that his ethical views are articulated in terms of virtue, for calling on virtues allows him to emphasize the importance of drives and passions in our ethical behaviour and to avoid the decadent psychology found in moral theories. Nietzsche chides both the utilitarian idea that we rationally calculate pleasure and happiness and act on those calculations, and Kant's appeal to pure practical reason, moral laws and respect. Kant in particular is, Nietzsche thinks, a fraud. His studied attempt to divorce ethical motivation from our actual psychology and to enshrine practical reason as the ground of ethical motivation is, for Nietzsche, nothing more than the most exquisite expression of a decadent's attempt to eradicate our passions. Kant is the philosopher who, after all, says in his *Critique of Practical Reason* that when we act from reason alone "the heart is freed from a burden that has secretly pressed upon it" because we can finally "release [ourselves] from the impetuous importunity of the inclinations."* Nietzsche's position is diametrically opposed to such a view. He thinks that Kant's practical reason is nothing but "a reason [designed] specifically for the case in which one was supposed not to have to bother about reason – that is, when morality, when the sublime demand 'thou shalt,' makes itself heard" (*AC* 12). Our passions and drives – our inclinations – make us who we are and their proper cultivation makes our life an instance of either a flourishing life or a decadent life. A person engaged in expansion of influence is *healthy* and a person who either denies that such

---

* I. Kant, *Critique of Practical Reason*, L. White Beck (trans.) (Indianapolis, IN: Bobbs-Merrill, 1981), AK 161.

expansion is healthy or is incapable of it, either through ill-constitution or corruption by decadence, is *diseased*.

One of the benefits of the category of virtue is that it straddles moral and psychological contexts perfectly, thus supporting Nietzsche's evaluative naturalism. Any moral explanation that ignores our quirky, messy and complicated psychology is for him a complete non-starter, and focusing on virtue quickly brings us down from the decadent heights of practical reason to the proper place of drives and inclinations. As drives and passions, virtues share the structure of all intentional psychological activity; namely, that of being conscious or unconscious drives to realize particular intentional objects. So when it comes to explaining action and explaining which actions are good actions, the explanatory economies afforded Nietzsche are apparent.

It is a good thing that Nietzsche's naturalism has some benefits, for there is an immediate problem with articulating Nietzschean virtues. It appears on all accounts that virtue must satisfy two inconsistent considerations: first, the goal of all virtue cultivation – Nietzschean health – must be augmenting influence; secondly, Nietzschean health must be realized in a large number of ways, some of them contradictory to one another. Nietzsche puts the point as follows in *The Gay Science*:

> There is no health as such, and all attempts to define a thing that way have been wretched failures. Even the determination of what is healthy for your *body* depends on your goal, your horizon, your energies, your impulses, your errors, and above all on the ideals and phantasms of your soul. Thus there are innumerable healths of the body; and the more we allow the unique and incomparable to raise its head again, and the more we abjure the dogma of the "equality of men," the more must the concept of a *normal* health, along with a normal diet and the normal course of an illness, be abandoned by medical men. Only then would the time have come to reflect on the health and illness of the *soul,* and to find the peculiar virtue of each man in the health of his soul. In one person, of course, this health could look like its opposite in another person.          (GS 120)

An obvious rejoinder to Nietzsche's position here is this: if there is no health as such, then there is no flourishing as such, and if there is no flourishing as such, that can only mean that there is no good as such, and especially no *Nietzschean* good as such.

How then can Nietzsche insist that the great divide between people is that there are those who are and those who are not healthy, well-constituted and powerful? For example:

> Everywhere the struggle [is] of the sick against the healthy – a silent struggle as a rule, with petty poisons, with pinpricks, with sly long-suffering expressions, but occasionally also with that invalid's Phariseeism of *loud* gestures that likes best to pose as "noble indignation". (*GM* III 14)

To be even more blunt, if there is no good as such, then Nietzsche's claim in *The Anti-Christ* that "what is good" is "all that heightens the feeling of power, the will to power, power itself in man" (*AC* 2) has to be wrong.

Amazingly enough, Nietzsche's position is consistent. He can affirm both that there is no good as such and that power is the good. That this is not inconsistent demands careful explanation, for it appears to be so on any obvious reading. We know that there have to be distinct kinds of virtues because there are distinct healths, and we know that only after we determine what a particular health of the soul is can the virtues of that health be specified. Clearly, then, there are virtues determined by distinct healths of body and soul. These are *specific virtues*. But there are also virtues that all specific kinds of health share, and hence some passions and drives that are ubiquitous across species of health, even though they are never realized except in a specific health. These are *pervasive virtues*. Pervasive and specific virtues are related. A given passion or drive is a specific virtue only if the kind of life in whose service it is cultivated is pervasively virtuous (i.e. a kind of health). So it is possible that a given passion or drive is both specifically virtuous *and* specifically vicious, for a passion or drive cultivated in the service of a virtuous life is a virtue but that same passion cultivated in the service of a vicious life will make it a vice. Likewise, since there are distinct virtuous lives there may be specific virtues in one healthy life that are not specific virtues even in another healthy life.

That there are both pervasive and specific virtues, and that a particular drive or passion can be both virtuous and vicious, are admittedly unusual consequences for an ethical outlook. We are accustomed to thinking that virtue is good and that its goodness is universalizable. Nietzsche rejects this assumption. Moreover, rejecting the universalizability of virtue is, despite its counter-intuitiveness, an immediate and consistent implication of Nietzsche's perspectivist views on truth and justification. Just as there are statements true in many perspectives and others true only in some, so too there are virtues exemplified in every healthy life and virtues exemplified only in some healthy lives. And, just as justification of some particular statement in one perspective is consistent with that same statement not being justified in some other perspective, so too the virtuousness of some particular drive or passion in one kind of healthy life is consistent with that same drive or passion not being virtuous in some other kind of healthy life.

These strange consequences require elaboration. Some examples may help. Nietzsche evaluates a number of different healthy lives – the new philosopher/free spirit, the noble, the master, and the artist – and for each there is both a set of specific virtues unique to that kind of life and a set of pervasive virtues shared by every one of them. *All* kinds of Nietzschean health imply form-giving and self-overcoming; that much follows from the priority of will to power. So there is a core set of passions and drives – the pervasive virtues – whose cultivation leads to health and which, once cultivated, are that in which health consists. Among them are separation and love of solitude, spiritual independence, discipline, disdain for equality of humans and courage. There may be other pervasive virtues – love of enemies, pride, being beyond good and evil, self-overcoming – but those listed are shared by all healthy souls.

Calling these passions and drives pervasive virtues means that it is through their cultivation that health is achieved and the contrary of health – *ressentiment* and decadence – are avoided. So their cultivation must have augmenting power as a consequence. Consider, for instance, discipline and love of solitude. Nietzsche repeatedly asserts that discipline is a virtue of the powerful, primarily because:

> from out of that there always emerges and has always emerged something for the sake of which it is worthwhile to live on earth, for example virtue, art, music, dance, reason, spirituality – something transfiguring, refined, mad and divine.           (*BGE* 188)

Discipline conserves and allows greater realization of power and conveys to its practitioner the uniqueness that apprenticeship in that specific health entails. Likewise, solitude directs our focus away from the herd and on to our unique condition, thereby reinforcing the specificity of our kind of health and the desirability of its peculiar cultivation. Just as cultivation of discipline and solitude helps us augment our power, so too do they help us reject *ressentiment* and decadence, for they reinforce the "tonic emotions which enhance the energy of the feeling of life" (*AC* 7) and so prevent resentment of others and those decadent traits that dispose us to conserve suffering based in weakness.

Virtues such as self-discipline and solitude are found in every healthy life. That is, after all, what makes them pervasively virtuous. But there are also virtues peculiar for each kind of flourishing life. Consider the contrasting virtues of new philosophers and the nobility. New philosophers realize independence and solitude by being sceptical, honest and contrary to their culture, and they realize self-overcoming by cultivating chastity, humility and poverty. In the nobility, on the other hand, independence is realized by adopting playful attitudes towards the herd and by being unrelentingly polite to them, and solitude is realized by being contrary only to the herd. Moreover, the nobility practise neither chastity, humility nor poverty. Indeed, they take pleasure in the company of the opposite sex, they are prideful and they do not think poverty is required.

As these cases exemplify, there are species of health for which chastity, humility and poverty are virtues and others for which they are not. More than that, however, chastity, humility and poverty can also be vices when they are cultivated in the service of a pervasively vicious goal. Chastity, for example, is vicious when cultivated in a Christian context but virtuous when cultivated in the context of the new philosopher, for in the former it is no more subtle than hatred of one's own and others' sexuality, whereas in the latter it is a condition of "the highest and boldest spirituality" (*GM* III 7). For the new philosopher, chastity is directed toward realizing self-overcoming, and the character traits with which it affiliates – intellectual independence and scepticism, solitude, courage, humility – enable the new philosopher to give form to an experimental life. In Christianity, on the other hand, chastity affiliates with *ressentiment* and decadent character traits and is cultivated in the service of goals antithetical to self-over-coming.

Cultivating Nietzschean virtues leads to a life that is recognizable as a healthy life, albeit one at odds with commodity capitalism, Christian-influenced morality and socialism. Much of what motivates the herd animal will be absent in new philosophers: they will not resent others' success at grabbing political or economic power; they will not resent others' attempts to insult and injure them; they will not acquiesce in the false dilemma of either eliminating passion altogether or being helplessly lewd; they will not shun actions and practices because they might cause suffering; they will not act from anger or emotional excess; they will not be motivated by unsatisfiable desires to be happy. Instead, they will be motivated by desires for particular states of affairs that enrich their interpretive stances toward ourselves and others; they will view the rat race of political and economic power-grabbing with bemused detachment; they will shrug insults off as unimportant; and they will take a stance toward themselves in which they view themselves as the locus of many forces with disparate aims and interests.

That some of the specific virtues of the new philosopher can be vices when exemplified by a diseased kind of life should not be taken to imply that new philosophers are healthy by simple dint of will. In fact, new philosophers are dependent upon the time in which they live for the peculiar character of their health. Part of what makes new philosophers praiseworthy is that they contradict the age in which they live: "by laying the knife vivisectionally to the bosom of the very *virtues of the age*, they [the new philosophers] betrayed what was their own secret: to know a *new* greatness of man, a new untrodden path to his enlargement" (*BGE* 212). Because their focus is inwards rather than outwards, the philosophers' power is self-directed rather than other-directed, self-ravishing rather than other-ravishing, self-overcoming rather than other-overcoming. In the new philosopher, above all, the cruelty once directed towards others has been turned inwards as "a kind of cruelty of the intellectual conscience and taste which every brave thinker will recognize in himself" (*BGE* 230). Of course, being *dependent* upon their age does not make new philosophers *determined* by that age. What new philosophers inherit from their culture is used as a text to interpret and with which to experiment:

> philosophy, as I have hitherto understood and lived it, is a voluntary quest for even the most detested and notorious sides of existence. From the long experience I gained from such a wandering through ice and wilderness, I learned to view differently all that had hitherto philosophized: the *hidden* history of philosophy, the psychology of its great names, came to light for me. "How much truth can a spirit *endure*, how much truth does a spirit *dare*?" – this became for me the real standard of value.
>
> (*WP* 1041)

New philosophers affirm will to power by reinterpreting tradition and investigating its darker sides, thereby exemplifying in themselves that they are experiments in self-overcoming. Hence, to be a new philosopher is to be someone who "lives 'unphilosophically' and 'unwisely', above all *imprudently*, and bears the burden and duty of a hundred attempts and temptations of life – he risks *himself* constantly, he plays *the* dangerous game" (*BGE* 205). By risking themselves, new philosophers risk even "the possibilities of the most fundamental nihilism" (*WP* 1041). However, if successful in their engagement with nihilism, new philosophers cross over to a "Dionysian affirmation of the world as it is, without subtraction, exception, or selection" (*WP* 1041).

That new philosophers can affirm the world as it is includes, of course, being able to affirm their own ignominious beginning as not yet capable of affirming the world as it is. This is just to say that successful new philosophers can, having realized their goal, will *amor fati*. As a consequence, they undergo a radical psychological transformation and reach a point at which they transcend virtue as we understand it. For, in their cultivation of their peculiar health, new philosophers will, if successful, realize the ability to will that they could not have been other than who they once were and become who they now are. With that ability secured, there is no further call for developing virtue. Once we can affirm everything with respect to our own life there is no further need to *develop* virtue, for the distinction between traits that are and traits that are not worthy of cultivation is overcome. Those who cultivate virtue but cannot yet affirm their own lives are creating themselves as selves with the right to view their lives as necessary for the self they will become. Once *amor fati* is willable, however, the earthly life of Dionysian affirmation is no longer a goal but a source of action and thought. A person for whom willing *amor fati* is actual is beyond good and evil, someone who affirms all sides of existence as necessary, and someone for whom there are no more goals of which the cultivation of virtue is a component. That person's habits, passions and thoughts are henceforth *designated* as virtues. For such a one, it is not "happiness follows virtue"; rather, her happy state is "first designated … as a virtue" (*WP* 1026). Hence, in so far as the Dionysian life of affirmation and eternal return is a human goal, its successful realization culminates one kind of life and inaugurates another kind of life, one beyond humanity altogether, the life characteristic of an *Übermensch*.

None of us will ever become an *Übermensch*. That status is reserved for some individual in the future, someone from whom all traces of *ressentiment* and decadence have been flushed, in whom every pervasive and specific virtue has been so finely honed that *amor fati* and eternal recurrence can be willed without residue. What is available to us moderns is something short of the self-overcoming of the species; we can "turn out well". Nietzsche describes such a person in *Ecce Homo*:

> What is it, fundamentally, that allows us to recognize *who has turned out well*? That a well-turned-out person pleases our senses, that he is carved from wood that is hard, delicate, and at the same time smells good. He has a taste only for what is good for him; his pleasure, his delight ceases where the measure of what is good for him is transgressed. He guesses what remedies avail against what is harmful; he exploits bad accidents to his advantage; what does not kill him makes him stronger. Instinctively, he collects from everything he sees, hears, lives through, *his* sum: he is a principle of selection, he discards much. He is always in his own company, whether he associates with books, human beings, or landscapes: he honors by *choosing*, by *admitting*, by *trusting*. He reacts slowly to all kinds of stimuli, with that slowness which long caution and deliberate pride have bred in him: he examines the stimulus that

approaches him, he is far from meeting it halfway. He believes neither in "misfortune" nor in "guilt": he comes to terms with himself, with others; he knows how to *forget* – he is strong enough; hence everything *must* turn out for his best.

(*EH* "Why I Am So Wise" 2)

Perhaps once there is a critical mass of well-turned-out persons, the social conditions necessary for the cultivation of the virtues constitutive of being an *Übermensch* might materialize. Until then, the best we can hope for, and it is, I think we have to admit, an extraordinarily stringent standard, is to live as dangerously as Nietzsche himself lived, to live diametrically opposed to mediocrity and baseness, to risk nihilism, to be an experiment within oneself.

## Politeness, politics and orders of rank

Nietzschean virtues are admittedly individualistic and self-centred. It is tempting to infer from this that he is interested in nothing but the cultivation of individual excellence and that he thinks that virtue can be cultivated equally well in any sociopolitical setting. All we have to do is open up his books to see that neither of these claims is true: he has plenty of criticisms of social and political organizations and institutions, and he repeatedly offers to specify how societies ought to be structured so that human flourishing can best be structured. Many of his criticisms are unpleasant in various ways, and all his positive proposals are meritocratic, inegalitarian and anti-democratic in certain ways. Denying these elements is fatuous. However, even here there are other tendencies. Nietzsche's primary targets in his criticisms are then-contemporary European social and political organizations and his positive proposals are offered primarily as counterpoint to what surrounds him. That makes it at least possible to remove some of the sting from his barbed attacks. After all, it is consistent to attack nineteenth-century democracies, capitalisms and socialisms as then instantiated and praise other, better, exemplifications of such organizations. Surprisingly, sprinkled throughout Nietzsche's work are passages suggesting that at least some forms of democracy and at least some kinds of egalitarianism are partially salvageable.

We shall unpack Nietzsche's political views by focusing on one of the few specific virtues that is explicitly social in character: politeness. Now, we might laugh at the idea that politeness is a specific virtue for anyone, but for Nietzsche in particular to suggest that politeness is a virtue seems patently ludicrous. We are accustomed to thinking of politeness as a conventional phoniness, a *persona* we adopt in certain circles, anything *but* a virtue, and nothing we have covered herein prepares us for thinking that Nietzsche would endorse as a virtue something conventional. However, we are mistaken, both about the possibility that politeness can be a virtue and about Nietzsche. Grant that politeness is conventional, part of the mores of a society. The missing premise here – that what is a social convention is incompatible with a flourishing life and cannot be a virtue – is false, at least if Nietzsche is right. For it is an amazing thing that, for all his well-deserved notoriety and for all his contempt for the herd, Nietzsche routinely endorses the "will to mere appearance, to simplification, to masks, to cloaks, in short, to the surface" (*BGE* 230) and actually endorses politeness as a virtue in the nobility and free spirits. For example, he insists that to understand honour, it is "essential" that:

> one insists unconditionally on good manners on the part of everyone with whom [we] come in contact (at least, when they do not belong to "*us*"); that [we are] neither familiar, nor genial, nor merry, nor modest, except *inter pares*; that [we] *always maintain poise*. (*WP* 948)

Another example of the close relation between morality and manners is found in the early sections of *The Gay Science*. Nietzsche claims here that anyone who wants to understand moral matters must take up a study of immense proportions, a study in which "all kinds of individual passions have to be thought through and pursued through different ages, peoples, and great and small individuals; all their reason and all their evaluations and perspectives on things have to be brought into the light" (*GS* 7). Once we have completed this monumental task, "the most insidious question of all would emerge into the foreground: whether science can furnish goals of action after it has proved that it can take such goals away and annihilate them" (*GS* 7), for our actions, passions and desires would then be subject to "centuries of experimentation that might eclipse all the great projects and sacrifices of history to date" (*GS* 7). In addition to histories and studies of law, history, avarice, work schedules, festivals, monastic life, marriage, friendship and food, Nietzsche poses a question about, of all things, manners and customs. He asks, "Have the manners of businessmen, artists, or artisans been studied and thought about? There is so much in them to think about" (*GS* 7). Here, the word "manner" serves double duty as deportment and as socially customary behaviour. What he has in mind for this study is what social customs reveal about the person who displays them. Surprisingly, not everything revealed by displaying social customs is negative.

One thing that social customs of any kind reveal is the fetishization of our own lives. Customs, mores, manners and the like are self-consciously adopted ways of behaving that expose our conviction that we are different from some and equal to others. As long as there have been social customs of any kind, they have been affiliated with aristocratic classes, for their perfection has always been a way for the aristocracy to distinguish and distance itself from business people, trades people, artisans and farmers. Classes excluded by the aristocracy also develop their own customs, often as a way of mimicking the aristocracy. Even in societies in which the aristocracy has eroded or was never in place to begin with, most social interactions are governed by social customs and codes of civil and correct behaviour. Whether it be social cards or business cards, such codes both identify us as a member of a particular class and, in virtue of that membership, distinguish us from those who are not members.

Another aspect of conventional codes of behaviour that is of interest to Nietzsche is that they are idiosyncratic, peculiar and arbitrary. Nietzsche is undeniably correct about this. In American business circles it is condescending to hold a woman's chair at the table; in social circles it is polite to hold a woman's chair at the table. In the United States, it is rude to avoid eye contact during conversation; in Thailand, it is rude to make eye contact during conversation. In some African countries, arriving on time for a meeting is rude; in the United Kingdom, it is expected; in Italy, your arrival should be on time even though your host will probably not show up for an hour; in China your host's entourage will arrive 15 minutes early to help you prepare. In Australia, praising someone's watch might provoke a "thank you"; in Saudi Arabia, praising someone's watch will provoke the watch itself as a gift. In the United States, handshakes between men last three to seven seconds; in many Muslim countries, handshakes between men frequently morph into hand-holding. In the United States, giving someone a "thumbs-up" sign or an "okay" sign is permissible; in other countries, both are the crudest possible references to sex. Conversely, in the United States, giving someone the finger is rude; in other countries, it is meaningless.

In their idiosyncrasy, peculiarity and arbitrariness, social conventions and mores display in an obvious way the perspectivity that characterizes all evaluation, and so, too, the evaluation found in ethics and morality, that is, the particular ethical evaluation found in the herd. Although it would be too strong to say that morality is nothing but bad manners, it is not too strong to say that morality is a point on a continuum with other social conventions and that, as such, morality never escapes the idiosyncrasy, peculiarity and arbitrariness of those codes. An argument to the contrary premised on the claim that morality, unlike social conventions, is universalizable is completely out of place in the context of Nietzsche's ethical reflections, for he denies that there are universal moral principles. With that denial, he rejects the idea that any ethical standard, virtues among them, must be found in *everyone* to be a standard for *anyone*. There is, however, a better argument that social conventions cannot be specific virtues. Conventional codes of behaviour are simply the customary designation of certain behaviours and habit formation as socially acceptable; virtues, on the other hand, are autonomously chosen codes of behaviour and habit formation. But even this difference is not sufficient for disqualifying socially acceptable behaviour as a specific virtue because the conventionality of a psychological ability is consistent with it nevertheless being instrumental in cultivating a pervasive virtue. That is how it is with virtues such as politeness. Politeness is a specific virtue because it helps the healthy cultivate pervasive virtue. Likewise, although typically followed rather than adopted from choice, nothing prevents politeness from being so adopted. And that is how the nobility and free spirits use politeness; they don it as one of the masks they wear.

That politeness is a specific virtue entails that there are ways of flourishing in which the opposite of politeness – rudeness – is also a virtue. And Nietzsche says exactly this in *Ecce Homo*: "You see, I don't want rudeness to be underestimated: it is by far the *most humane* form of contradiction and ... one of our foremost virtues" (*EH* "Why I Am So Wise" 5). There are two ways to interpret this passage, both of which make the point that politeness is a specific virtue. First, we can say that there are kinds of health for which rudeness is a virtue and politeness not, and kinds of health for which politeness is a virtue and rudeness not. Secondly, we can say that rudeness and good manners are *both* virtues in some kinds of healthy lives. Nietzsche says both.

Look again at the passage from *Ecce Homo*: "I don't want rudeness to be underestimated: it is by far the *most humane* form of contradiction and ... one of our foremost virtues." To whom does Nietzsche refer with this "our"? Nietzsche is speaking here, as he often does in *Twilight*, *The Anti-Christ*, and *Beyond Good and Evil*, to those he considers his equals, other free spirits and those who have, as has Nietzsche, struggled to overcome resentment and avoid decadence. Free spirits are, as noted above, intellectual sceptics, honest, and opposed to the culture of which they are members. Rudeness is a virtue for the free spirit or new philosopher because it is a more humane way to express their contradiction to their culture than, say, silence or going on murderous rampages. Yet Nietzsche nowhere claims that rudeness is the *only* way for a free spirit to express opposition to her culture or that it is always the *best* way to express that opposition. A free spirit is not encouraged to be virtuously rude at any time to anyone who is a member of the culture to which she is opposed. After all, the free spirit's opposition to the culture does not always take the form of contradicting it. She may express her opposition by arguing against it, by offering alternatives to it or by withdrawing from it. None of these expressions of opposition require rudeness and for none of them need it be advocated.

Compare the free spirit to the nobility. For the nobility, rudeness appears *never* to be a virtue. Instead, politeness characterizes the restraint typically found among noble peers in their relations with the herd. It is to be admitted that Nietzsche is a little equivocal on the use of manners by the nobility towards the herd. In *Beyond Good and Evil*, for example, he characterizes the delicacy of the relations between members of the nobility as a kind of "good manners" (*BGE* 259), but claims that outside their own company, the nobility may behave towards the herd as they please. In *The Anti-Christ*, on the other hand, he claims that, "When the exceptional human being treats the mediocre more tenderly than himself and his peers, this is not mere courtesy of the heart – it is simply his *duty*" (*AC* 57). This passage may go a little far, but not by much, for Nietzsche frequently requires the nobility to treat the herd with courtesy. For example, in *Daybreak*, he calls relentless politeness, honesty towards our friends and ourselves, bravery towards enemies and magnanimity towards the defeated, the four cardinal virtues (*D* 556). Nietzsche also chastises industrial culture for its egalitarian elimination of higher manners. He notes in *The Gay Science* that, contrary to noble military culture, there is in capitalism a serious "lack of higher manners", which, together with "the notorious vulgarity of manufacturers with their ruddy, fat hands give [the common man] the idea that it is only accident and luck that have elevated one person above another" (*GS* 40).

We have, then, a contrast between the role of politeness and rudeness in free spirits and in the nobility. Being rude on occasion to those who are members of the dominant culture against which the free spirit sets herself off is permissible, but for the nobility to be rude to the herd is not permissible. That is because the nobility is not opposed to the entire culture of which it is a part but only to its herd component, whereas the new philosopher is opposed to the culture that has had its social stratification destroyed already by the herd. Aristocratic culture presupposes an established position for the noble and herd classes, whereas the culture from which the free spirit emerges is one in which social stratification has been abolished by the slave revolt. Given a secure position in the order of rank, the nobility dons the mask of politeness towards the herd to keep it away and protect itself from commonness. Politeness also displays to the herd the beneficial characteristics found in their noble and healthy life with its surplus of power. The noble human being, replete with a "feeling of fullness, of power that seeks to overflow" knows how to speak and be silent and wants to help the unfortunate herd, "but not, or almost not, from pity, but prompted more by an urge begotten by excess of power" (*BGE* 260).

Free spirits, on the other hand, emerge from societies in which the external order of rank has been lost or destroyed. In such a society, the traditional conditions for displays of aristocratic power have been fundamentally corrupted or eliminated altogether. Those who strive to be free spirited live in societies in which the noble self-experience of being the "*meaning* and highest justification" (*BGE* 258) of society has been lost. Individuals who carry within themselves an internalized order of rank have replaced external orders of rank that have the nobility as the heart and soul of a society. The best members of contemporary societies replicate inside what aristocratic societies once displayed to all, a rank order of passions and drives, the noblest of them subjecting the most vulgar to discipline, sublimation and cultivation. Thus, we moderns are called to be kind and polite to ourselves, to accept that our own drives and passions, as ignoble and humble as many of them are, serve us in our experimental lives as the herd once served the aristocracy. We gladly accept that, without the hierarchical welter of drives that constitute who we are, we would not now be the person who seeks to go beyond them. But towards those who relish the collapse of the aristocracy – whether external or internal – by wallowing in the common, we are entitled on occasion to contradict with rudeness what no other means of opposition can successfully accomplish. Some are so entrenched in mediocrity and suffering that no education, argument or persuasion is sufficient to expose to them the waste their fondness for vulgarity makes of their own lives. Something is needed to jolt them; rudeness can, on occasion, be that jolt.

Why do free spirits bother to contradict their culture at all? Why not, as in the case of the nobility, retreat behind a mask of indifferent politeness toward the herd? Here, too, an answer is that free spirits emerge in a context in which the conditions for the nobility's benign indifference are lacking. Free spirits are members of the class to which they are opposed. Their disciplining of their passions and drives, and their own self-overcoming, are not reserved only for a lucky aristocratic few. They care just enough about their fellows to oppose their vulgarity and, on occasion, to contradict it. Of course, free spirits also love solitude, so we can forgive them when, after confronting the intentionally common, they, too, don the mask of politeness again and return to their solitude.

There is one final feature of politeness that is of interest. Politeness towards the herd is the only thing to be found in Nietzsche that approximates social reciprocity. Traditionally, it is respect that philosophers advocate as the social glue of morality and democracy. In both Kant's moral theory and utilitarianism, for example, each person is equal to all others – either, as in Kant, because each person is equally a rational agent, or, as in utilitarianism, because every individual's utility is equal in the calculation of moral goodness – so we have a duty to respect each other. In fact, admitting that respect is a motivating affect is the closest Kant ever comes to admitting a moral passion into his theory. (Respect is designed to take the place of sympathy, which is for other moralities the fundamental passion that binds us together. Kant rejected sympathy because it was intermittent, not shared equally across everyone, and, as an inclination, impetuous and unpredictable. Respect is, in contrast, stable and universal, and, where it is not exemplified, there may we level moral condemnation for it not being so.)

As we should expect, Nietzsche thinks Kant and the utilitarians get it wrong. Respect is misguided not just because it mistakenly presumes that we are all alike rational agents – Nietzsche thinks no one is rational in that sense – but because it mistakenly presumes that we are ethically equal with one another on *any* criterion we might choose. *That* assumption is false, malicious and decadent. Especially in the hands of democrats, who think we all have equal rights, the end result of that assumption is a downward spiral, "until finally a smaller, almost ridiculous type, a herd animal, something eager to please, sickly, and mediocre has been bred, the European of today" (*BGE* 62). Then it is true that we are equal: equally pathetic. Nietzsche's free-spirited vivisection of European society demands that he assert the opposite of equality, an order of rank of individuals, some more powerful than others, and a rank order of treatment based on that order of rank. Where there is equality, namely, between the powerful, there we may have respect, but where equality is lacking, as between the powerful and the herd, respect is completely out of place. There politeness replaces respect.

Politeness is also the best Nietzsche can muster as a check on the otherwise unconstrained behaviour of the nobility to the herd. No doubt those higher in rank are sufficiently refined, disciplined and well-mannered to refrain from violence against the herd. It may even be, as *The Anti-Christ* suggests, a duty to be gentle to those lower in rank, and not just a matter of politeness. But if it is a duty of the exceptional human being to "handle the mediocre more gently than he does himself" (*AC* 57), that duty is one the nobility bear to themselves as exceptional human beings, and not to the mediocre as their equals. Gentility to the mediocre could never be a duty that the nobility bear to them, for we have duties only to those who are our equals, and the mediocre are never the equal of the nobility. Noble politeness is *noblesse oblige*, the obligation to conduct oneself always as is befitting nobility, nothing more. (Nothing less either, admittedly:

aristocratic societies whose upper classes have a well developed sense of *noblesse oblige* have, in certain historical circumstances, actually introduced some democratic institutions in some important ways.) Noble politeness is a gift to the herd, not a binding duty on them. They could, without fault, retract their generosity at the drop of a hat.

Such haughtiness makes most tongues cluck. We can reasonably ask whether noble politeness is any consolation to the poor and oppressed. The nobility's tasteful restraint of their power is, after all, not what condemns the poor to poverty; it is the assumption that the poor are in their proper place that does it. Thinking that the oppressed have much to fear from the nobility's occasional eruptions of careless violence is akin to thinking that capitalism succeeds only because there is a conspiracy to keep the means of production out of the hands of the proletariat. No conspiracy, either of the capitalists or of the nobility, is ever required to keep social inequities going. What condemn the poor to poverty are the capitalist's capitalist activity and the nobility's nonchalant apathy towards both the capitalist and the working poor. To this, Nietzsche's response is to side with the nobility and to accept it as a given that some are there simply to serve the noble class:

> To be a public utility, a cog, a function, is a natural vocation: it is *not* society, it is the kind of *happiness* of which the great majority are alone capable, which makes intelligent machines of them. For the mediocre it is happiness to be mediocre; mastery in one thing, specialization, is for them a natural instinct. It would be quite unworthy of a more profound mind to see an objection to mediocrity as such. It is even the *prime* requirement for the existence of exceptions: a high culture is conditional upon it.
>
> (*AC* 57)

These servants to the nobility include the capitalists, by the way; Nietzsche does not think that people are noble because they are rich or can buy many works of art or have read all F. Scott Fitzgerald's books. What makes a person noble is their manner of augmenting their power. Spending millions on a house and its furnishings so as to provide a spectacle for others to admire does not amount to much.

Passages such as the one just quoted are not difficult to find, so we must finally confront Nietzsche's unabashed anti-egalitarian elements. With only a few exceptions, Nietzsche's hostility to egalitarianism and democracy is consistent. He has two basic complaints against egalitarian democracy. The first is that, *pace* democracy, we do not all have equal rights; the second is that democracy entails mediocrity. Both complaints follow from his commitment to individual human health as continuous growth and power enhancement. Where such a view of health operates, the democratic principle that everyone is equal cannot but be false, for, as we have seen, holding that we are all equal would entail that the sick and decadent count for the same as the healthy and flourishing. Such a view is anathema to Nietzsche, who believes to the contrary that "A people is a detour of nature to get to six or seven great men" (*BGE* 126). Likewise, acting on the principle that we are all equal condemns any social organization to undermining the conditions that allow these few great exemplars ever to emerge, a view never more succinctly expressed than in this *Nachlass* note: "Democracy represents the disbelief in great human beings" (*WP* 752).

Even if we take a wide view of democracy as that form of social and political organization in which dominating political power is regulated and limited, in which political power is mobile across individuals and economic classes, and in which political positions must survive the public scrutiny of debate and deliberation, Nietzsche nevertheless objects to it. His objection is not to the increase in independence that democracy cultivates or to the diminished role that the rich play in a democracy. He is prepared to admit that democracy is preferable to any wealth-based aristocracy or oligarchy:

> Democracy wants to create and guarantee as much *independence* as possible: independence of opinion, of mode of life and of employment. To that end it needs to deprive of the right to vote both those who possess no property and the genuinely rich ... It must likewise prevent everything that seems to have for its objective the organization of parties. For the three great enemies of independence ... are the indigent, the rich, and the parties. – I am speaking of democracy as something yet to come.
>
> (*HAH* 383)

Moreover, Nietzsche actually admires the rough and tumble exchange of political ideas found in democracies, for this aspect of democracy recalls the *agôn*, or contest, of ancient Greek culture. The problem is rather that the character of democratic contests is embarrassingly and unalterably mediocre. Democratic debate focuses on persuading the most incompetent and winning in the short term rather than on persuading the worthy and thinking of the long-term health of society. As democratic ideology spreads through a society, this feature becomes more pronounced: "One lives for today, one lives very fast – one lives very irresponsibly: it is precisely this which one calls 'freedom'" (*TI* IX 39). In the hurly-burly of democratic life, we lose patience, reflection and the ability to think in the long term. This is contrary to what is required for political health. As he continues in this passage from *Twilight of the Idols*, "for institutions to exist there must exist the ... will to tradition, to authority, to centuries-long responsibility, to *solidarity* between succeeding generations ... The West has lost those instincts" (*TI* IX 39).

Nietzsche's fundamental assumption is that democracy and egalitarianism are inconsistent with the enhancement of our power. Here is how he puts it:

> Without that *pathos of distance* which grows out of the ingrained difference between strata – when the ruling caste constantly looks afar and looks down upon subjects and instruments and just as constantly practices obedience and command, keeping down and keeping at a distance – that other more mysterious pathos could not have grown up either – the craving for an ever new widening of distances within the soul itself, the development of ever higher, rarer, more remote, further-stretching, more comprehensive states – in brief, simply the enhancement of the type "man," the continual "self-overcoming of man ..."     (*BGE* 257)

Nietzsche clearly states that social stratification is necessary for cultivating the psychological capacities necessary for achieving a healthy, flourishing life. Without that social stratification, those psychological capacities cannot, he thinks, develop. Nietzsche is probably wrong about this. All we have to do is come up with individuals who, having inhabited a non-stratified society, nevertheless cultivate Nietzschean virtues. There are such individuals, Nietzsche among them. Moreover, if this claim were true, it would follow directly that cultivation of Nietzschean virtues would be ruled out for anyone brought up in a democracy. Nietzsche might be willing to draw this conclusion, but then all *his* positive proposals about that healthy life are as interesting as the braying of a donkey. Why write books describing the good life when the good life is ruled out to begin with? Of course, Nietzsche waffles on just this point, for he also admits that, "we all still have bad instincts, the Christian instincts, somewhere within us" (*AC* 59), but does not condemn us to the herd on this score alone.

We reject, then, the claim that social stratification is necessary for health. It is not sufficient either. After all, there are plenty of dissolute aristocrats who squander everything life has afforded them in oscillations between orgies of petty self-indulgence and lethargic ennui. So inhabiting a stratified society is neither necessary nor sufficient for achieving a healthy life. No doubt it is *easier* to live a good life in a stratified society, at least if we are lucky enough to be in the stratum where such a life is possible, so a stratified society may be a contributory factor to a healthy life. But that society is not ours. Ours is the mediocre, live-for-today society that exemplifies what goes wrong with democracies. Achieving a healthy Nietzschean life may be more difficult for us decadent democrats than for those lucky enough to have been brought up as members of the highest strata of a caste system. All things considered, however, we should take our chances as modern egalitarian democrats, for the likelihood that any of us would be a member of the highest stratum of a caste system is vanishingly small, of the same order of likelihood as having been a prince or princess in a former life. We are much more likely to be or to have been a grimy peasant sharing the straw with our milk cow.

Still, some are willing to roll the dice even on this kind of game, knowing full well that their chances of coming out on top are minuscule. The question is, is Nietzsche one of them? He would like to be, but he must suspect that he is not. For all the aspirations we may have as new philosophers to find our own values, to create values and to legislate for the future, we are also social animals who have inherited several hundred thousand years' worth of social instincts. The *Übermensch* is a long way off. Even the exceptional human being who is a law-giver and commander of the future will always be the exception. The sedimentation of the herd in all of us is so thorough, and the cost of reorganizing society so as to allow more exceptional human beings to bubble up is so horrible, that it will never happen. The level of self-respect that makes a life composed of being nothing more than a social cog abhorrent is, for better or worse, also one of the legacies of democracy, and it will not vanish simply because it quashes the chances for there being more exceptional human beings. Once in place, the self-respect of the mediocre herd animal, however unjustified, will ruin any proposal for undoing it so that we might have more destinies such as Nietzsche's. We can, I suppose, always console ourselves with the thought that although herd morality has succeeded in breeding the mediocre person of contemporary democracies, we nevertheless came up with *one* Nietzsche. Perhaps it is only the herd speaking to give voice to the worry that societies that could routinely come up with *more* than one Nietzsche might very well not survive the encounter.

# Guide to further reading

## Nietzsche's works

### Collected works in German

*Werke: Kritische Gesamtausgabe Briefwechsel*, G. Colli & M. Montinari (eds), 24 vols, in 4 parts (Berlin: Walter de Gruyter, 1975).
*Sämtliche Werke: Kritische Studienausgabe in 15 Bänden*, G. Colli & M. Montinari (eds) (Berlin: Walter de Gruyter, 1988).

### Works in English translation

There is no reliable collection of Nietzsche's works in English currently available. Such a collection is under construction by Stanford University Press, under the general editorship of Ernst Behler. I have listed the available volumes of this as yet incomplete edition below along with other reliable English translations of Nietzsche's books.

*The Anti-Christ*, W. Kaufmann (trans.), in *The Portable Nietzsche*, W. Kaufmann (ed.) (New York: Viking Press, 1968).
*The Anti-Christ*, R. J. Hollingdale (trans.), in *Twilight of the Idols and The Anti-Christ* (New York: Penguin, 1968).
*Beyond Good and Evil*, W. Kaufmann (trans.) (New York: Random House, 1966).
*Beyond Good and Evil*, M. Faber (trans.) (New York: Oxford University Press, 1998).
*The Birth of Tragedy*, W. Kaufmann (trans.) (New York: Random House, 1967).
*The Birth of Tragedy and Other Writings*, R. Speirs (trans.) (New York: Cambridge University Press, 1999).
*The Birth of Tragedy*, D. Smith (trans.) (New York: Oxford University Press, 2000).
*The Case of Wagner*, W. Kaufmann (trans.) (New York: Random House, 1967).
*Daybreak: Thoughts on the Prejudices of Morality*, R. J. Hollingdale (trans.) (New York: Cambridge University Press, 1982).
*Ecce Homo: How One Becomes What One Is*, W. Kaufmann (trans.) (New York: Random House, 1967).
*Ecce Homo: How One Becomes What One Is*, R. J. Hollingdale (trans.) (New York: Penguin, 1979).
*The Gay Science, with a Prelude of Rhymes and an Appendix of Songs*, W. Kaufmann (trans.) (New York: Random House, 1974).

*The Gay Science, with a Prelude in German Rhymes and an Appendix of Songs*, J. Nauckhoff (trans.), poems A. Del Caro (trans.), B. Williams (ed.) (New York: Cambridge University Press, 2001).

*Human, All Too Human: A Book for Free Spirits*, R. J. Hollingdale (trans.) (New York: Cambridge University Press, 1986).

*Human, All Too Human, I*, G. Handwerk (trans.), volume 3 of *The Complete Works of Friedrich Nietzsche*, E. Behler (ed.) (Stanford, CA: Stanford University Press, 1997).

*Nietzsche Contra Wagner*, W. Kaufmann (trans.), in *The Portable Nietzsche* (New York: Viking Press, 1968).

*On the Genealogy of Morals*, W. Kaufmann & R. J. Hollingdale (trans.) (New York: Random House, 1967).

*On the Genealogy of Morals*, D. Smith (trans.) (New York: Oxford University Press, 1996).

*On the Genealogy of Morality*, C. Diethe (trans.) (New York: Cambridge University Press, 1994).

*On the Genealogy of Morality*, M. Clark & A. Swensen (trans.) (Indianapolis, IN: Hackett, 1998).

*Philosophy and Truth: Selections from Nietzsche's Notebooks of the Early 1870s*, D. Breazeale (ed. and trans.) (Atlantic Highlands, NJ: Humanities Press, 1979).

*Philosophy in the Tragic Age of the Greeks*, M. Cowan (trans.) (Chicago, IL: Henry Regnery Company, 1962).

*Thus Spoke Zarathustra*, W. Kaufmann (trans.), in *The Portable Nietzsche* (New York: Viking Press, 1968).

*Thus Spoke Zarathustra*, R. J. Hollingdale (trans.) (Harmondsworth: Penguin, 1969).

*Twilight of the Idols*, W. Kaufmann (trans.), in *The Portable Nietzsche* (New York: Viking Press, 1968).

*Twilight of the Idols*, R. J. Hollingdale (trans.), in *Twilight of the Idols and The Anti-Christ* (New York: Penguin, 1968).

*Twilight of the Idols*, D. Large (trans.) (New York: Oxford University Press, 1998).

*Unfashionable Observations*, R. T. Gray (trans.), volume 2 of *The Complete Works of Friedrich Nietzsche*, E. Behler (ed.) (Stanford, CA: Stanford University Press, 1995).

*Untimely Meditations*, R. J. Hollingdale (trans.) (Cambridge: Cambridge University Press, 1983).

*The Will to Power*, W. Kaufmann (trans.) (New York: Random House, 1967).

## Books about Nietzsche and his philosophical views

I have listed books and collections of essays available in English. Books on Nietzsche in German and French are listed in the bibliographies of many of the listed books. Journal articles concerning ongoing scholarly debates are also listed in the bibliographies of many of the listed books.

### Biographies and reminiscences

Chamberlain, L. *Nietzsche in Turin: An Intimate Biography* (New York: St. Martin's Press, 1999).

Gilman, S. L. (ed.) *Conversations with Nietzsche: A Life in the Words of his Contemporaries*, D. J. Parent (trans.) (New York: Oxford University Press, 1987).

Hayman, R. *Nietzsche, a Critical Life* (New York: Oxford University Press, 1980).

Hollingdale, R. J. *Nietzsche: The Man and His Philosophy*, 2nd edn. (New York: Cambridge University Press, 1999).

Hollingdale, R. J. *Nietzsche* (New York: Routledge and Kegan Paul, 1973).

Pletch, C. *Young Nietzsche: Becoming a Genius* (New York: Free Press, 1991).

Safranski, R. *Nietzsche: A Philosophical Biography*, S. Frisch (trans.) (New York: Norton, 2002).

Salomé, L. *Nietzsche*, S. Mandel (ed. and trans.) (Redding Ridge, CT: Black Swan Books, 1988).

Stern, J. P. *A Study of Nietzsche* (New York: Cambridge University Press, 1979).

## Nietzsche's philosophy as a whole

Ackermann, R. *Nietzsche: A Frenzied Look* (Amherst, MA: University of Massachusetts Press, 1990).

Allison, D. *Reading the New Nietzsche* (Lanham, MD: Rowman & Littlefield Publishing, 2000).

Aschheim, S. *The Nietzsche Legacy in Germany, 1890–1990* (Berkeley, CA: University of California Press, 1992).

Bataille, G. *On Nietzsche*, B. Boone (trans.) (London: Athlone Press, 1992).

Conway, D. *Nietzsche's Dangerous Game: Philosophy in the Twilight of the Idols* (New York: Cambridge University Press, 1997).

Danto, A. *Nietzsche as Philosopher: An Original Study* (New York: Columbia University Press, 1965).

Deleuze, G. *Nietzsche and Philosophy*, H. Tomlinson (trans.) (New York: Columbia University Press, 1983).

Fink, E. *Nietzsche's Philosophy*, G. Richter (trans.) (New York: Continuum, 2003).

Heidegger, M. *Nietzsche, Vol. I: The Will to Power as Art*, D. F. Krell (trans.) (New York: Harper & Row, 1979).

Heidegger, M. *Nietzsche, Vol. II: The Eternal Recurrence of the Same*, D. F. Krell (trans.) (San Francisco: Harper & Row, 1984).

Heidegger, M. *Nietzsche, Vol. III: Will to Power as Knowledge and as Metaphysics*, J. Stambaugh & F. Capuzzi (trans.) (San Francisco: Harper & Row, 1986).

Heidegger, M. *Nietzsche, Vol. IV: Nihilism*, D. F. Krell (trans.) (New York: Harper & Row, 1982).

Jaspers, K. *Nietzsche: An Introduction to the Understanding of His Philosophical Activity*, C. F. Wallraff & F. J. Schmitz (trans.) (South Bend, IN: Regentry/Gateway, 1979).

Kaufmann, W. *Nietzsche: Philosopher, Psychologist, Anti-Christ*, 4th edn (Princeton, NJ: Princeton University Press, 1974).

Magnus, B. & K. Higgins (eds). *The Cambridge Companion to Nietzsche* (New York: Cambridge University Press, 1996).

Müller-Lauter, W. *Nietzsche: His Philosophy of Contradictions and the Contradictions of His Philosophy*, David J. Parent (trans.) (Urbana, IL: University of Illinois Press, 1999).

Richardson, J. *Nietzsche's System* (New York: Oxford University Press, 1996).

Richardson, J. & B. Leiter (eds). *Nietzsche* (New York: Oxford University Press, 2001).

Schacht, R. *Nietzsche* (New York: Routledge & Kegan Paul, 1983).

Sedgwick, P. (ed.). *Nietzsche: A Critical Reader* (Oxford: Blackwell, 1995).

Solomon, R. (ed.). *Nietzsche: A Collection of Critical Essays* (New York: Anchor Books, 1973).

Solomon, R. & K. Higgins. *What Nietzsche Really Said* (New York: Shocken, 2000).

Solomon, R. & K. M. Higgins (eds). *Reading Nietzsche* (New York: Oxford University Press, 1988).

## Morality

Berkowitz, P. *Nietzsche: The Ethics of an Immoralist* (Cambridge, MA: Harvard University Press, 1995).

Foucault, M. *Language, Counter-Memory, Practice: Selected Essays and Interviews by Michael Foucault,* D. F. Bouchard (ed.), D. F. Bouchard & S. Simon (trans.) (Ithaca, NY: Cornell University Press, 1977).

Havas, R. *Nietzsche's Genealogy: Nihilism and the Will to Knowledge* (Ithaca, NY: Cornell University Press, 1995).

Hunt, L. *Nietzsche and the Origin of Virtue* (New York: Routledge, 1991).

Leiter, B. *Nietzsche on Morality* (New York: Routledge, 2002).

May, S. *Nietzsche's Ethics and His War on "Morality"* (New York: Oxford, 1999).

Ridley, A. *Nietzsche's Conscience: Six Character Studies from the* Genealogy (Ithaca, NY: Cornell University Press, 1998).

Schacht, R. (ed.). *Nietzsche, Genealogy, Morality* (Berkeley, CA: University of California Press, 1994).

Sleinis, E. *Nietzsche's Revaluation of Values* (Urbana, IL: University of Illinois Press, 1994).

Wilcox, J. *Truth and Value in Nietzsche: A Study of His Metaethics and Epistemology* (Ann Arbor, MI: University of Michigan Press, 1974).

## Religion

Fraser, G. *Redeeming Nietzsche* (New York: Routledge, 2002).

Golomb, J. (ed.). *Nietzsche and Jewish Culture* (New York: Routledge, 1997).

Jaspers, K. *Nietzsche and Christianity*, E. B. Ashton (trans.) (Chicago: Regnery, 1961).

Kaufmann, W. *Nietzsche: Philosopher, Psychologist, Anti-Christ,* 4th edn (Princeton, NJ: Princeton University Press, 1974).

Kee, A. *Nietzsche Against the Crucified* (London: SCM Press, 1999).

Kellenberger, J. *Kierkegaard and Nietzsche: Faith and Eternal Acceptance* (New York: Macmillan, 1997).

Mistry, F. *Nietzsche and Buddhism* (Berlin: Walter de Gruyter, 1981).

Morrison, R. *Nietzsche and Buddhism* (New York: Oxford University Press, 1997).

Roberts, T. *Contesting Spirit: Nietzsche, Affirmation, Religion* (Princeton, NJ: Princeton University Press, 1998).

Santaniello, W. *Nietzsche, God, and The Jews: His Critique of Judeo-Christianity in Relation to the Nazi Myth* (Albany, NY: SUNY Press, 1994).

Yovel, Y. *Dark Riddle: Hegel, Nietzsche, and the Jews* (Cambridge: Polity Press, 1998).

## Nihilism

Darby, T. *et al.* (eds). *Nietzsche and the Rhetoric of Nihilism* (Ottawa: Carleton University Press, 1989).

Gillespie, M. A. *Nihilism Before Nietzsche* (Chicago, IL: University of Chicago Press, 1995).

Havas, R. *Nietzsche's Genealogy: Nihilism and the Will to Knowledge* (Ithaca, NY: Cornell University Press, 1995).

Janaway, C. (ed.). *Willing and Nothingness: Schopenhauer as Nietzsche's Educator* (New York: Oxford University Press, 1998).

Magnus, B. *Nietzsche's Existential Imperative* (Bloomington, IN: University of Indiana Press, 1978).

Müller-Lauter, W. *Nietzsche: His Philosophy of Contradictions and the Contradictions of*

*His Philosophy*, D. J. Parent (trans.) (Urbana, IL: University of Illinois Press, 1999).

Schacht, R. *Making Sense of Nietzsche: Reflections Timely and Untimely* (Urbana, IL: University of Illinois Press, 1995).

Schutte, O. *Beyond Nihilism: Nietzsche Without Masks* (Chicago, IL: University of Chicago Press, 1984).

## Truth and language

Clark, M. *Nietzsche on Truth and Philosophy* (New York: Cambridge University Press, 1990).

Cox, C. *Nietzsche: Naturalism and Interpretation* (Berkeley, CA: University of California Press, 1999).

Foucault, M. *Power/Knowledge: Selected Interviews and Other Writings, 1972–1977*, C. Gordon (ed. and trans.) (New York: Pantheon, 1980).

Hales, S. & R. Welshon. *Nietzsche's Perspectivism* (Urbana, IL: University of Illinois Press, 2000).

Magnus, B., S. Stewart, J.-P. Mileur (eds). *Nietzsche's Case: Philosophy and/as Literature* (New York: Routledge, 1993).

Schacht, R. *Nietzsche* (New York: Routledge and Kegan Paul, 1983).

Schacht, R. *Making Sense of Nietzsche: Reflections Timely and Untimely* (Urbana, IL: University of Illinois Press, 1995).

Wilcox, J. *Truth and Value in Nietzsche: A Study of His Metaethics and Epistemology* (Ann Arbor, MI: University of Michigan Press, 1974).

## Epistemology and philosophy of science

Babich, B. E. *Nietzsche's Philosophy of Science: Reflecting Science on the Ground of Art and Life* (Albany, NY: SUNY Press, 1994).

Babich, B. & R. S. Cohen (eds). *Nietzsche, Theories of Knowledge and Critical Theory: Nietzsche and the Sciences I* (Dordrecht: Kluwer, 1999).

Babich, B. & R. S. Cohen (eds). *Nietzsche, Epistemology, and the Philosophy of Science: Nietzsche and the Sciences II* (Dordrecht: Kluwer, 1999).

Cox, C. *Nietzsche: Naturalism and Interpretation* (Berkeley, CA: University of California Press, 1999).

Grimm, R. *Nietzsche's Theory of Knowledge* (Berlin: Walter de Gruyter, 1977).

Hales, S. & R. Welshon. *Nietzsche's Perspectivism* (Urbana, IL: University of Illinois Press, 2000).

Moles, A. *Nietzsche's Philosophy of Nature and Cosmology* (Berlin: Peter Lang, 1990).

Moore, G. *Nietzsche, Biology, and Metaphor* (New York: Cambridge University Press, 2002).

Wilcox, J. *Truth and Value in Nietzsche: A Study of His Metaethics and Epistemology* (Ann Arbor, MI: University of Michigan Press, 1974).

## Metaphysics

Cox, C. *Nietzsche: Naturalism and Interpretation* (Berkeley, CA: University of California Press, 1999).

Green, M. *Nietzsche and the Transcendental Tradition* (Urbana, IL: University of Illinois Press, 2001).

Haar, M. *Nietzsche and Metaphysics* (Albany, NY: SUNY Press, 1996).

Hales, S. & R. Welshon. *Nietzsche's Perspectivism* (Urbana, IL: University of Illinois Press, 2000).
Houlgate, S. *Hegel, Nietzsche, and the Criticism of Metaphysics* (New York: Cambridge University Press, 1986).
Poellner, P. *Nietzsche and Metaphysics* (Oxford: Oxford University Press, 1995).
Stambrough, J. *Nietzsche's Thought of Eternal Return* (Baltimore, MD: Johns Hopkins University Press, 1972).

## Psychology

Chappelle, D. *Nietzsche and Psychoanalysis* (Albany, NY: SUNY Press, 1993).
Golomb, J. *Nietzsche's Enticing Psychology of Power* (Ames, IA: University of Iowa Press, 1989).
Nehamas, A. *Nietzsche: Life as Literature* (Cambridge, MA: Harvard University Press, 1985).
Parkes, G. *Composing the Soul: Reaches of Nietzsche's Psychology* (Chicago, IL: University of Chicago Press, 1994).

## Politics

Ansell-Pearson, K. *Nietzsche Contra Rousseau* (Cambridge: Cambridge University Press, 1991).
Ansell-Pearson, K. *An Introduction to Nietzsche as Political Thinker* (Cambridge: Cambridge University Press, 1994).
Appel, F. *Nietzsche Contra Democracy* (Ithaca, NY: Cornell University Press, 1999).
Conway, D. *Nietzsche and the Political* (New York: Routledge, 1997).
Detwiler, B. *Nietzsche and the Politics of Aristocratic Radicalism* (Chicago: University of Chicago Press, 1990).
Golomb, J. & R. S. Wistrich (eds). *Nietzsche, Godfather of Fascism? On the Uses and Abuses of a Philosophy* (Princeton, NJ: Princeton University Press, 2002).
Hatab, L. *A Nietzschean Defense of Democracy: An Experiment in Postmodern Politics* (Chicago, IL: Open Court, 1995).
Love, N. *Marx, Nietzsche, and Modernity* (New York: Columbia University Press, 1996).
Owen, D. *Maturity and Modernity: Nietzsche, Weber, Foucault and the Ambivalence of Reason* (New York: Routledge, 1994).
Owen, D. *Nietzsche, Politics, and Modernity* (London: Sage, 1995).
Strong, T. *Friederich Nietzsche and the Politics of Transfiguration*, expanded edn (Berkeley, CA: University of California Press, 1988).
Thiele, L. P. *Friedrich Nietzsche and the Politics of the Soul* (Princeton, NJ: Princeton University Press, 1990).
Thomas, R. H. *Nietzsche in German Politics and Society, 1890–1918* (Manchester: Manchester University Press, 1983).
Warren, M. *Nietzsche and Political Thought* (Cambridge, MA: MIT Press, 1988).
Yovel, Y. *Dark Riddle: Hegel, Nietzsche, and the Jews* (Cambridge: Polity Press, 1998).

## Feminist interpretations

Burgard, P. (ed.). *Nietzsche and the Feminine* (Charlottesville, VA: University of Virginia Press, 1994).
Diethe, C. *Nietzsche's Women: Beyond the Whip* (Berlin and New York: Walter de Gruyter, 1996).

Krell, D. F. *Postponements: Women, Sensuality, and Death in Nietzsche* (Bloomington, IN: Indiana University Press, 1986).

Oliver, K. *Womanizing Nietzsche: Philosophy's Relation to the "Feminine"* (New York: Routledge, 1995).

Oliver, K. & M. Pearsall (eds). *Feminist Interpretations of Friedrich Nietzsche* (University Park, PA: Pennsylvania State University Press, 1998).

Patton, P. (ed.). *Nietzsche, Feminism, and Political Theory* (New York: Routledge, 1993).

## Other interesting books on Nietzsche's philosophical thought

Abbey, R. *Nietzsche's Middle Period* (New York: Oxford University Press, 2000).

Allison, D. B. (ed.). *The New Nietzsche: Contemporary Styles of Interpretation* (Cambridge, MA: MIT Press, 1985).

Blondel, E. *Nietzsche: The Body and Culture*, S. Hand (trans.) (Stanford, CA: Stanford University Press, 1991).

Bloom, H. (ed.). *Modern Critical Views: Friedrich Nietzsche* (New York: Chelsea House Publishers, 1987).

Derrida, J. *Spurs: Nietzsche's Styles*, B. Harlow (trans.) (Chicago, IL: University of Chicago Press, 1979).

Gillespie, M. A. & T. Strong (eds). *Nietzsche's New Seas: Explorations in Philosophy, Aesthetics, and Politics* (Chicago, IL: University of Chicago Press, 1988).

Higgins, K. M. *Nietzsche's Zarathustra* (Philadelphia. PA: Temple University Press, 1987).

Higgins, K. *Comic Relief: Nietzsche's Gay Science* (New York: Oxford University Press, 2000).

Hoy, D. C. *The Critical Circle: Literature, History, and Philosophical Hermeneutics* (Berkeley, CA: University of California Press, 1978).

Irigaray, L. *Marine Lover of Friedrich Nietzsche*, G. C. Gill (trans.) (New York: Columbia University Press, 1991).

Jung, C. *Nietzsche's* Zarathustra, J. L. Jarrett (ed.) (Princeton, NJ: Princeton University Press, 1988).

Klein, W. *Nietzsche and the Promise of Philosophy* (Albany, NY: State University of New York Press, 1997).

Klossowski, P. *Nietzsche and the Vicious Circle* (London: Athlone, 1993).

Koelb, C. (ed.). *Nietzsche as Postmodernist: Essays Pro and Con* (Albany, NY: SUNY Press, 1990).

Kofman, S. *Nietzsche and Metaphor*, D. Large (trans.) (Stanford, CA: Stanford University Press, 1993).

Krell, D. F. *Infectious Nietzsche* (Bloomington, IN: University of Indiana Press, 1996).

Krell, D. F. & D. Wood (eds) *Exceedingly Nietzsche: Aspects of Contemporary Nietzsche Interpretation* (New York: Routledge, 1988).

Lampert, L. *Nietzsche's Task: An Interpretation of* Beyond Good and Evil (New Haven, CT: Yale University Press, 2001).

Lampert, L. *Nietzsche's Teaching: An Interpretation of* Thus Spoke Zarathustra (New Haven, CT: Yale University Press, 1987).

Löwith, K. *Nietzsche's Philosophy of the Eternal Recurrence of the Same*, J. Harvey Lomax (trans.), foreword by B. Magnus (Berkeley, CA: University of California Press, 1997).

Mandel, S. *Nietzsche and the Jews* (New York: Prometheus Books, 1998).

Megill, A. *Prophets of Extremity: Nietzsche, Heidegger, Foucault, Derrida* (Berkeley, CA: University of California Press, 1985).

Morgan, G. *What Nietzsche Means* (New York: Harper and Row, 1941).

Nehamas, A. *Nietzsche: Life as Literature* (Cambridge, MA: Harvard University Press, 1985).

Parkes, G. (ed.) *Nietzsche and Asian Thought* (Chicago, IL: University of Chicago Press, 1991).

Pasley, M. (ed.) *Nietzsche's Imagery and Thought: A Collection of Essays* (Berkeley, CA: University of California Press, 1978).

Pavur, C. *Nietzsche Humanist* (Milwaukee, WI: Marquette University Press, 1998).

Porter, J. *Nietzsche and the Philology of the Future* (Stanford, CA: Stanford University Press, 2000).

Rosen, S. *The Mask of Enlightenment: Nietzsche's* Zarathustra (New York: Cambridge University Press, 1995).

Sallis, J. *Crossings: Nietzsche and the Space of Tragedy* (Chicago, IL: University of Chicago Press, 1991).

Schacht, R. *Making Sense of Nietzsche: Reflections Timely and Untimely* (Urbana, IL: University of Illinois Press, 1995).

Schrift, A. *Nietzsche's French Legacy: A Genealogy of Poststructuralism* (New York: Routledge, 1995).

Schrift, A. *Nietzsche and the Question of Interpretation: Between Hermeneutics and Deconstruction* (New York: Routledge, 1990).

Schrift, A. *Why Nietzsche Still? Reflections on Drama, Culture, and Politics* (Berkeley, CA: University of California Press, 2000).

Scott, C. *The Question of Ethics: Nietzsche, Foucault, Heidegger* (Bloomington, IN: Indiana University Press, 1990).

Shapiro, G. *Alcyone: Nietzsche on Gifts, Noise, and Women* (Albany, NY: SUNY Press, 1991).

Shapiro, G. *Nietzschean Narratives* (Bloomington, IN: Indiana University Press, 1989).

Silk, M. S. & J. P. Stern. *Nietzsche on Tragedy* (Cambridge: Cambridge University Press, 1981).

Simmel, G. *Schopenhauer and Nietzsche*, H. Loiskandle, D. Weinstein & M. Weinstein (trans.) (Urbana, IL: University of Illinois Press, 1991).

Small, R. *Nietzsche in Context* (Aldershot: Ashgate, 2001).

Stack, G. *Lange and Nietzsche* (Berlin: Walter de Gruyter, 1983).

Stack, G. *Nietzsche and Emerson: An Elective Affinity* (Athens, OH: Ohio University Press, 1993).

Staten, H. *Nietzsche's Voice* (Ithaca, NY: Cornell University Press, 1990).

White, A. *Within Nietzsche's Labyrinth* (New York: Routledge, 1990).

Young, J. *Nietzsche's Philosophy of Art* (New York: Cambridge University Press, 1992).

Yovel, Y. (ed.). *Nietzsche as Affirmative Thinker* (Dordrecht: Martinus Nijhoff Publishers, 1986).

Yovel, Y. *Dark Riddle: Hegel, Nietzsche, and the Jews* (Cambridge: Polity Press, 1998).

# Index